"Neagley combines a personal memoir with the history of a well-known tourist site. The author presents the reader with two fascinating stories...a personal account of growing up in a Russian immigrant family and coping with her parents' alcoholism. She then recounts how...she developed a professional career in interior design that brought her into contact with the Webb family of Vermont's Shelburne Farms...This admixture of personal history and chronicle of the Shelburne Farms estate is engaging to read. . .a fascinating and worthwhile account of what happens when a family estate must reinvent itself."

—*Kirkus Reviews*

"Marilyn Neagley's memoir addresses issues so critical now: how to take care of our natural world, of each other, of ourselves—we need magic attics of imagination and stories that inspire our activism. In addition her book touches on a beloved place in Vermonter's hearts, and by extension all the beloved places on our planet home we have neglected for far too long!"

–Julia Alvarez, Dominican-American poet, novelist, and essayist

"A very compelling memoir written in a unique style that covers Marilyn Webb Neagley's fascinating life, which has myriad inter-sections, including her role as a leader of Shelburne Farms, as well as her own experience as a champion and steward of the environment. The memoir is also intensely personal and projects a narrative that extends beyond her career commitments into her own troubled childhood and her own spiritual evolution. This is a book that will resonate with a broad range of readers."

" of *The Lamoille Stories* and other novels

"*Attic of Dreams* is a memoir of vivid vignettes held together by the golden thread of Marilyn's indomitable spirit. These small chapters, sparkling with intimate detail, reveal a strong-willed, vulnerable, and reflective woman who overcame a troubled childhood to emerge as a leading voice in the Vermont conservation movement and a driving force behind the creation of one of our greatest treasures, Shelburne Farms. Reading Marilyn's book is like having a deep and revealing conversation with a remarkable woman about love, life, and passion."

–Susan Ritz, author of *A Dream to Die For* and
feature writer for *Vermont Woman*

"Marilyn's memoir reads like a very personal journal. It is rich in images, as if she turned her life upside down in a snow globe and let stories filter onto the pages. From her dark childhood reminiscences of her mother's alcoholism to her legacy as one of the formative leaders of Shelburne Farms, Marilyn describes in detail the hard work of growing up, marrying into a storied family, and contributing to her life's greatest mission: to help children feel connected to nature and animals. Her humble roots honed her dogged determination to make a difference in ways that countless people will continue to benefit from. This book is a testament to resilience and will inspire others to overcome their own challenges in favor of doing good in the world."

–Eileen Rockefeller, author of
Being a Rockefeller, Becoming Myself

ATTIC OF DREAMS

ATTIC OF DREAMS

A Memoir

Marilyn Webb Neagley

For Kitty —
With warm wishes,
Marilyn

Rootstock Publishing

Montpelier, VT

Release Date: 09/05/23

Softcover ISBN: 978-1-57869-131-9
Hardcover ISBN: 978-1-57869-132-6
eBook ISBN: 978-1-57869-133-3

Library of Congress Control Number: 2023902692

Published by Rootstock Publishing

www.rootstockpublishing.com
info@rootstockpublishing.com

Quote by John O'Donohue from *To Bless the Space Between Us* (Penguin Random House, 2008). Reprinted with permission.

Quote by Diane Dewey from *Fixing the Fates* (She Writes Press, 2019). Reprinted with permission.

Interior by Eddie Vincent, ENC Graphic Services
(ed.vincent@encirclepub.com)

Cover Art: Tom Absher, "Lost Art Comes Home," found objects and mixed media box, ©2022. Photographed by Juliana Jennings.

Author photograph: Amanda H. Herzberger

For permissions or to schedule an author interview, contact the author at marilynwneagley@gmail.com.

Printed in the USA

For Mark, my children, and my grandchildren.

Author's Note

When knitting together the strands of a life, dropped stitches create holes. Writing about the past picks up stitches to mend the holes. Memoir, a collection of remembered moments, helps to redeem and heal, to find meaning in one's life story, for the author and the reader.

Many of the recollections in this memoir can be tied to existing records. Those that are otherwise from my memories are my personal truth, even though I fully recognize that memories can trick us. We remember from our individual vantage points.

Quotations are, of course, paraphrased according to my memory. In rare instances, timelines may be slightly inaccurate. Some names have been changed to protect anonymity.

Once dust of stars,
for earth I yearned,
then to the stars returned.

PART ONE

Spring Peepers

I'm five. It's my bedtime, but Mom and Dad want to take me for a walk. They say the restaurant isn't busy, so they can leave for a while. We cross Route 5 and turn toward a dirt road that has no name and no lights. The road is wet and spongy. The air is full of steam. My whole world seems soft and safe.

"Listen for the spring peepers," they whisper. At first, I hear nothing. Then, as we near a pond, I shout, "I hear the peepers!" We stop to listen. My parents' quiet sounds tell me they are smiling. I inhale their happiness with one big breath.

We walk a mile or so, hand in hand. It's dark. Even the stars are hidden, but I feel safe and happy.

We turn toward home. There, ahead, I see our restaurant's neon lights. A mist has lifted their red glow to warm the blackened sky.

Safe Places

I'm not quite old enough to go to school. In the early mornings, I go to Mom and Dad's bed to lie in the warm crib of their blanketed legs. I pull a separate cover over myself and snuggle in. This is my safest place.

On Sunday mornings, while Mom and Dad are sleeping, I sit on the rug in front of our console radio and listen to Puck the Comic Weekly Man read the funnies. His voice makes me smile.

In our living room, I sometimes cover a card table with a canvas cloth painted with two windows and a door. This tiny home, my hideaway, is warm and homey, especially when I add a lamp.

Silver Radiators

Our house is small, nothing fancy. It sits only a few feet from the restaurant. Mom calls it a bungalow. I think it's just the right size for an only child. The white clapboard siding, black shutters, and picket fence are inviting, especially when the lilacs and mock oranges are in bloom.

Inside, we have linoleum floors and flowery wallpaper. There are two bedrooms and a bathroom. A kitchen sink and stove join the dining and living rooms.

The sunporch, with its varnished beadboard walls, is my favorite room. I sometimes sleep there next to my mother's hope chest. On special days, Mom allows me to open it to gaze at the treasures she has so carefully arranged.

In the winter, our house feels cozy. Silver-painted radiators hiss warm steam, making a frosty coating on the windows. I kneel on the sofa for a closer view of the lacy frost patterns. The radiator in the living room, behind the sofa, is where I dry my snow caked woolen mittens.

All day and night, a drip of spring water fills a large wooden cistern in the cellar. The sounds of hissing and dripping are like familiar friends. I'm comforted by their steadiness.

We have one of the first televisions and electric washing machines in our village. We don't have a refrigerator, though, partly because the restaurant is only a few steps away. I eat most of my meals there.

Our house and the restaurant sit on busy Route 5 in the village of Ascutney, Vermont. We own a grocery store across the parking lot, on the same side of the road. The Connecticut River runs east of us. Mount Ascutney stands to the west.

Mom and Dad named their restaurant The Top Hat, but, at home, we call it The Club. The Club has a glow at night. Unlike my house, it has colorful lights, music, and people . . . good food too.

The Club doesn't always glow though. It sometimes causes darkness during daylight hours.

Jaundice

I'm in first grade now. The school day has ended. While playing outside our house, I hear unusual sounds. They're coming from our living room. I hurry inside to see what's happening. Dad and my mom's brother, my uncle John, are supporting Mom. She's twisting in pain. Her body, clothed in a black crepe dress with sparkles, is bending toward the floor like a beautiful black bird falling from the sky. Mom's crying out for help. They struggle to prop her up enough to move her into a car and to the nearest hospital. I'm afraid for her, but I just watch, and try to understand what's happening.

Dad and I are walking through a bleak hallway in Windsor Hospital. A patient is wheeled past us. She's lying on a gurney so her face passes near my eyes. I tug on Dad's sleeve. "Look! That looks like Mom." "It *is* your Mom" is all he says.

Her eyes and skin are yellow. I can't believe that this is my mother. And she is too sick to recognize me. Dad explains, "She has jaundice."

Mom needed abdominal surgery, something to do with the gallbladder and pancreas. She has since returned home with an ostomy, a tube and sac that fills with brown bile. I don't like looking at it, but she won't need it for too many days. (And yet, two more surgeries follow.)

Bottles and Keys

My friend Linda and I are waiting to ask Dad a question. He and his business partner, Uncle John, are having a serious conversation on the path between our house and The Club. "I'm telling you, Tommy, this much is gone from the bottle." He shows Dad a measurement of several inches with his thumb and forefinger.

Uncle John is saying that he marked the liquor bottles in The Club to prove that Mom has been drinking during the days. Dad scowls and nods. He clears his throat, catching a moment to think. "I had a feeling she was up to something. Damn it. I didn't think it was this bad."

Uncle John suddenly notices Linda. He bends toward her and scolds, "What are you doing, listening to this? Stop being so nosy. You go home right now. Go on!" Linda is timid to begin with. She walks home in tears.

I don't like that he has spoken to my friend in this way. We weren't trying to listen. We were just waiting for a chance to ask if we could play in Dad's car. What's the big deal anyway? Didn't they know that Mom had been drinking?

I've known for a while. She hides liquor bottles in the dirty clothes hamper, or in the closet. Mom must be so happy whenever she finds one of her hidden bottles, the way a dog finds a buried bone.

My stomach tightened the first time I found a hidden bottle. It looked strange. I didn't understand why it was there and wondered whether I should worry. But then I got used to finding bottles. Keys were sometimes hidden next to them. Hiding keys from Dad has become Mom's favorite game. If Dad is upset, she has won the game.

I don't talk about these things. I mostly observe and move on.

Stardust

The Club at night is a child's wonderland. At the corner of the dance floor, a jukebox sparkles with color and sound. From the center of the dance floor, a recessed light beams up to an ornate fixture made of multihued mirror glass. As the fixture turns, bubbly rainbows of light dreamily drift around the room.

On the nights when there aren't many customers, Dad teaches me to dance to "Stardust." I feel his hand on my back signaling me to step forward and backward. He coaches with "Let me lead. You relax and follow."

Nat King Cole's voice is rich and soothing. It glows like the room. Feeling safely protected by my father, I glide along, humming fragments of "Stardust."

Perfumes and Gladioli

My friends and I explore The Club when it's closed to the public. We girls sing hit songs through the bandstand's microphone and explore the restrooms. A newly installed urinal in the men's room is quite amusing. And in the women's restroom, we're delighted by a pink perfume machine that offers Shalimar, Tabu, Tweed, and Chanel N°5 for only ten cents a squirt.

When open at night, The Club smells like beer, french fries, lobster, cigarette smoke, and perfume. There's a bar and lounge area. On one end of the bar are potato chips, beef jerky, boiled eggs, and Mom's homemade dill pickles. A television sits at the other end. Behind the bar are tiers of liquor bottles and wall mirrors. Dollar bills cover large areas of the wall in case a customer has "a rainy day" and needs an extra buck.

Dad and I usually eat in the lounge area next to the bar. If he's busy, I eat in the kitchen, using the ice cream chest freezer as my table. Or, if tired, I nap there, on top of the freezer.

Four to six musicians play big band music on the weekends. I like to stand between the upright bass and piano to request songs for the musicians to play. Ralph, the bass player, is my favorite. He's a kind man who sings like Nat King Cole.

Tonight, twin waiters dressed in tuxedos, the Hemming Boys, step up to the microphone. They call me to the bandstand. I shyly move toward them. They place a bundle of gladioli, my birth flower, into my arms. I look down at long stems of red, yellow, pink, purple, orange, and white blossoms. The band plays as a hundred or so customers sing "Happy Birthday" to me. I feel warm all over.

Cast of Characters

The Club has a colorful cast of characters. Chefs, waitresses, bartenders, cleaners, and customers, even delivery truck drivers, interest me. They are messengers from the outside world.

The bread and dairy trucks come almost every day. I climb into them and see what is new. Their truck bodies smell of yeasty flour or soured milk. A seafood truck comes from Maine every Friday. I keep a bit of distance because of the odor, but know that fresh seafood is something to be happy about.

Lobster, shrimp, and steamed clams are delicious treats. Dad has taught me to dunk the lobster and clams in broth, then in melted butter. We use bowls of warm water and lemon to clean the butter from our fingertips.

Mom likes to say that she's proud of her clientele: "doctors, lawyers, merchants, chiefs." For them, The Club is *the* place to be. Most customers are local, from a fifty-mile radius, but others are just passing through.

A rug salesman sometimes stops in. One night, he teetered into the kitchen, smelling of liquor. With sanpaku eyes and fleshy lips, he leaned down to kiss me. I turned my head away. He snickered, then paused to light a cigarette. His body wavered unsteadily as he tried to strike a match. The "safety" matchbook caught fire and burned his fingers. I was glad and didn't feel guilty. He never tried to kiss me again.

During the first five or so years of owning The Club, Dad or Uncle John were the cooks. Now that Uncle John has moved away, a new chef, Pappy, has been hired. Dad wants me to meet him.

I stand at a worktable in the kitchen, across from Pappy. He has a rascal smile that makes me happy to have him on our team. I study his beady eyes, tattooed forearms, and trimmed gray mustache. He prepares for work by unrolling a black leather case. It's about six feet long and is lined with red fabric. My eyes widen. There are so many knives in all shapes and sizes that I think, *He must be very good at his job.*

In a gravelly voice, Pappy says, "Here's a cutting board, a knife, and some vegetables. Slice these. They're for tossed salads. After that, you can put butter on pads and fill the creamers."

My parents never give me chores but I often volunteer. Helping Pappy makes me feel like a grown-up.

Waitresses arrive and begin to organize their workstations. I've finished my chores and am waiting for Dad, so we can eat supper together. He's at our house, changing into work clothes. One waitress takes a moment to show me how to draw a cat and a candle. She shows me how to make the candle "glow" by drawing lines that radiate from the flame.

Dad arrives wearing his usual outfit: a dress shirt, tie, and trousers. I can see that he is frustrated. One waitress has refused to shave her legs. Dad has asked more than once. He complains to me, "Seeing matted black hair through nylon stockings is disgusting. It's like finding a hair in food."

Mom had once mentioned that this waitress was a Jehovah's Witness. I can't help but wonder whether that has anything to do with her not shaving.

Running Errands

The school year has ended. Dad and I are driving to nearby Windsor to shop for The Club's groceries and liquor. He's singing "The Twelve Days of Christmas" in the middle of summer. He says, "Darn it," and laughs. "I can't get that song out of my head." We both laugh and begin to sing "I've Been Working on the Railroad."

Dad breaks in with "Wanna a hot dog?" I nod. We pull over to a favorite roadside stand and order. The hot dogs arrive in rolls deliciously grilled in butter.

A little farther down the road we stop at a natural spring for a cold drink. Dad makes his usual fuss over the fresh taste of the ice-cold water. "There's nothing like it!" I agree.

In Windsor, Dad stops at the American Legion to have a few drinks with his friends. This is my least favorite part of our trips to town. Sitting alone in a cavernous lounge area with leather furniture and navy blue walls, I watch *Tarzan* on television while eating Good & Plenty candies. Their pink and white sugary coating melts away to the sharper taste of licorice. I savor each morsel. It isn't so bad . . . waiting like this . . . for a while.

Now it has been a *long* while. I've watched a couple more television shows. It's time to walk to the bar. I plead with Dad, "How much longer? Can we *please* go now?"

We've finally left. Our first stop is the butcher shop. A refrigerated room is filled with hanging carcasses that smell of fat and blood. Dad and the butcher talk about different cuts of meat. It reminds me of the day we went to a slaughterhouse. I was so sad. The cows were brought out of a shed and made to stand in a doorway. They were shot, one at a time. I never again went to a slaughterhouse.

Dad asks me to get into the car. It's time to shop for liquor and groceries before going home. While driving, I recall other days when the errands were more fun.

We often go to an enormous warehouse across the river in Claremont, New Hampshire. There, ceiling-high shelves are loaded with salt and pepper shakers, napkins, and place mats—everything needed for a restaurant. I enjoy looking at all the choices. Glass or metal teapots. Coffee urns. Plates.

From there we go to a chilly barn to buy ice. The entrance is dark except for ribbons of daylight that angle through gaps between the wallboards. Inside, damp floors are covered with sawdust. In the dim light we can barely discern large blocks of ice. We bring smaller ice blocks back to The Club where, with a metal pick, Dad chips ice for cocktails.

Today, we've stopped at a greenhouse to buy flower arrangements. Sunlight pours through the glass walls and ceilings. The air is warm and fragrant. I walk among beds of roses, cloaked in the scent of spice and tea.

Bedtime Stories

Dad is the nurturer in our home. He regularly checks my temperature during the usual childhood ailments like measles, German measles, chicken pox, colds, flu, plus poison ivy and sunburns. If needed, he comforts me with ginger beer or a cup of freshly squeezed warm lemonade sweetened with honey. Confinement can be difficult, but lying in bed under a satin puff, getting all that love and attention, is quite pleasant.

At night, Dad usually breaks away from work to tuck me in and read a bedtime story like *Mother West Wind Stories*, *Heidi*, or *Black Beauty*.

Tonight he apologizes with "I'm sorry, Peanut. We're very busy tonight, and shorthanded. I can't read to you."

"Please. Just one chapter?" I beg. Dad says, "I can't. I have to go back to work." I refuse to kiss him goodnight. Disappointed, he shrugs his shoulders with a sigh and turns to leave, trying to hold the line. He then turns back, sits on the edge of my bed, and reads one short story.

My need for reassurance is unusual. I've never tested Dad's love for me in such an impish way. Has this day been more difficult? Not sure, but I feel much better now.

New Year's Eve

I'm nine. It's New Year's Eve, 1955. Mom is dressing to greet customers at the front door of The Club. I'm standing in the doorway of her bedroom waiting to ask a question. She looks pretty in a quilted skirt and velvet top. Both are coral pink. The scoop neck top exposes a gold necklace that matches her earrings. Her medium-length brown hair is neatly combed. She seems to be okay, sober and ready to go to work. I'm relieved.

Glamorous dancers soon arrive. They crowd the bedroom where Mom was dressing moments earlier. I stand in the same doorway to observe the commotion. These women have come from New York. They are excited about performing. Fantastic cosmetics and costumes spill from their luggage onto my parents' bed. The dancers step into netted stockings and skimpy satin coverings. They huddle before the large mirror of Mom's vanity table to color their eyelids and attach false eyelashes.

One of the dancers hands me a small package of pastel figurines—marzipan candies, straight from the big city. I'm at first wide-eyed, then thrilled by these exotic strangers.

My job tonight is to be the coat-check girl. Mom's youngest brother, Uncle Eugene, has come to help out. His jobs are to park cars and help me hang the heavy woolen coats. I run ahead to The Club. Customers will soon be arriving. I want to be ready for them.

The Club is abuzz. Customers are pouring in, dressed in their best clothes. The dance floor shimmers with color as the band begins to play. Now that everyone has arrived, I sit near Mom to watch the show.

An emcee steps up to the mic. He tells off-color jokes. One of the waitresses covers my ears before each punch line. That embarrasses me, but for only a minute. There are so many other things to think about. A magician confuses everyone with his tricks. The fancy dancers finally appear. Everyone, especially the men, claps and hoots.

The show has ended. Everyone has eaten. The band begins again. Couples swarm the floor like dancing bees. Women step out of their high heels. Some dance so freely that they tear through their seamed stockings. This kind of pleasure is beautiful to see.

As midnight approaches, the dancers stop to hold hands. They encircle the dance floor. At exactly midnight the band begins to play "Auld Lang Syne." Everyone sings along. As the music ends, couples kiss. Enveloped by the warm, bubbly light, they are wishing each other a happy New Year. And they mean it.

Mom whispers, "A lot of complicated things are happening out there." I don't know what she sees. Happiness, the kind that makes you smile with your whole body, is all that I can see, and feel.

Dancing Lovebirds

The Hitchcocks come to The Club once a year, likely on their wedding anniversary. Although they are in their eighties, the other dancers stand back and let them go. He is surprisingly strong. Her skirt flares as he spins her in circles. They read each other's signals, like lovebirds. Bobbing and twirling, they become one lively whirligig.

Like me, the other customers are proud of them, happy for them. They still have each other, and can dance like that in their later years.

Skitchewaug Trail

Dad likes to get an early start for road trips. He awakens me after closing The Club. Sometimes, like tonight, the trip is short. He simply wants to share his mother-in-law's hospitality with friends. I'm awakened after midnight and loaded into the car. Off we go to Springfield.

We take the back way along Skitchewaug Trail. Lying on the back seat, foggy from sleep, I watch the passing treetops as we speed along. They, in their leafless state, look as eerie as marching skeletons.

Grammy, my Russian grandmother, doesn't seem to mind our arrival. She rises from bed, approaches with slightly waddling steps, and greets everyone with a smile. She then descends into the passageways of her musty cellar. Grammy soon returns, breathing heavily. Her arms are full of liquor bottles. She removes homemade breads, cheeses, and sausages from the refrigerator and places them on a long table.

Dad thinks his mother-in-law is a wonder. She refers to him as her prince.

I don't know how or when I'll go home. I usually curl up somewhere, like a favorite carpeted place behind Grammy's sectional sofa. There, a floor lamp has a light at its base, making it a comforting place to fall asleep. My guess is that Dad will later carry me to the car, return home, and tuck me into bed.

When we arrive late, the two doors are sometimes locked by Mom. Dad opens a window for me to climb through and unlock one of the doors. On those nights, Dad usually makes home fries and scrambled eggs. Comfort food.

Mom may or may not have been with us on this night at Grammy's, because of her drinking. I don't remember. Late one other night though, she and two of her girlfriends took me on the same trip. One of the friends drove. All of them had been drinking. At a T in the road, we screeched through a stop sign and into a sharp turn. I held on for dear life in the back seat. Fortunately, there were no other cars on the road at that late hour. (There were no seat belts then.)

Broken-Wing Act

Dad loves the outdoors. Whenever we walk in the woods, he says, "Pay attention. Try to discover something you've never seen before." Sure enough, I'll find something like a porcupine quill or pine cones torn open by squirrels. Otherwise, I'd have gone along, inside my head, seeing nothing at all.

I have a fishing pole, a bow with arrows, and a .410 shotgun, all gifts from Dad. Together we go to fall turkey shoots. Using the .410, I target clay pigeons. I've never shot a living creature, though, and to my knowledge, neither has he, although he did trap animals as a boy. I sometimes come home from school to find surprise gifts from him, like pet dogs, fish, wild raccoons, and woodchucks.

Dad tells great stories. One is about his father, Thomas, who lived in Shelburne, Vermont. A jack-of-all-trades, he owned a couple of grocery stores, sold insurance and real estate, was an active member of the Masons, and was a school director, town auditor, tax collector, and constable.

As the local lawman, Thomas was once called to break up a KKK meeting in a neighboring town. Dad was allowed to ride along. When they arrived, he was told to stay in the car as his father approached the crowd. Dad was almost too afraid to watch.

As he describes the nightmarish scene to me, I imagine hooded figures illuminated by fire like a spooky swarm of giant white moths.

Dad's an honest man, but I doubt that story, mainly because I've never witnessed anything to support it.

(It turns out that KKK activity did exist. At that time in Vermont, Catholics and Jews were the primary targets.)

Dad tells another story about a mother partridge and how she fools humans with a broken-wing act. By pretending she can't fly, she attracts predators to her, giving her babies time to take cover. Dad goes on to describe baby partridges as "fluffy and yellow, the size of tennis balls." He says, "They hide by holding a leaf over themselves, like an umbrella."

I'm delighted by that story, whether the last part is true or not. He embellishes stories in a way that feeds my imagination.

On the night that Dad was too busy to read me a bedtime story, I had impishly refused to kiss him good night. Perhaps, for emotional protection, that was my own broken-wing act.

Water, Please

My life with Mom is different. We don't have regular outings, partly because she never got her driver's license. Mom always comes through for my birthdays though. Friends are invited to celebrate by having dinner in The Club, a picnic at the beach, or a cookout on top of Mount Ascutney. So soon after World War II, times are tough for many families. Birthdays like mine are unusual.

Mom does well with epic events like traveling by train to Boston. We stay at the Parker House hotel, near the department stores. Highlights for me are shopping for clothes and seeing the Ice Follies. In the summer, we go to Hampton Beach.

At home, usually in the heat of summer, we see hobos walking along Route 5. When they stop at our house, Mom asks what they want. "Water, please" is the usual response.

Mom goes into The Club to pack a lunch for them: a club sandwich, chips, and a jar of spring water.

She's equally generous with the children in our neighborhood.

When they tease for treats, she gives them ice cream cones or potato chips. I'm proud of her generosity. But if she's inebriated, I resent the children's teasing. They find it amusing to take advantage of her. I find it humiliating for her, and for me.

Hope Chest

Mom sometimes allows me to play with her collection of salt and pepper shakers. Or, as a special privilege, she permits me to open her hope chest. I ceremoniously lift the heavy lid. A pleasant cedar fragrance drifts into the room. The chest is lined with rosy-blond wood. Mom's wedding gown is carefully stored at the bottom. Upper shelves, covered with red velvet, hold my bronzed baby shoes and Mom's ornate wedding candles.

Hope chests usually store items for the future. In Mom's case, the contents of her hope chest are luminous symbols of her past. They're beautifully arranged reminders of what once was . . . and what could still be. When viewing these contents, I feel delight, and a spark of hope.

Tiny Stones

My uncles transport me to the Russian Orthodox Church, twenty-two miles away in Springfield. I'm taking Russian language lessons taught by the priest, Father Peter. He is a kind, erudite man whom I greatly admire. Russian Orthodox priests are allowed to marry.

Perhaps having his own family makes him comfortable with children. I feel a bond with him.

During today's visit, Father Peter is preparing the church for Easter. He hurries off to his upstairs apartment and returns with an envelope of stone bits. They had been given to him by a friend. As he extends the envelope, he explains, "This is from the tomb of Jesus Christ. Easter, you know, is the highest of Christian holidays. I want you to have this."

Father Peter shows me a simple wooden model of Jesus's tomb that he had built. It stands in the center of the sanctuary, impressively blanketed with flowers. A thick Bible, made of wine-colored velvet and brass, heavily sits on a drawing of Jesus.

I take all of this to heart. But I do wonder, for a minute, whether Father Peter had been fooled by his friend. The tiny stones look like gravel found along a roadside. They don't look special.

I carry the envelope home, anyway, to my own "hope chest," a small cedar-lined box of my most treasured artifacts.

Losing Faith

Dad is leaving early this morning for a hunting trip. "I'll be home tonight, after supper," he says, as he kisses me on the cheek.

It's now midmorning. Mom is passed out in bed. I try to rouse her but she doesn't move. In my young mind, she will be closer to waking when she changes her position. I stand and wait for what seems a very long while. . . . Each time she makes a sound or turns I yell, "Mom! Wake up! Wake up!" I shake her.

Her bed is now nearly soaked. A pissy odor, sweet and sickening, fills the room. My stomach turns upside down. My chest tightens. Time is passing. I retreat to my bedroom, then return to her and try again. Nothing changes. I'm afraid that she might be dying.

Darkness is settling in. An uncle stops by. I'm relieved to see him. He gives me a Devil Dog and a banana. "Mom won't wake up. She's been like this all day." He looks in on my mother, his sister. I think, *Maybe he can fix this.* He sighs, shakes his head, and leaves.

It is now my bedtime. Mom is still in her bed. I climb between the sheets. *Please, Dad, come home.* I focus on a small iconic picture of Mary and Jesus tacked to the wall next to my bed. It's from the day when I, as an infant, had been baptized in the Russian Orthodox Church. Mary's countenance is gilded with love for her child.

Uncovered, I now kneel on my pillow. Looking over the headboard through venetian blinds, I see cars pass by on Route 5. I think, *Maybe if I count one hundred cars, Dad will come home.* Finally, after counting one hundred cars again and again, I see headlights and a blinking turn signal.

It worked! Dad's home. I hurry to the door. One of his friends has stopped to say that my father won't be home until the next morning

Back in bed, I look up at Mary and begin to cry. Barely able to breathe, I rip her and Baby Jesus off the wall. I tear the picture into tiny pieces and sob, "I hate you, God. I *hate* you!"

Human Anatomy

Mom spends much of her time in four New England hospitals. She is home now, for a while. We have redecorated my bedroom with a new desk, lavender wallpaper, and a matching bedspread.

My friends are attaching pictures of teen idols and movie stars to their bedroom walls. I display pictures of the human body. Truly. Brains, hearts, and digestive systems cover the lavender wallpaper.

Instead of perfumes on my dresser, I have "medicines," like rubbing alcohol and iodine. I hope to be a doctor, a surgeon. Perhaps I want to understand Mom's moods and the cause of her drinking. Maybe I can fix her.

Tape Recording

Dad has come in from The Club to say good night. He tells me that he's filing for a divorce. Feeling both sadness and relief, I ask, "Where will we live? When will this happen?" It sounds like the right decision, but I wonder who will take care of Mom. Where will she live?

At nine, I'm probably old for my years and overly responsible. No matter how bad things get with Mom, I worry about her. We three have formed a complicated triangle.

As Dad prepares for divorce court, he has decided to document Mom's behavior with a reel-to-reel tape recorder. Early this evening, Mom walked through the kitchen's swinging doors and stepped onto the empty dance floor of The Club. Fifty or sixty customers were seated at their respective tables. They watched as she took center stage.

I push open one of the swinging doors to peek from the kitchen. Fully intoxicated, she's loudly slurring her words, "Sure, Bry, I know what you want. Look at you, you whoremaster. All you want is this. I know you."

She's grabbing her own pelvic area, to make the point. Whenever she drinks, *only* when she drinks, her behavior is obscene. I feel ashamed, but also sad to think that Dad is recording Mom. She's been ambushed. And what should have been her shame has somehow transferred to me.

I don't know what will happen to the three of us.

Scarlet Ribbons

I fortify myself in odd ways. I find solace in my baby book. Mom had written all the details of my birth and early childhood in a pink satin-covered book. Her words: "She's our bundle of joy." I memorize these words for reassurance. I can see, though, that Mom was uncomfortable with a more intimate word like "love."

I need more talismans like the baby book. One is a vinyl record of Jo Stafford, Mom's favorite female vocalist. The song "Scarlet Ribbons" strikes a chord with me. The lyrics of a little girl. The words suggest that good things can mysteriously arrive from somewhere beyond.

Chicken and Biscuits

I find the idea of a mysterious beyond from the Russian Orthodox Church. Its rituals, gilded icons, polished brass, incense, and chants stir my imagination.

Mom's family is strictly Russian Orthodox, and Dad's is Episcopalian. Neither parent is a regular churchgoer. (Although they did send me to a summer Bible school at age five, perhaps to make up for the fact that kindergarten was not yet offered in Ascutney.

The bible school was held in a Congregational church. There in the sanctuary, we napped in the pews on red cushions. The cushions were soft, but smelled musty. For fun, we children formed a line with hands on the shoulders of peers; we sang "Down by the Station" as we chugged along, a train of "little pufferbellies." As silly as it sounds, there was comfort in that, especially for an only child.)

Independently from my parents, I, at age nine, become a member of that same Congregational church, the only obvious faith group in our village. When I sing in the children's choir, or serve chicken and biscuits at church suppers, I feel a warm sense of belonging.

Dream Attic

I find a surprise stairway in our house. It's in the sunroom, the room with varnished beadboard walls and Mom's hope chest. I climb the stairs and lift a trapdoor. I step into an inviting attic-like room. It too has varnished beadboard walls, like those in the sunporch. But this dream attic is more beautiful, with high ceilings, beams, and low windows. Was this room here all along? If so, why hadn't I found it until now?

This has been my recurring dream for two or so years. It doesn't come to me every night but comes often enough. I'm certain that this dream attic exists in real life each time that I awaken. Yet when I search our sunporch, there is no stairway to an attic.

I beg Dad to let me prove that my dream attic exists. He occasionally sighs and says, "Oh, all right." There is only one way to our attic. Dad props a ladder against a stoop at the rear entrance of our house.

I climb the ladder, open a small door, and look inside. Crestfallen, I see only a low, gray, and windowless crawl space. The wood is unfinished. There are no varnished beadboard walls. Dad's abandoned violin and tennis racket lie on the dusty floor, like scabs that have fallen from a wounded life. I see nothing that resembles my beautiful dream attic.

Each time this happens, I am disappointed and saddened. It doesn't make sense. How can my dream be so vivid, so believable, and not be true?

I don't know why I'm so deeply convinced and disappointed. I dream of flying above it all, looking down at my neighbors' houses, and smiling at the sensation of gliding. I yearn to climb Mount Ascutney. If only I can reach its peak, I will see beyond my home. I'll be able to look out at the rest of the world.

Mom's drinking has become more intense. Perhaps when I awaken from my attic dream, I can more easily imagine escaping . . . to a more beautiful home.

Pencil Dots

In our village of about four hundred people, there are three or four rich families and about the same number who are poor. The rest of us are members of the middle class, some upper and some lower. We kids are aware of who has more or less, but we don't feel divided.

It's so soon after the war that times are difficult for most. I'm lucky to enjoy certain luxuries like meals in The Club. It's rare to be invited to eat in neighborhood homes. There's seldom enough food for an added person. I feel pleased and honored whenever I'm invited to share in a lunch that may consist of no more than saltines and milk or fried green tomatoes. To me, these are special treats, and it's pleasant to be in the company of other families.

Being an only child, I love my village. I mean the *whole* village. A favorite pastime, especially when sick in bed, is to draw a village of roads, buildings, and people. I tell a story aloud to myself, showing how the people move from place to place using the dots of my pencil point.

I know my village in ways that grown-ups don't. I know the nooks, crannies, and smells of homes. Each family has its own characteristics. I learn about the kind parts and the not-so-kind parts, people's differences and similarities. I wouldn't trade my village life for anything.

Cod Liver Oil

In the fall, we children raise money for our school by selling cod liver oil pills. The honey-colored gels, placed in small cellophane bags, look like nuggets of gold. They are meant to help prevent winter colds and flu. I believe we're doing a good thing as we go door-to-door, first taking orders and, later, delivering the packets of pills.

In midwinter, we sell packets of seeds for our neighbors' gardens. These packets have colorful images of flowers and vegetables-to-be. Seeds are our happy reminders that spring isn't far away.

A school contest is held every spring to help save our trees. Whoever finds the most tent caterpillar egg cases wins a prize. The egg cases look like crusty bands of silver that blend with the gray bark of twigs and branches. Perfectly camouflaged, they are difficult to find.

One classmate, Herman, lives on a dairy farm. He knows to look for the egg cases on apple and cherry trees. No matter how hard the rest of us try, Herman always finds the most egg cases. This year, his prize is a cactus that our teacher had brought home from a vacation in Arizona. He probably doesn't feel it's much of a prize, but he is proud of winning.

Life is simple here, at least in these ways.

Mud Season

During mud season, Linda and I ride our bicycles to a family's farm where sugaring is underway. With only one speed, we struggle to pedal uphill on muddy roads.

The farm family warmly welcomes us into their sugarhouse. Maple steam makes the air soft and sweet; toasty too. The children offer us tastes of delicious syrup. One grade is the color of honey. Another reminds me of molasses.

The children dash into their house and return with big smiles and a surprise plate of maple-frosted cake for us to taste.

One winter night, I stand on a stool over their kitchen stove. The mother explains how to make custard, step by step. We children take turns stirring the hot, scented pudding. With each breath, I absorb the sweet ambience of life in their home.

Hunter-Gatherers

Friends and I spend hours building forts in the woods, usually in places where fallen pine needles make a perfect floor. We use tree branches for brooms and dig make-believe firepits. Sometimes we pretend to be hunter-gatherers. Our "food" is made by crushing berries, leaves, and mosses with stones.

We bring wildflowers home to be pressed and labeled. Aunt Ede, Dad's oldest sister, has given me a book about nature. I've been using it to learn the names of wildflowers, birds, and trees.

On our way home from school, friends and I find butterflies and birds along Route 5. They, our first encounters with death, have usually been struck by a passing truck or car.

When the ground isn't frozen, I bring them home to be buried under the maple tree next to my house. In this miniature cemetery, I mark each burial with a cross made of two Popsicle sticks.

Oiled Leather

Wednesdays are the best days. The bookmobile arrives with new books for our library. Friends and I hurriedly bike there to get first pick. Our library has an air of dignity, causing us to whisper inside. I love the scent of its waxed floors and oiled leather. Whenever there, with all of these books, I feel a sense of importance.

Biographies of Clara Barton, Benjamin Franklin, George Washington Carver, and others enlarge my world. Nancy Drew mysteries and novels like *Lorna Doone*, *Little Women*, and *Uncle Tom's Cabin* carry me to new places and ideas.

On our way to the library, my girlfriends and I keep our eyes peeled for returnable bottles. Loose change comes in handy at Marston's Store. For a nickel or dime, we can buy a comic book or candy bar. We sit outside on the edge of the porch with legs dangling over the sides. I look down at my young girl legs. Shins are scraped and bruised from playing hard. Today, we and a few boys have just played a game of touch football on the village green.

Mother's Milk

School is out of session. I feel a bit lonely when there are more hours to fill. But I mostly feel free. Friends and I are happy to do nothing, especially when it's hot and humid. We lie on a grassy lawn and gaze up through the treetops. Clouds puff along in the sunny blue sky. We search for shapes of people or animals in the clouds. We thread daisies into chains or call out the model and year of a passing car. Our lazy kind of fun matches the slow-moving, languid days of summer.

I enjoy spending time next door at the Curtis farm. The Curtis grandchildren and I gather warm eggs in the henhouse. We shuck golden kernels from dried ears of corn to feed the chickens, or we weed a huge vegetable garden. Weeding in the hot sun is hard work.

I watch a cow give birth. That's hard work too. She lay still for quite a while, breathing slowly. Her big belly was heaving with each breath. When her calf was finally born, that cow was such a good mother. She licked her baby until it could stand on its own. The calf was wobbly, but knew right where to find its mother's warm milk.

One day Mr. Curtis asks me to drive a hay truck while others load the bales. Dad has let me drive his car around The Club's parking lot before, so I know a little about driving. But, at not quite ten, I doubt that I can reach the pedals. Mr. Curtis reassures me. "All you have to do is stay in first gear."

I climb into the truck, wrap my hands around the steering wheel, and extend my legs toward the pedals. While stretching my neck to see over the dashboard, I gently press on the gas pedal. The truck inches forward.

Mr. Curtis offers to pay me with a hay ride. Now that the busy harvest season has ended, we head out into the crisp and clear night air. My friends and I snuggle down into the hay. Our noses are cold but we sing and laugh as the wagon rolls along. The stars, tiny pinpoints of light, form our familiar constellations. We happily call out their names.

Marston's Store

After climbing several steps to a broad porch, I enter Marston's Store through a large screen door. Stepping inside onto wide unfinished floorboards, I'm greeted by a mixed aroma of canned coffee and spoiling vegetables. A white cat is sleeping inside the glass candy case.

Granny Marston is also napping, behind the woodstove. When up and about, she fusses with the merchandise, slowly moving from here to there. Her figure is slim and stooped. Her white hair is drawn back in a knot. Rimless eyeglasses slip down on her nose.

Her son is seated in the far corner. Wearing a green visor and glasses, he's sorting and placing mail in postal boxes. The black-and-brass postal boxes are the fanciest part of the store.

I once paid Granny Marston a dime for a classic comic book. Halfway home, I remembered that classic comic books cost twenty-five cents. I turned back to give her the extra fifteen cents. She wasn't known for her friendliness, but, with a slight smile, she handed me a small paper bag and said, "Choose any candy you want." It's safe to say that we young people regard this old general store as the heart of our village.

Enchanted Forest

Friends and I decide to explore the woods across the road from Marston's Store. We knock on the door of a vine-covered cottage that looks as though it belongs in a fairy tale. We assume the owners of the property live here. Two women come to the door. We ask for permission to traipse through their woods. Both smile. One says, "Yes, you may."

While meandering through the trees, we arrive at a clearing that's beautifully carpeted with pine needles. As though in a dream, we've come upon child-sized wooden structures: a castle, a church, a cabin, and a stage! We at first doubt what we are seeing, but soon fall into the whimsical world of imaginary play.

(I've since learned that some years earlier, perhaps before I was born, those two women had created a summer camp for children who were blind or visually impaired. That's how our village is, in part.)

Singing Sparrow

At Linda's home, we browse through books of anatomy. Photographs of skin ailments scare us in the way that kids like to be scared.

We read Rudyard Kipling's poem "If," wishing it spoke to a daughter as well as a son. Less interesting to me are afternoon television shows like *The Mickey Mouse Club* or *American Bandstand*. I prefer to head outdoors to one of our three favorite trees where we carve our initials, swing from branches, or climb to a tree house.

Beth, Linda's mother, is one of my two surrogate mothers during these grade school years. She drives me to church, where she plays the piano and leads the choir. She often takes me into her home on the nights when I can't sleep in my own home because of Mom's drinking.

Beth is a short, sturdy woman with working hands. She has raw strength, the way country women often do. Not many mothers work outside the home, but she does. At home, Beth takes care of a sizable vegetable garden, four children, and a grandmother or two.

Saturday is washday. Linda and I venture down to the basement. At the bottom of the stairs, sauerkraut and salt pork are aging in large crocks. Beth and her elderly mother-in-law are pushing wet clothes through a wringer on the back of a washtub. We follow Beth outside to help hang the laundry. Each garment is secured to the line with wooden clothespins. The clean clothing smells as fresh as a summer breeze.

On warm days, Beth hangs the laundry or works the garden wearing only a small padded bra and shorts. She sings like a little sparrow.

Total Woman

Village life isn't always pleasant. Like my life, there are good parts and bad parts. The mother of my friend Marie is what's facetiously called a "total woman," meaning she'll do anything to please her man. Pretty, with soft blue eyes, she reminds me of a kitten. She doesn't wrap herself in Saran Wrap for her husband's arrival at the end of the workday, but she does change into outfits like an angora sweater, fitted skirt, and heels.

When we arrive there after school, she is dutifully preparing dinner and baking cookies. In a motherly way, she allows us to bake a batch. She teaches us to dip fork tines in sugar and press them into the top of each peanut butter cookie. The sweet granules then bake into a scrumptious topping.

Today, Marie greets me at the front door. I can see that she is sad. Her "total woman" mother is lying behind her on the sofa, facing the flames of their fireplace. She has just learned that her husband molested Marie, his own daughter, my friend. The mother's tears are like tiny mirrors. The fire, and her pain, flicker in them. She looks both beautiful and broken.

While her mother was away having heart surgery, Marie was told to sit on the arm of her father's easy chair. Girls' pants had side zippers. She told me that her father had reached into her pants and touched her. He went to her bedroom during nights. Now that her mother has returned from the hospital, Marie has told her everything.

I can see how devastated they are, but I don't know what to do or say. The family is being torn apart. I didn't know that a father would ever do something like that. I'm angry with Marie's father, sad for her and her mother, and grateful to have my own dad.

Marie has two younger sisters. The middle daughter has an altar in her bedroom where, as a Catholic, she prays so much that I have wondered whether she might someday be a nun. I now wonder whether her father has harmed her too.

My friend and her family, including the father, have rather quickly moved away, to the other side of the state. I miss her terribly.

Red Woolen Blanket

Two other friends live at the opposite end of our village. One is from a family of three girls with a gentle mother and a strict father. He once scolded me for beginning to hum a tune at the breakfast table. Even so, I enjoy spending the night at this family's house.

Sitting around the breakfast table, we read cereal boxes and look at photos of missing children on milk cartons. We talk about kidnapping. I silently devise plans for clever ways of escaping if someone should ever nab me.

A river runs through a ravine outside my friend's bedroom window. At night, I listen to the soothing babble of the river from the bottom bunk bed. A wall lamp reflects the red color of my woolen blanket, making it a warm place for me to nestle.

Prayers are important to this friend. Each of us, lying in her own bed, recites a whole series of them to ourselves: "Our Father . . ." "Now I lay me . . ." "God bless so and so." When we ask for blessings, we try to outdo each other with long lists of people. We then compare notes. I feel clever to have thought of "God bless President Ike and his wife, Mamie."

Telephone Operator

The other friend at the opposite end of our village lives with her mother and brother. Her mother is in the process of divorcing the father, or is he the stepfather?

I've been invited to sleep over. We are allowed to watch one television show before going to bed. The room is dark except for the television's eerie blue light. We hear a noise outside and, looking through the nearest window, see a man crouched in the darkness. He stands to look at us. We duck behind furniture, out of his view.

My friend calls to her mother. I hear glass breaking. The father, or stepfather, is trying to ruin the television. Having covered my head, I can't see whether he has entered the house or has thrown something through the window. The mother calls our local constable. In about twenty minutes, the angry father, or stepfather, is taken away.

That mother is a telephone operator. To place a call, I simply lift the receiver to my ear. A voice asks, "Number please?" When I give the number, she is often on duty and speaks to me. "Marilyn, honey, is that you? How are you today?"

We have a special connection. I know that mother isn't far away, if I should ever need her help. But tonight, when she needed our help, we children didn't know what to do.

Two-Room Schoolhouse

My first and second grades are being taught in a two-room schoolhouse. Next year, when we outgrow this one, we will move to a new three-room school. Three teachers, Madames Trafton, Stillson, and Hilliard, rather than two, will then teach eight grades.

I love this two-room school. We children take turns pulling the long rope of a tower bell that announces the end of recess. A wall of windows lets the outdoors in. Clever bees find their way into the classroom through cracks in the wood.

How I look forward to each new school day. Learning is fun. Reading is an act of freedom. With books I can go anywhere in time and place. I can meet anyone and everyone. Math is a basic tool. Art makes me happy.

Women prepare hot lunch in a room behind the green chalkboard wall. Our stomachs growl as the aromas of salmon wiggle, or scrambled eggs and bacon, fill the room. School feels safe, homey.

I never wonder what the teachers and my classmates think about me missing school on Monday mornings. They must think something though. One teacher sometimes invites me to her house after school to do art projects.

Another teacher once invited me to a PTA meeting to hear a Vermont artist speak. I was the only child there. That same teacher allows me to leave my desk once in a while. She seems to understand that I need free creative time.

It's satisfying to work with powder paints. I'm surprised when each new color appears by simply mixing this with that.

Monday Mornings

Dad is the primary cook in our family. When The Club is closed, he might say, "If you can make an omelet and a roux, you can learn to cook just about anything." He then teaches me how to make both.

Each fall, Dad puts on a wild game dinner for friends. And for Christmas dinner, he prepares roast beef and Yorkshire pudding, his mother's English tradition, although I've never seen her cook.

When Mom is not in a hospital, she remains sober long enough to make a healthy breakfast and sometimes pack my lunch for school. After that, she completes the bookkeeping for The Club. Mom is then free to drink.

She does have outside help with housecleaning. I somehow have nice clean clothes to wear. Mom must see to that task. In my earlier years, she boasted that she washed and ironed fifteen shirts a week for Dad and Uncle John.

On Sundays, when the restaurant is closed, Mom drinks all day. I almost never attend school on Monday mornings. I'm just too tired. Mom will have carried on all night by coughing and moaning in bed, complaining that medicines are the problem. Or she may have challenged Dad to a fight.

School report cards verify my regular tardiness. Slipping into class late is normal for me. I think little of it.

Brick Mansion

Dad wants to visit Shelburne, Vermont, his hometown. He and Mom have invited my friend Vicki and her parents to join us. Our first stop is the Shelburne Museum, where Vicki and I are treated to rock candy. That is what I most remember about the museum.

Dad drives by the house where he was raised. We then stop at the Shelburne Country Store, where an old man sits next to a cold woodstove, sipping a bottle of beer. Dad chuckles, "Ol' John Tracy is still around." They briefly greet each other.

From there we drive through the nearby Webb estate, where Dad had caddied as a boy. Well into the property, near the lakeshore, we spot a brick mansion. I ask, "Dad, why don't you go to the door? Tell them how you caddied here." He answers with "I can't do *that*." "Why not?" I persist, still excited. He shakes his head and murmurs something about bad manners.

I don't understand. It seems like a good idea.

Moss Gardens

We now own a **summer cottage on Lake Sunapee** in New Hampshire. Dad drops Mom and me off to stay for a week at a time. He joins us on Sundays, or may spend an entire weekend with us.

I love being at the lake. My friend Vicki sometimes stays with us. Mom brings her bookkeeping from The Club. She teaches us to count coins and bills for bank deposits. We reconcile waitress slips and sort invoices by date and consecutive number. This helps our math skills. Mom can use her business training while teaching us. She had always dreamed of being a teacher.

On rainy days like this, we read, mold clay, or play cards and board games by the fire. A stone fireplace in the living area and a screened sleeping porch are my favorite features of the camp.

Mom is reading that the actress Grace Kelly has become a princess. Vicki and I are ten-year-olds. We smile at this real-life fairy tale as we head outdoors to design moss gardens. Careful not to obscure shiny bits of mica, we spread kelly green mats of moss over granite rocks. In our minds, the thin mica crystals are jewels.

After lunch, we boil water and hurriedly wash the dishes by hand. We can't wait to get down to the dock and jump into the clear, clean lake water. Lost in our imaginary world, we play mermaid among the fish, pretending to speak French, mostly underwater.

Strep Throat

During this visit to **the lake, only Mom is with me.** I'm in bed with a sore throat and burning fever. The flannel sheets are uncomfortably warm against my hot skin. I drift in and out of sickened sleep. Mom says I'm hallucinating. She tells me that I'm saying crazy things.

Three days pass. Mom uses a neighbor's phone to call Dad. He quickly arrives and drives us back to Ascutney. As our family doctor enters the house, I hear him say "Strep throat. I can smell it." He injects me with an antibiotic.

The doctor explains that, if not treated, my illness could have become quite serious. It's a relief to know that I'm not dying.

White Sweater

Mom and I have just returned home from buying my first bra at Houghton & Simonds department store in Claremont. I've hung the new purchase on the doorknob of my closet, visible from my bed.

I awaken early, pull on blue seersucker short shorts, and proudly sport my new bra under a white sweater. My girlfriends and I, when younger, had wadded and stuffed socks under our blouses, pretending to have breasts. I no longer have to pretend.

It doesn't occur to me that the sweater and bra might send a signal to the outer world. I am thinking only of myself. A friend asks me to go for a walk. We sit at the edge of the woods on a stone wall. He crudely makes verbal advances toward me. My throat tightens. "No, I don't want to do this." He's agitated. "C'mon. Why not? I've got a rubber." Thinking this might be the real thing, my mind scans images of all I'd heard about sexual intercourse. My voice changes. "No—I *don't* want to do it."

Sensing that he could be mean, I start to walk away. Thankfully, he doesn't force the issue. Disgruntled and disappointed, he leaves me to walk home alone. I am no longer a tree-climbing tomboy. As my body is changing, my world is changing.

On Becoming

Dad considers travel of any kind to be important for learning. During the winters of the mid-1950's, we vacation in Florida. Sometimes we drive to Washington, D.C., and fly from there. This year we are driving the entire way. I've settled into the back seat. The book *On Becoming a Woman* absorbs most of my attention.

Heading farther south, I notice a surprising landscape of brick-red soil. We stop at a restaurant along the way. A sign on the front door reads NO COLORED ALLOWED. WHITES ONLY. I ask my parents what this means. They try to explain but it makes no sense to them or to me. How can it be? Why? I've known of bullying and unfairness, but this is different. This has the stench of cruelty.

Goulden Ridge

Back at home, a woman named Florence has been hired to clean The Club. She has a daughter who is ten, a year younger than I am. While Florence cleans and when there is no school, her daughter, June, and I play for hours.

Florence and her husband, Bill, own Goulden Ridge, a poultry farm on the outskirts of Ascutney. Their hill farm is in foreclosure because of high grain costs. They are saddened by the loss of their sprawling white house, their green pastures, and mountain views.

I sometimes spend a weekend at their farm. In cold weather, June and I sleep in an unheated upstairs. We lie there under heavily layered horsehair blankets. The air chills my nose. Beagles bark and whine outside. A full moon makes their prey more visible.

In good weather, June and I are allowed to drive her father's car on the grassy farm roads. Only once did we accidentally drive into a ditch.

Today, we wander down to a neighbor's home. The neighbor, Helen, is a woman of the world by our standards. I'm intrigued by her newly built barn with floor-to-ceiling racks of magazines. There are thousands of them. Helen makes a good living by selling graphics from her magazines to New York advertising companies.

We've finished eating supper. June's parents are drinking too much. I guess they are drowning their sorrows. Florence sings, or tries to sing, "On top of old Smokey . . ." Bill asks "Junie" to tap-dance. As Lawrence Welk's music bubbles up from the television, June taps away like an organ-grinder's monkey. Although she is very good at it, I feel sorry for her. She'll do whatever her parents ask of her, to make life better. It is what I, another only child, would do.

The evening ends with a bowl of ice cream. We have our choice of caramel, chocolate, or strawberry toppings. I guess the dessert is our reward . . . for going along with everything.

Crushed Eyeglasses

Mom and Florence have brought June and me to our Sunapee camp, just for the day. "Go on down to the dock, girls, but don't swim without us. We'll be there in a few minutes."

June and I have waited for a very long time. We finally return to the cottage by climbing the hundred or so stone steps. Florence is inebriated. She has fallen onto the gray porch floor and is attempting to speak but is gurgling instead. Her head has crushed her eyeglasses. Mom is drunk too, but still standing.

Because Mom never learned to drive, we are depending on Florence for a ride home. Florence finally stands unsteadily. She insists on driving us back to Ascutney, a forty-five-minute trip. I can't understand a word she is saying.

We climb into the car. Florence, with damaged eyeglasses, tries to steer but we are weaving all over the road. Halfway home we spot an oncoming car. It stops. We stop. Both of our fathers walk toward us. They are angry and let our mothers know it. I wonder how they found us. I know that I will never again get into a car with a drunk driver.

Dad says he wants to sell the cottage soon, before I enter high school.

White Maggots

Our home life is difficult. Mom's alcoholism is worsening with each year. On the nights when she's inebriated, she spies on Dad. He keeps his car parked behind The Club. She opens the driver's seat door and stands on the rocker panel of his Rambler. From that perch, she can view Dad working at the bar.

Mom blows the horn until the battery runs low or dies. I try to stop her but she keeps on, convinced that Dad is with some woman or other. I've never seen or heard of that to be true. Dad is handsome and charming. There might be women who want to know him. But to me, he is the best, most trustworthy father that a daughter can have.

I adore him.

I just met up with Mom on the path between The Club and our house. While arguing with Dad, she punched her arm through a door window because he'd locked her out of The Club.

Her upper arm is cut open. I stare at exposed muscle and fatty tissue. *Fascinating*, I think. The fat looks like white maggots in the garbage cans behind The Club. I'm worried for Mom but at the same time, curious to see the inside of an arm.

I run to find Dad. He wraps the gaping wound with a towel and drives her to the hospital.

Yellow Bird

The Club isn't yet open for business. I'm in the kitchen. The swinging door to the dining area is ajar. I peek through the narrow gap. Mom is sitting alone next to the jukebox, on the other side of the dance floor. I can see that she is crying. "Yellow Bird" has just stopped playing. She drops another coin into the jukebox slot . . . and then another.

Mom is so drunk that she can barely insert the coins. She mumbles to herself, shaking her head as the song drones on with words of loneliness. The Club loses its glow on days like this.

There are other days when Mom needs a sad song to mark her place in the world. She begs me to sing the hymn "Rock of Ages." Depressing, yes, but I usually do it. Like the organ-grinder's monkey, I will do just about anything to help her feel better. I think, *This might make my life easier*. Although it never does.

Mom lives under a rock, in a bottomless pit, missing the best parts of life. I'm right there with her. Maybe sharing this hymn reveals our mutual wish to be saved.

Boiling Over

My parents have never hit me, but Mom and Dad have knock-down, drag-out fights. One Sunday night though, I got caught in the middle. Dad and I were watching *Charlie Chan*. Mom turned off the television. When he turned it on again, she threw hot coffee at us.

Mom will often blame Dad for something when he comes in from work. She'll throw things at him, or hit him, and, after a while, he hits back. I feel safe with Dad. He has never harmed me. Yet he does hit Mom when his patience thins. I understand that, but a man shouldn't hit a woman. I often try to stop them. At other times, I just listen from my room to the yelling and crashing, and worry that one or both of them could die.

After a fight, Mom lies in bed, sometimes bruised, fake coughing, or mumbling to herself in a drunken stupor, "No, no. It's not right." *Cough*. "I can't, can't. No. No. I'm sick. Ohhh, I'm sick." *Cough, cough.* "It hurts. It hurts. My medicines. It's my medicines." *Cough*. "I can't breathe. No, nooo. This is terrible. I'm dying. It's not right." *Cough*. *Cough*. "See? It's not. It's not right."

With eyes half closed and lips pressed into a line, she carries on, shaking her head and wincing. "I'm dying." She rambles on, sometimes for hours, not only after a fight. This is a regular part of her routine, but never when she is sober.

She often accuses Dad. "Look at you, Bry. Sure, Bry. You and your

Osgood's nose," referring to a drunkard's red nose. Or she says, "Look at the catarrh. I see that white in the corners of your eyes. It's catarrh. It's your drinking. I know."

At other times, Mom changes her tune with, "Everything is copacetic." She seems to find pleasure in words like nonchalant and copacetic.

Liver

Because Mom never acquired her driver's license, I refer to the family car as Dad's. His parked car is my safe getaway from weather-related thunderstorms, and from a stormy home life.

Dad has taken a day off to golf out of town. He carpooled with friends. I guess he forgot, or was not told, that I had a dental appointment five miles away in Windsor. Mom has announced that she is going to drive me in his car.

"Get in. I'll take you," she slurs. "No, I'm not going with you." I had never stood up to her, or any grown-up, but I had promised myself to never again ride with a drunk driver. She demands that I get in. I refuse and go into the house to call a taxicab.

I explain the situation to the taxi service and promise that my father will pay the driver when he comes home. Because we live in a small town, my request is granted. The taxi soon arrives. Mom tries to prevent me from leaving. She's angry with me and the driver, but we ignore her.

I arrive in time for my appointment. The dentist's door seems to be stuck. I impishly convince myself that the office is closed. In my mind, this is a cruel dentist. His manner is gruff and he doesn't use anesthesia.

My friend Vicki lives only a few blocks away. I walk to her apartment and call home to tell Mom where I am. A neighbor answers the phone. He explains that my mother has been in a car accident less than a mile from our house. "She collided with a telephone pole. She has facial injuries. Several neighbors are here with her, waiting for a doctor to arrive." Vicki's mother, Peg, drives me home.

Windsor is fortunate to have four family doctors. Three make home visits and know a lot about each family. Dr. Krause, whose wife also suffers from alcoholism, cares about my mother. He arrives on the scene and treats her with compassion. Dr. Krause pulls me aside. He softly says, "I'll make arrangements for someone from Alcoholics Anonymous to visit her."

Alcoholics Anonymous is a relatively new program. When the AA man arrives with a priest from Windsor's Episcopal Church, Mom is furious. She orders both men out of the house.

Dr. Krause returns to examine Mom. He leans toward her. With hooded blue eyes, he warns, "Mary, if you're going to keep drinking like this, at least eat liver and drink milk. You've got to protect your liver."

I usually bring suppers to her from The Club. She most often requests calves' liver . . . or swordfish.

Family Mythology

Mom has returned home from one of her hospital stays. I notice that she seems more serious, less childlike. Without admitting that

44

she has a problem with alcohol, she implies that she wants to be well. I desperately hope that she can find the strength to do so.

Three or four days pass. I'm in my bedroom when, out of nowhere, I hear Mom shrieking with terror. I run to her bedroom. Wild-eyed and shaking, she's recoiling from thousands of snakes surrounding her bed. I see nothing. Then, outside her bedroom window, she hallucinates a man with red hair. Mom is hysterical.

I run to find Dad in The Club. What happens next is a blur. Someone explains that Mom is experiencing DTs, or delirium tremens, caused by withdrawal from alcohol. Seeing snakes can be a common hallucination during DTs. I wonder why.

(Decades later, my eighth-grade son, Sam, offered a believable explanation. According to his newly found knowledge of Greek mythology, Ser, or Seth, a redheaded god, played a vital role in repelling the serpent of chaos. In Egyptian mythology, Set was a less positive god. The hieroglyph for him was found in words like illness, turmoil, confusion, and rage. The snakes, the redheaded man, and her experience of them were archetypal in nature, transcending time and space.)

Sumac Leaves

Weeks pass. Hospital visits come and go. Linda and I make our usual stop at my house after school. We can't find Mom anywhere. Linda follows me down to the cellar. I think, *Maybe Mom is doing the laundry.* "Mom, are you down here?"

We hear a moan from behind a birchbark cocktail bar at the far end of the cellar. My parents use it only for storage. Discarded furniture is stacked on top of the bar, draped in cobwebs. Mom can't be there, on the floor, in that dingy corner.

I bend down to look behind the bar. Sure enough. She's barely visible, lying in darkness on the damp cement floor. Mom is curled into a fetal position and is groaning like a wounded animal.

I run to the restaurant to see if anyone has arrived for work. Chef Stan has just parked his car. He reaches Dad by phone, and before I know it, the two of them are hauling Mom out of the cellar and into bed. I walk Linda partway home, then hurry back to our house.

Mom is standing unsteadily in our dining room, trying to call out on a business phone that only receives calls. I can barely decipher her garbled, incoherent speech.

A puddle of urine begins at her feet and slides across the already dismal yellow of our linoleum floor. The shock of it is visceral, as though coursing through my blood. *Really?* I think. *This is the person who potty trained me?*

I leave the house feeling disgusted and ashamed. Angry too, and likely sad, really sad, beneath it all. But I don't cry. My chest and stomach are tight. I keep everything in. Under stress, it's fight, flight, or freeze. I flee—and then freeze.

Dad had made a long rope swing for me behind The Club. I find myself standing there, next to a clump of sumacs. Time slows. I blindly stare toward the neighbor's dairy barn below. My hand reaches for a sumac branch. I shave its leaves with one downward movement. The leaves gather into my hand. I let go. They fall somewhere....

I sense a shadow. My quiet Russian grandfather is standing next to me. He has come from Springfield with Grammy. She must be tending to Mom. Tears stream down Grampy's rugged cheeks and jawbone. His lips quiver against the ruthlessness of grief. What has become of his beautiful daughter? He says nothing. He does nothing. He simply stands there, trying not to sob.

I look over my shoulder toward the house. Mom is being lifted into an ambulance. She is lying on a gurney, in a straitjacket.

Dad tells me that she is going to Waterbury, the state mental hospital. I don't know what that means. I'm simply relieved that others are helping us.

Mom will come home in two and a half months, near the end of summer vacation, as I enter eighth grade.

I sometimes wonder why no adult ever holds and reassures me with "Everything will be all right." Although, my grandfather did stand with me. He offered all that he had in that moment--his presence, and his own vulnerability.

The Elders

Reverend Cantwell pulls me aside after church. He says, "Our church elders have chosen you to attend a summer camp." I feel quite special, being singled out like that.

(Although I now realize the elders may have known that Mom was in the state hospital. Either way, it's good for a kid to feel special.)

Summer vacation is just beginning. The Reverend is driving me to Camp Wihakowi in Northfield, Vermont. We talk about the weather. He muses, "If we didn't have rainy days, we wouldn't appreciate sunny days." That sticks with me. My life, like many lives, is a mixture of trying days and pleasant days.

In church this minister once explained how to pray. He advised not to ask for anything in particular. "We might get what we ask for and that might not be what we need." He continued, "God knows best what we need so we should ask only for God's wisdom. Even with prayer, we have to do the work. We can't just sit back and expect things to come to us."

I like the way he talks, the way he makes me think, and wonder.

Sit Spot

I was nervous about camp. Will I like the girls in my cabin? Will they like me? Will I pass the swim test?

Well, I've passed the swim test and I like the girls in my cabin. We cover many topics as we talk into the night. Even though it's a church camp, we mostly talk about our changing bodies.

Each morning we go to an amphitheater made of rough logs. We sing out across a green valley. After that, we find our own "sit spot" in the woods, to be with our thoughts. This seems strange, at first. I, an only child, have spent a lot of time alone with my thoughts. But here it is different. I'm *choosing* to do this. Sitting on the ground, in the woods, I feel a part of something greater than myself.

At sunset we return to the same outdoor amphitheater for vespers. Two girls with beautiful voices lift our songs up and across the hills. After dinner we'll sing again, around the campfire.

This is our last evening. As we sing in a large circle, I cry at the thought of leaving, of saying goodbye.

Island Scrimshaw

With Mom still at the state hospital, my next stop is Nantucket Island. Dad's sister, my aunt Ede, lives there with her husband, Harold. This trip to Nantucket isn't my first. We have visited during other summers. One Christmas, when I was younger, Dad chartered a flight here. This time though, I'm without my parents.

Ede and Harold never had children of their own, perhaps because she, as a child, was the victim of a polio outbreak in Vermont. They instead have two springer spaniels. She dotes on them, and on me.

I look forward every year to her Christmas gifts. They arrive in a large box that might contain an entire set of the Bobbsey Twins books, a wristwatch, and a gold ring with my birthstone. She always sends a new holiday dress that I'm allowed to open on Christmas Eve. The one I most liked had a black velvet bodice and a red plaid skirt of satin.

Life here is quite different from my life in Ascutney. Ede is tall and elegant. I counted her shoes one day. There are sixty-five pairs in her closet. Her hair is done each week by a male stylist whom she adores. She comes home during her lunch break to wallpaper a bathroom, bake a cake for Harold's nightly snack, or do a load of laundry.

Their home, with its beautifully coordinated furnishings, was featured in a magazine. Aunt Ede is an above-average cook. She serves "the best wild rice," ordered by the case from Gokey's in Minnesota, with bluefish baked in milk, "because it's an oily fish." Roasted Canada goose is prepared with a prune-and-walnut stuffing. When we dine at home, my task is to carefully extinguish the candles with a brass snuffer.

Harold, a rugged outdoorsman, is a native islander. He has a deep, melodic voice and a broad, toothy grin that perfectly fits his square jaw. When he walks into a room, the whole place lights up. Harold and three other men own a 634-acre game preserve known as Ram

Pasture. He and I take the dogs there for a morning run and scatter food for the waterfowl. There, in an old Jeep, he's teaching me to drive standard shift. When I stall and want to quit, he patiently laughs with "Can't never did anything."

Preparations for a tricentennial celebration are underway. To include me in the festivities, Aunt Ede is having me fitted for a long red-and-white gingham dress. It's to be worn with an apron and a broad-brimmed straw hat.

She and Harold have rented a bicycle, giving me freedom to explore the town. I spend hours at the workshop of Jose Reyes. He's well-known for weaving Nantucket lightship baskets.

On weekends, Aunt Ede and I take long beach walks. She and my grandmother, Mimi, are turning me into a lifelong lover of walking.

We frequently dine out. The famous Opera House restaurant has menu items that I've never heard of, like Chateaubriand and Baked Alaska. We celebrated my thirteenth birthday there. Aunt Ede presented me with a bracelet of silver charms to remind me of my time on Nantucket. One of the charms is a silver peanut that opens and closes. It's meant to be a reminder of Dad. He calls me Peanut.

Aunt Ede introduced me to Haydi, a girl of my age. We sometimes sail in her boat across Nantucket Harbor to Coatue Beach. There, in the summer sun, we wade into shallow water and discover nearly imperceptible objects. Treasures to us. Moon snails have made rubbery paper-thin sand collars shaped like the neck of a bottle. When dried by sun and air, the egg masses crumble into grains of sand. As much as we want to bring our trophies home, we quickly learn to leave them in their natural place.

Ralph Waldo Emerson explains our sentiment with these words:
> I fetched my sea-born treasures home;
> But the poor, unsightly, noisome things

Had left their beauty on the shore,
With the sun, and the sand, and the wild uproar.

I again find it difficult to say goodbye. Nantucket is a place of cobblestone streets, whaling artifacts, sand dunes, weathered wood, and salty air. These impressions, like the island's scrimshaw, are now engraved in me.

Effie's Bread

Dad has driven me to Lake Willoughby in northeastern Vermont. Here, I'll spend my last two weeks of summer vacation. During the first week, I'm with his brother's wife, Aunt Betty, and their son, Rick.

Their red cottage extends over crystal-clear water with a direct view of two steep mountains, Pisgah and Hor, each on one side of the glacially carved lake. A large sleeping porch abuts an overhanging deck. A white birch tree grows through the wooden deck.

This dreamy getaway shares a sandy beach with a few other cottage owners. Frigid mountain water streams through one end of the beach. A swing set and a pit for regular bonfires occupy the other end.

An annual regatta provides a great source of entertainment for the children. Some decorate rowboats or adapt homemade masts and bedsheets for sailing. Aunt Betty's father delights us once each summer by walking into the lake until he and his burning cigar are submerged.

Three girls of about my age summer here. One friend, Carol, and I spend time horseback riding, playing with plastic horses on rocky outcroppings, or competing in games of Monopoly.

I sometimes spend the night at Carol's cottage. Her mother, who also suffers from alcoholism, sings a bedtime lullaby to both of us. I love that she sweetly includes my name. "Go to sleep, little Carol and Marilyn, go to sleep and good night...."

Each morning, Rick and I walk a dirt road in search of wild berries. A local woman, Effie, bakes bread in her home. We place Effie's bread in an old-fashioned toaster with sides that open and close. The sides press our slices against heat coils, slightly blackening the bread. This toast, spread with butter and jam, along with cereal and freshly picked berries, makes a breakfast fit for royals.

During my second week at the lake, Aunt Betty's sister Doris is taking her turn to stay at the family's cottage. Aunt Betty is leaving. Rick and I are staying on.

Both sisters are lovely and intelligent. They are gifted conversationalists, and quite stunning. Their hair prematurely whitened in their twenties. Doris, being taller, with perfect teeth and dark eyebrows, was once a professional model. She's a people person. I'm more comfortable with Doris, and though she is related only by marriage, I adopt and adore her as my aunt.

At the end of three weeks, I'm again struggling with my goodbyes, yet I can't wait to see Mom. She has returned home. I miss her. We have never been apart for such a long time. With so many days spent in the hospital, I am quite sure that she will finally be well.

Aluminum Ashtray

Dad is driving me home from the lake. I ask, "Can we stop at a gift shop to buy a present for Mom?" We soon stop at a 1950s souvenir shop. I choose two gifts: a little log cabin that burns balsam incense and a painted aluminum ashtray in the shape of Vermont.

Although Mom rarely smokes, and does so only in the privacy of our bathroom, I think she'll like the ashtray. Like most homes, ours has a container of cigarettes in the living room in case a guest wants to smoke. Ashtrays are positioned on the various tables.

We've arrived. Mom looks clear, as though deep in thought. She isn't smiling. I hug her and eagerly hand her my two gifts. She seems fragile. I move about ever so carefully, but with great hope.

A few days have passed. Mom is expressing anger by throwing the "cheap" ashtray across the room. She says she hates the gifts I've given her. That hurts at first, like a punch in my stomach, but what was I thinking? She seldom smokes, and why would she want a log cabin that burns incense? Will this make her drink again? I'm walking on eggs and have already broken one. I again feel that tightness, a defensive shield, in my chest and stomach.

To make matters worse, Mom is hurt because Dad and I never visited her in the hospital. My guess is that visitors weren't welcome during treatment. I surely didn't know that visiting was a possibility. I would have given anything to see her. And worse, Mom had endured electroshock therapy. She now blames Dad and me for her suffering.

Mom has returned home . . . to alcohol.

Maternal Notes

I will digress here to briefly describe my family history. It helps to see how previous generations pass on their struggles until the patterns are exposed, and hopefully changed.

My maternal grandparents, Joseph and Tatiana Siliski, are Russian immigrants from the area of Minsk. During the unrest that eventually led to the fall of the tsar, my grandparents fled their respective homes, leaving parents and younger siblings behind. Tatiana and Joseph arrived at Ellis Island as teenagers, later met, were married, and lived in Springfield, Vermont. They had thirteen children, only nine of whom reached adulthood. Seven of their nine adult children, including four of my aunts, attended college.

Their first home was a run-down apartment house, but they soon bought a dairy farm in Hard Scrabble, a district on the south side of town. Tatiana, Grammy to me, raised the children, tended and harvested the gardens, made the clothing, did the laundry, prepared meals, and delivered dairy products from a horse-drawn wagon. She later became an enterprising businesswoman.

I figure Grammy was either pregnant or nursing for twenty-two consecutive years. She is 5'2" and weighs about 250 pounds. She has a beautiful face. In the style of the old country, her smile reveals fine dentures with intentional gold crowns. Unless there's a special occasion, Grammy prefers to wear a traditional cotton print dress, a babushka tied behind her head, and small gold hoop earrings.

At about 5'9", my grandfather is a lean, muscular, and good-looking man. Grampy worked the farm by day. He then walked several miles into town to work night shifts as a molder at the Foundry. My grandparents' motto was "Work hard." They leaned upon their children to help with the farm and household chores. The family was held together by hard work, the Russian Orthodox Church, and a spirit of celebration.

Grampy doesn't drive or use the telephone. He quietly stays in the background. Lacking fluency in English, he relies on body language.

I've had only one conversation with him that was more than a basic greeting. It was about the importance of hard work. For emphasis, he thrust his fist into the air, a gesture he repeats whenever Nikita Khrushchev appears on television. Grampy scowls at the Soviet leader, uttering what must be Russian profanities.

My mother, a middle child, grew into a stylish brunette of medium height. Although somewhat shy and lacking in confidence, Mom can be playful and warm, even toward strangers.

She wanted to be a teacher, but attended a business college, likely because her parents thought that was a better idea.

My parents were married soon after both had completed business school. They met when working for the same company in Bellows Falls, Vermont. Dad's manager asked him to give Mom a ride home so that she would be willing to cover a night shift.

They stopped along the way to listen to spring peepers. Four months later, they were married but spent only ten days together. Dad entered the air force and was stationed in the South Pacific as a cryptographer. Mom saw him only once until the war ended. Dad's first love letter to her said, "It won't be long, Hon." They waited for three and a half years to reconnect!

Dad speaks little of his time overseas but has told me of army ants, cannibals, and diving into a foxhole for cover. I can imagine that decoding enemy messages added to the stress.

Mom claims that he returned from the war a changed man. He honorably completed his tour of duty, but medical records indicated that he had been hospitalized months before being discharged. His diagnosis: "Psychosis. Psychoneuroses. Severe anxiety type." He was 27.

I was born in August of 1946, ten months after Dad's homecoming. Eighteen months later, Mom and Dad, with her brother John, bought the restaurant in Ascutney, with financial support from Grammy and Grampy.

Paternal Notes

On my paternal side, Grandmother Alice, Mimi to me, was born in Liverpool, England. She often speaks of the River Mersey, where her father owned a successful shipping company. His early death meant that, according to tradition, the only son of four children would inherit the estate, including the business. The son, I was told, drove the business into the ground.

Mimi's widowed mother struggled to support her children's previous lifestyle. At sixteen, Mimi, in search of a more glamorous life, came to America, alone, with the equivalent of five dollars in her pocket.

She found work, first in a textile business, then as a model in New York City. Having naturally high color in her cheeks, as Englishwomen sometimes do, she was ridiculed with "Paint your cheeks, huh?" Although Mimi didn't wear "paint," or makeup, she was harassed with accusations of cheapness. Pallor was the preferred style. At that time, white women often carried parasols to block the sun.

Disillusioned, she moved to Richmond, Vermont, to live with a cousin. In search of new work, Mimi responded to an ad placed by my grandfather, Thomas M. Thompson, nicknamed TT.

I have no memory of Grandfather Thomas. He died when I was four. He was a successful businessman from Shelburne, Vermont. His first wife died after only nine years of marriage, leaving him with a son named Mark. He hired my grandmother, Mimi, to keep house and help raise young Mark.

A year later, Thomas and Mimi were married. Because she was nine years younger, they may have felt the need to marry to legitimize appearances. They went on to have six children, two of whom died in infancy.

Tragedy struck yet again. Young Mark was crushed in a gravel slide accident the day before his eighteenth birthday. Mimi often tells me how much she loved that boy, and what a fine young man he had been. My dad, their next-to-youngest child, was born the following year, in August of 1917. He was named Bryson but, until his later years, preferred to be called Tommy.

Dad grew from an undersized boy into a slender, handsome man. He's often compared to the actor Tyrone Power. If he has a physical flaw, it's that his teeth are slightly crowded, but he has a smile that accentuates his cheekbones. Whenever Dad smiles, I feel as though I'm in on something of importance. He smiles often.

As a boy, Dad explored the McCabe Brook. He enjoyed sleigh rides to his grandparents' 140-acre farm in Shelburne and horse-drawn trips to Montreal. His summers were spent with siblings at their family camp on Cedar Beach in Charlotte, Vermont.

As I mentioned earlier, Dad caddied on the sprawling Webb estate in Shelburne. He told of "the Madame," Lila Vanderbilt Webb, rewarding the caddies with hot pecan pie after a round of golf. The boys would run home by way of the greenhouses. Alexander Graham, the estate's gardener, treated them to luscious fruit grown for the Webb household, and for travelers on the Rutland Railway.

When Dad was about sixteen, his parents, Thomas and Mimi, were divorced. Divorce was uncommon and frowned upon in those years. I was told that Mimi had to justify every cent she spent. Thomas kept a detailed log of expenditures. For a woman who had been so self-reliant, her loss of freedom might have been challenging enough to drive her away.

But isn't it often true that when a child dies, the marriage may struggle to survive? The ongoing tragedies in both of their lives may have made them emotionally unavailable to each other. And I wonder whether Thomas was able to take the emotional risk of loving his new sons as he had loved Mark, his firstborn.

Without the support of counseling in those times, people often suffered in silence. Most endured. But Mimi, with a stiff upper lip, had already learned that she could survive on her own. She left.

The younger children moved to Springfield, Massachusetts, with her. Ede, the eldest, had already left home and was in pursuit of her career. She helped support her siblings so they could attend college. Their father, Thomas, refused to help. I assume he resented his children for moving away with their mother, even though they returned for visits with him.

Dad wanted to be a doctor, and would have been an excellent one, but now could only afford Bay Path, a three-year business school. When my grandfather died, his will stated something like: *One may think I have forgotten my children, but I have not. Other than my youngest daughter, Jean, my children shall receive nothing from my estate.*

I don't know why my aunt Jean was included in his will. Perhaps she was too young to have rebelled against her father.

This must have been very painful for Dad and his siblings. The divorce was not their fault. But children often assume that they are somehow to blame for their parents' problems.

Soothing Tea

I'm fortunate to have my grandmothers. They fill some of the gaps in my life.

Mimi usually lives with us between mid-September and mid-December. Today, I'm looking forward to her annual arrival at the Windsor train station. She appears in a teal-colored suit tailored to her slender, almost frail body. A violin pin, made of inlaid beads, is fastened to her lapel. Her wavy gray hair has a streak of natural white.

Scarlet fingernails are perfectly manicured, although the fingers of her right hand are stained with nicotine.

Mimi isn't one to express her feelings, but being with us seems to make her happy. She customarily adopts a living room chair that no one else can use. There, she drinks many cups of tea (later, coffee), solves crossword puzzles, knits, and smokes incessantly.

Even though I am a child, Mimi sometimes makes tea for me. Last night I was awakened by sounds in the house. I peered through my window blinds. The northern sky was blood red. Mimi appeared. She explained that a poultry farm was burning and Dad was there as a volunteer firefighter. Afraid for his safety, I couldn't sleep. Mimi soothed me with a warm cup of tea that she had mixed with milk and sugar.

As far as I know she no longer attends church, but Mimi did give me my first and only Bible, which zips shut. Attached to the zipper is a small glass globe that holds a mustard seed, to symbolize faith.

Mimi plays the piano on days when The Club is closed, and I am her only audience. Tchaikovsky's Concerto No. 1 is her favorite. She also enjoys "Look for the Silver Lining." That's her outlook on life. She has learned one song for each of her children. Cole Porter's "Begin the Beguine" is Dad's song.

I have two of Mimi's poems, written by her hand. One begins with "Child of today what have we done / that your favorite toy must be a gun." The other, "Give Me the Simple Things in Life," praises the beauty of nature, "which is free for all to enjoy."

Mimi loves to walk for exercise. Walking also feeds her spirit. When she finds the air to be especially clear, or the sunset unusually stunning, she calls me out to walk with her. Her enthusiasm spills over to me. It fills me.

When walking, she says things like, "Always pay respect when passing someone doing manual labor. Don't ever think you are more important than another person." And along another vein, she tells me that judging people by their skin color is foolish and wrong. With her English accent, she instructs, "Put your hand on a white sheet, Marilyn. Your skin's not white. Everyone's skin has a different flesh tone, from light to dark. There are many beautiful skin colors, but no one is actually white."

When Mimi was a model in New York, people made fun of her pink cheeks, her natural skin color. As an immigrant, she was, at first, an outsider without status. Her pain must have made her sensitive to the pain of others.

Family Secrets

A family secret on my mother's side is that Grampy drank heavily in his earlier years. If inebriated, he brought out a shaving strop when his children told family secrets or disobeyed him.

In my mind, privacy is one thing, secrecy is another. Privacy is a choice, kept out of self-respect or respect for another. Secrecy usually begins with pressure from others: "Don't you tell, or else." Secrets are like lies. They can lead to shame, one of the deepest of wounds. A culture of secrecy, and shame, can be generational. I can see the rot growing in my own family tree.

My grandparents bootlegged on the farm during Prohibition. Two Russian immigrants who boarded with them helped make the alcohol. That family secret was told to me by the grandmother of my friend Vicki, not by a member of my own family.

Grammy and Grampy became successful enough to make loans to Russian immigrants who had been refused by local banks. Those loans were often not repaid. Even so, my grandparents could afford to send most of their sons and daughters to college.

They went on to make loans to some of their grown children, like my parents, to start their own businesses. Grammy and Grampy sold the dairy farm when their children began to leave home. They moved to a sprawling house in downtown Springfield. But Grammy kept one jersey cow and several pigs on land south of town, near the old farm.

Being five or six when Grammy and Grampy sold their farm, only these few memories are imprinted in me: The kitchen curtains were made of dotted Swiss fabric, red and yellow like strawberries in the field and dried corn tossed to the chickens.

On my grandparents' farm I tasted the wild redness of tiny strawberries picked in the morning sun. My small hands sifted through golden kernels that I gathered and tossed from the coolness of a white enamel bowl. Eager chickens bobbed and pecked with joy.

Adorable Pigs

Three immigrants rent rooms at Grammy and Grampy's new town home. Two live upstairs. Both are named Steve. Mrs. Sirotka lives near the kitchen, next to the indoor woodshed. My cousins and I laugh when she repeatedly murmurs "Oi, yoi, yoi," her only words to us. She has yellowing white hair that's waist length, or sometimes knotted in a bun. Her figure is bent. I'm a bit wary of her ghostly manner as she shuffles from her room to Grammy's kitchen.

During summers at the town house, I enjoy walking through an arbor entrance to Grammy's garden of roses. Vibrant begonias and other colorful plantings surround the front of the house. I'm elated by their exuberance and proud of Grammy's green thumb.

The house has a four-car garage, two living rooms, two kitchens, two pantries, eight bedrooms, and a jail next to the garage. The previous owner, a judge, evidently needed a jail. Each spring, my grandparents repurpose the jail to raise baby chicks. During spring visits, I go directly to the chicks. The jail, warmed by heat lamps, smells of powdery grain. Tiny chirps and the softness of yellow fluff are my pure delight.

The old kitchen has two windows that overlook vegetable gardens, a henhouse, and the town below. There's a small pantry, two soapstone sinks, and a wood-fired cookstove. Alluring aromas of burning wood and roasting meat fill the air.

I spend many days with Grammy in the old kitchen. Homemade butter, sausage, and bread are staples. A ball of curd, wrapped in cheesecloth, hangs over a deep sink, draining and firming to become farmer's cheese. Oilcloth covers the kitchen table where Grammy works. A mug full of spoons invites her sons, and others, to drop by for a cup of coffee or a bowl of kapusta, her hearty cabbage-based soup of vegetables and meat.

A pot of food scraps simmers on the back of the wood cookstove. This savory stew is meant for Grammy's pigs, but I'd be happy to eat it.

Grammy adores her pigs and her one jersey cow. They are precious to her, perhaps because they give her a reason to keep on farming, if only in a small way. The admiration is mutual. I watch the pigs smile whenever I join her in feeding them. She speaks sweetly to them and to her cow in Russian or broken English. They, in turn, nourish her with food, and their sweet affection.

The scent of Grammy's kitchen and the love of her animals somehow blend together with her love for me.

Life isn't easy for immigrant families. Russians aren't welcome. And yet Grammy has earned respect. With only rudimentary reading and writing skills, she has learned to drive, succeed in business, and help launch most of her children.

In Grammy's Russia, the people revered the Virgin Mary. Maybe that's why Grammy believes that she, as a woman, can be strong. But, like Mary, she is also burdened.

My Russian grandmother works hard. She rules the roost. Her family is matriarchal. My own family is not, at least not directly. Mom lacks Grammy's strength, but her drinking makes her the center of attention.

Spanish Flu

Aunt Valentina lives with Grammy and Grampy. As an infant, she was struck by the Spanish flu of 1918, leaving her with special needs. Although roughly the age of my parents, she is a sweet and cheerful companion for me whenever I stay with my grandparents. We sometimes share chores like changing beds or handwashing flat linens on a scrub board. Grammy inspects our work, including the beds' hospital corners. She expects perfection.

Valentina and I sometimes walk to the town's Polish bakery to buy fragrant loaves of rye bread. We sample a slice or two when we return to Grammy's kitchen. The chewy crust gives way to a soft center with melted homemade butter. Caraway seeds add bursts of delicate flavor.

Valentina and I are allowed to see today's matinee, my first grown-up movie. *Home Before Dark*, starring Jean Simmons, is the haunting story of a woman returning home from a mental institution after having had a nervous breakdown.

I feel upset and spooked by her behavior. The woman has lost her bearings. She's wearing smeared lipstick and ill-fitted clothing. This could be humorous but is, instead, embarrassing and sad, almost sickening. (Below the threshold of my consciousness, am I reminded of my mother?)

Yellow Cellophane

I'm relieved and happy **that we've returned to Grammy's kitchen. She** asks me to sort eggs in preparation for selling or giving them away. I go to the larger pantry that doubles as her dressing room. My job is to hold each egg over a light in search of embryos. I then buff each shell with fine sandpaper. How I love the pale color and fragile nature of an egg. Each oval shape fits so pleasantly in the palm of my growing hand.

On Saturdays, Grammy loads her Cadillac with meats, butter, cheese, bread, eggs, and vegetables. Unknown to the rest of her family, she delivers quantities of food to Russian immigrants who live in South View. I learn they are called displaced persons, or DPs.

When Grammy and I arrive today, children tumble out from behind the screen doors of humble homes. Grammy whispers to me, in broken English, that the father of this home wrote a bad check. He's in jail. That's why she's bringing food.

The children's big smiles make me happy! I smile back. They proudly reciprocate by offering me a bowl of hard candies. I reach into the glass bowl and take three or four candies. They are wrapped in brilliantly colored, mostly yellow, cellophane.

Breaking Eggshells

Grammy and Grampy host robust celebrations. This offsets hard times while preserving their Russian culture. Large groups gather in their four-car garage or in a rented downtown venue. Most often, though, the new kitchen and dining room are set up for smaller parties.

On white tablecloths, liquors and mixers form a centerline. A priest usually attends. Uncle Walt plays polkas on his accordion. I love that he wears a wistful expression when playing, as though he has gone to a better place. His music makes me happy. I'm frightened, though, by other men who drink enough to stumble or fall.

Easter celebration means homemade pastries and breads, bowls of vegetables, ham, pork sausages, beef, and chicken. Easter bread, kulich, made with eggs, golden raisins, and saffron, is topped with icing and rainbow sprinkles. The abundance is a wondrous thing.

Eggs boiled in onion skins are dyed terra cotta. We pass the eggs around the table. We tap the eggshells on our teeth to test their strength. Then, with a chosen egg firmly in hand, each person tries to break another's egg. The person with the last unbroken egg is the winner. Grampy usually wins. He knows his eggs.

When celebrations like this begin to wind down, my grandmother and other Russian women of her generation make themselves known. Satisfied with their splendid feast, they lay their burdens down and enjoy a few drinks.

From some corner of the room or lawn, a high-pitched haunting song arises. A hint of grief or longing resides in their voices. How I love that sound. Even though I don't understand the words, their emotion touches my heart.

Like wild birds refreshed by rain, these women are singing out. They are staking their claim on life, in the fullest sense of the word. I, a young girl, am their witness.

Asian Sage

It's around one in the morning. Mom and I are simultaneously awakened by strange dreams. Our bedrooms are side by side so we speak aloud about our dreams. For no good reason except a sense of dread, I feel that my dream is a bad omen. Russians can be superstitious.

My dream is of a white-bearded, white-robed Asian sage lying dead in a coffin. He abruptly sits up and looks around, startling me awake. (I eventually learned that dreaming of the color white can signify death.)

Later in the day, we receive a call. My aunt Valentina has unexpectedly died of a cerebral hemorrhage. There is a customary wake. Her body is laid out in my grandparents' home on the night before the funeral.

Grammy, for reasons unknown to me, asks me to spend that night in her house. I decline out of fear. She's visibly disappointed with me. I hope to make it up to her by attending the funeral the next day.

Paper Umbrellas

Valentina's funeral is my first open-casket experience, my first encounter with human death. I am unprepared for the shock of it.

Tradition calls for kissing the deceased goodbye. As I approach the casket, droplets of holy water resemble tears on Valentina's cheeks. She looks peaceful. Her chest appears to be rising and falling with small, quiet breaths, as though she is alive. I bend to kiss her forehead. My lips meet her stone-cold, hardened skin. A startling shock passes through me: This is death! I imagine my Valentina smothered by burial, suffocated by the peach-toned lining of her casket.

As everyone is leaving the funeral I, for some inexplicable reason, decide to walk back into the sanctuary. I ask the priest, "May I kiss the cross again?" We already kissed the cross while receiving Holy Communion. The priest seems pleased. He quickly fetches the cross and holds it so that I can again kiss Jesus.

I leave the narrow sanctuary for a second time. The surrounding walls support framed prints of saintly icons. I glance at their gilded beauty. In that moment, I am enveloped by a sensation of warm light. There's a peculiar sense of knowing. Knowing what, I can't say for certain. It feels like a greater force or presence than me, one that can't be seen or touched. As I step outside, the sensation disappears. A black hearse is rolling away, toward the cemetery, with Valentina on board.

The family sorts through Valentina's belongings. The bottom drawer of her dresser is lined with souvenirs like rhinestone rings and paper umbrellas used for cocktails. I recognize them as gifts from me. She had saved every one.

My heart breaks when Grammy instructs my aunts not to give the souvenirs to me. I don't want the gifts. I simply want my love for Valentina to shine. Grammy is rarely unkind. She usually spoils me. Her retribution is unexpected and confusing. My heart feels sore.

A fear of death has settled in. For many months I've been unable to sleep without a night-light. Not surprisingly, I'm seeking extra "illumination" by reading everything from the entire Bible to Eastern philosophy, admittedly with little depth of understanding.

I am now questioning the religion of my early childhood. Biblical stories offer great lessons for life but remind me of the telephone game. Truths can be distorted as they are passed from person to person over the centuries. To me, these stories are more useful as metaphors.

Beloved Dog

My first dog, Cinders, died when I was six. We adopted two other dogs. When they were gone, Dad promised that I could have one more. We're driving to the other end of the village, across a bridge, barely into New Hampshire. He's taking me to see a litter of newborn collies. I've been offered the pick of the litter. As we arrive, I can see that one little guy stands out. He's the one. I name him Sandy.

We form a sweet bond. I bicycle nearly every day to admire my new pup until he is weaned and allowed to come home with me.

Sandy is no longer a puppy. He is so loyal that he often runs away from home to find me at school. My little friend stands with his paws on the windowsill. He looks so pitiful that the teacher often lets him into the classroom. He chews through paper bags and devours the children's lunches stored on a bottom shelf. My teacher is increasingly unhappy with Sandy and his wandering ways. Mom is equally unhappy with him.

Summer vacation is ending. I'll soon enter high school. My home life is continuing to fall apart. I've spent much of the summer with a family that manages the Windsor Country Club. While there this afternoon, the local veterinarian calls. She asks to speak with me. "Your mother has hired me to euthanize Sandy. Do you want to say goodbye?"

The animal hospital is only a mile or two away. Someone drives me there. The veterinarian meets me at the door. She shakes her head and sadly says, "I'm so sorry. There's nothing I can do." My Dad is away for the day. I, a minor, have no authority over Mom's wishes.

I walk through a swinging door, straight into the kennel area. Sandy knows I'm here. He's wagging his tail, pacing, and whimpering with excitement. I climb into the crate and say my goodbye. My throat aches. I am trying so hard not to cry. Sandy can't see my sadness. I don't want him to be afraid.

Outside, my tears flow. I sob over the loss of my beloved dog, and the loss of my mother's loyalty. Why would she do that? Was she simply frustrated by his wandering, or was she jealous of my relationship with him?

I feel betrayed, but not angry. These days, anger is rarely my response. I attempt to rise above my emotions and, instead, stuff them deep inside.

Mud Puddle

It's the Larkin family that is managing the country club this summer. Dad must have asked if I could spend my days there to get me out of the turmoil in our house. Or perhaps the family invited me because they know about my family life. Two of the sons closest in age to me are protective, like brothers.

They're driving me home this afternoon. Turning into the parking lot of The Club, we see Mom lying facedown in a mud puddle. She must have passed out while trying to walk to the mailbox.

I freeze in the company of my two peers. Even though they are speechless, I can feel their sympathy. This deepens my humiliation. I hadn't felt embarrassed by my mother until now. At a younger age, when childhood friends witnessed Mom's drinking, it was simply part of my life. But now, as a teen, peer judgment is considerable. I feel deep shame.

Shame casts dark shadows on a person. And generations of shame can layer those shadows into an opaque darkness.

Belonging

Windsor High School requires freshmen to take a full course load. I've opted for two extra electives: art and general science. I've taken the advice of family friends who urged me to study Latin and run for student council.

In the middle of my first semester, Mom is again admitted to the state hospital—against her will. Not surprisingly, I've become ill with pneumonia. Perhaps my method of coping, the tightening of my stomach and chest, has interfered with the natural flow of my breath. I'm afraid to take it all in. Grief can suffocate.

Vicki's mother, Peg, the other of my two surrogate mothers, is a trained nurse but has never practiced, except in situations like this. She urged Dad to have me hospitalized.

Here I am, the only patient in a large ward with five empty beds. Thirty or more students from all four grades are trickling in to pay a visit. Perhaps a teacher or the principal suggested it. Regardless, I feel embraced by a sweet sense of belonging.

In lieu of my own mother, Peg has come to the hospital each day to massage my back. She is the same person who, two years earlier, sat me down in her living room and explained, "Your mother has a disease called alcoholism. Did you know that? No one knows what causes it and it's hard to cure. There's usually a lot of secrecy in homes where there's alcoholism. If you ever have the need to talk about it, get it out. Talk to someone. It's unhealthy to hold it in."

Sickness

Mom's and my simultaneous hospitalizations expose the sickness of our home. It had been a year or so since Mom first returned from the Waterbury state hospital. Now she's there again while I'm in Windsor Hospital with pneumonia.

Mom's drinking escalated and my family is in a state of crisis. I can see significant changes, mostly in Dad's character and, ultimately, in our lives. Perhaps he's distancing himself from me because I need him less than when I was a young child. Or does he want less responsibility, more freedom?

I've been so focused on my peers and the excitement of entering high school that I can't clearly see, or understand, the larger picture.

Clearing Wind

Peg's explanation of alcoholism was more than a breath of fresh air. It was a clearing wind. I had, in fact, been told repeatedly not to tell family stories. Mom never admitted that she drank. Her stumbling and slurring were blamed on her surgeries and medications, although everyone knew better. As I've said, secrecy abounded in her family, and continues in ours.

I'm not allowed to bring friends into the house if Mom is speaking Russian to her family members, usually by telephone. This reveals, in part, the fear and shame that immigrants experience. Sadly, their heritage has to be concealed in order to blend in, to be accepted.

Mom told me that one of her teachers had forced her to sit on the floor, on a sheet of newspaper, in the corner of her classroom. As a Russian immigrant, she wasn't worthy of a chair and desk.

Some townspeople prevented their children from playing with her and her siblings. It's no wonder that her family's church has become a gathering place to experience not only worship, but also community and belonging.

Suit of Armor

I'm going home after spending only a few days in Windsor Hospital. Mom's stay at the state hospital will be shorter this time. Grammy has requested, or demanded, her early release.

I am, for some reason, riding in Grammy's Cadillac with three of my aunts. Grammy is reprimanding me in broken English. She is angry. "Your mother no drink. Your father drink. She no be in hos-pi-tal. He put there. He is blame. He no good."

She's lashing out at me. Grammy usually coddles me. And isn't Dad her prince? What is happening? Does she know something about Dad that I don't know? Or perhaps Grammy is covering her own shame. Denial, strengthened by secrecy, is a dangerous mindset. Her changed behavior makes no sense.

I feel wounded, confused, and small in the back of that big car, but I don't cry. Teeming emotion is pushed way down. My heart and stomach tighten. Protective armor clicks shut.

Honey Mead

Mr. Pierce, my freshman science teacher, has invited a few of us students to his home. He talks about turtle soup and shows us his homemade honey mead. We somehow drift to the topic of alcoholism. He mentions that children can become unstable when coping with alcoholic parents. I ask, "Do you think I'm stable?"

He must know about my family. Following a pause, he gives a carefully drawn-out reply. "I would say that you are"—another long pause—"*desperately* stable."

In other words, I am holding on by my fingertips, trying not to drown.
Jolted by my teacher's honesty, I can no longer fool myself. I have to survive.

My healing process is helped by Peg's earlier encouragement to speak out. Telling stories of my home life, exposing the secrets, frees me. I begin to tell my story, again and again.

Dancing and Twisting

My classmates are close-knit. We consider our class to be the best ever. Our teen hangout is called the Cinderella Spa, a soda fountain with booths and a jukebox. Everyone meets there after football games, or whenever we can.

On Friday nights, we dance in Brownsville. On Saturday nights, friends and I dance in Claremont. Most of us arrive as singles and dance in large groups, rather than as couples. "Let's twist again. . . ." We meet up with our boyfriends when the dancing ends..

I guess we are exploring the meaning of relationship. I am, anyway, through dating, and a lot of it, but all benign. There's no promiscuity, partly because I can't shame Mom. She would disown me.

Iridescent Skies

One classmate, Helen, lives across the road from the artist Maxfield Parrish. She has taken me to his studio on a few occasions. He's a striking man with a shock of white hair, a cleft chin, and intensely blue eyes. "And so it goes, and so it goes" or "And so it is, and so it is" are his oft-repeated phrases.

His studio is like a tree house, the way it overlooks the woods. The main studio's deep green and brown walls display romantic paintings, his dreamworld of lithe young women and iridescent blue skies.

During this visit, Mr. Parrish is leading us on a tour of his property, called The Oaks. After winding through his grand home, we approach a broad concrete stairway to the garden. I reach out to steady him. He shakes me off, a bit annoyed that I would think him incapable, at age ninety or so, of descending the steps unaided.

I'm thoroughly inspired by his work and his style of life.

Healing Balms

Art has become one of my healing balms. A freshman classmate and I are taking private lessons with painter and illustrator Will Hollingsworth. Still life painting is teaching me to see ordinary objects with new eyes. A dab of white on the rim of a glass suggests reflective light. Shadows, I learn, aren't entirely black.

I'm becoming more philosophical. Friends and I spend hours discussing the meaning of life. Our school principal recently spotted me in the library. He asked what I was searching for. "Eastern philosophy," I replied. The collection of Eastern philosophy books was meager. He pulled from a high shelf *The Importance of Living* by Lin Yutang.

The book nudged my adolescent brain to take a step back, invoke humor, and notice the simpler aspects of daily life that I often take for granted . . . or don't notice at all.

Another healing balm is being outdoors in nature. I'm learning more about Ralph Waldo Emerson and Henry David Thoreau. My English teacher happens to be the waitress who taught me to draw a candle flame during one slow night in The Club.

Emerson's words, in particular, are like hearing my own language spoken while in a foreign country. He helps to cement my relationship with the natural world.

The Bahamas

Tenth grade is beginning with a bang. My grades are well above average. Student council and field hockey are underway. I met a guy with a dark crew cut and equally dark eyes at the Sophomore Hop. He's quickly becoming the "love of my life."

While I'm looking forward to the winter holidays and slalom racing, Dad announces that we are moving to the Bahamas. He explains that he and Mom are going to restart their marriage. "Why don't you get a divorce instead?" I ask. The idea of moving in the middle of my sophomore year feels like the end of the world, particularly if it means leaving my friends and the love of my life.

I'd never heard him mention the Bahamas. "The Bahamas? Why?" I ask. "And why are you giving Mom another chance now?" He shrugs and murmurs, "I don't know. I guess I love her."

I can't argue with that.

The Club is sold. It's January of 1962. We're living in Pompano Beach, Florida, where I'll complete my school year. When my parents receive payment from the sale of The Club, we will move to the Bahamas.

Mother Turtle

My sprawling Florida school has open-air hallways. Assemblies warn us of STDs and marijuana. Our country is in the midst of the Cuban Missile Crisis and I am reading *On the Beach* by Nevil Shute, wondering whether I would end my life in the event of a nuclear war. I'm also reading news of possible test-tube babies. Might I be seeing the end of the world, or am I seeing the end of my world?

Mom and Dad, for the first time, have forged a wall of solidarity known as codependency. In the past, when Dad's drinking was under control, he sought help for Mom. They now encourage each other to drink. He is drinking more heavily and becoming noticeably less stable, more distant toward me. This change, added to homesickness, doubles my sadness.

My walks home from school aren't like walks in Vermont. When I'm barefoot, the Florida pavement scorches and blisters my feet. Lawns prick my feet with sandspurs. I despise all the limos and miss my mountains. Cars spew exhaust into the muggy atmosphere. People seem to be less grounded than Vermonters, more caught up in materialism. After school, almost every day, I cry in the shower, without being seen or heard.

Payments from the sale of The Club have not yet arrived. For extra cash, Mom works at Nettie Milgrim's, a women's fashion store. Dad is the interim manager of a cheesy pink motel. Its cheesiness reflects the downturn in their lives, and in mine. The motel's small courtyard has a mango tree with rash-producing sap drippings. Monstrous palmetto bugs hide in our drawers of clean laundry.

Dad awakens me at midnight. He wants to search for sea turtles. After searching the beach for about ten minutes, we spot a large form on the high side of the beach. Here, in the moonlight, we have found a spectacular turtle. She is digging a pit with her rear flippers. Her size takes my breath away. We stand next to her while she drops precious eggs into the hole.

Mother turtle, again using her flippers, buries her clutch with sand. This ancient-looking, solitary figure, lighter now, turns and slowly plods across the beach into the vast ocean. She doesn't know whether any of her offspring will survive, but she has done her best.

Green Mountains

Soon after school lets out for summer vacation, Dad's only brother Shirl dies from a self-inflicted gunshot to the head. He had been a reticent man. During hunting trips in Vermont, he would remain near the car rather than venture off into the woods. The other hunters teased him, but shooting a deer, or any animal, was unfathomable to Uncle Shirl.

Dad makes plans to attend the funeral in Connecticut. I announce, in no uncertain terms, that I intend to go with him. He agrees. Mom will stay behind to operate the cheesy motel. Dad and I will drive to Vermont after the funeral.

We leave Connecticut. My heart swells as we cross the Massachusetts/Vermont border. The Green Mountains soon come into view. Oh, they are beautiful! I am home again.

Peg, my surrogate mother, invites me to spend the summer with Vicki and the family. I've somehow convinced my parents that I should return to Windsor High School.

Mom's and Dad's sales agreement must have been faulty. They have not yet been paid for the sale of The Club. Their savings have been depleted. They've also depleted my meager but not insignificant savings. Mine were from government bonds and cash gifts, mainly from Grammy and Aunt Ede.

Dad returns to Florida without me.

Hotel Moody

Mom and Dad return to Vermont as I'm entering my junior year of high school. They are planning to operate The Club again. How fortuitous it will be for them to return to their liquor supply!

We have temporarily rented an attractive townhouse on the outskirts of Windsor. It has high ceilings, a near view of the Connecticut River, a fireplace, and French doors that separate our spacious kitchen from the living room.

Grandmother Mimi is living with us this fall. She has become more uppity in her later years. The immigrant work ethic of my mother's family does not blend well with the more aristocratic roots of my grandmother.

One of Mom's guests today sits in Mimi's living room chair. Mimi stomps on the guest's feet. Mom now regards Mimi as her enemy. Dad has no choice but to move his mother to the Hotel Moody in Claremont, where he has taken a temporary bartending job.

Dad seems to have reached a low point during these months. The sale of The Club has failed. His plan to move to the Bahamas has failed. He must be both embarrassed and depressed about the loss of their savings.

Mom whispers that she fears he, like his brother, might take his life. She tells me that he is, at this moment, in the cellar with a gun. I haven't seen signs of this and don't know whether to believe her. Although some part of him *has* changed, broken. Dad's now like an empty shell.

We have moved back to The Club. Our new home is not our original home. It's the apartment across the parking lot, behind our Laundromat, the former grocery store.

I spend the night with my friend Vicki and her family. The phone is ringing. It's after midnight. When Mom is on a drinking spree, she often plagues their household with late phone calls, particularly when I'm here. I vaguely hear Vicki's mother, Peg, answer the call. She lowers her voice. I fall asleep until morning.

Peg tells me that my parents were driving two waitresses home from The Club during a snowstorm. A tractor-trailer truck carrying a load of Christmas trees jackknifed in the road. The truck's taillights were invisible. Dad's car collided with the truck. Peg will take me to the hospital to see them.

Dad is receiving blood transfusions. Mom has suffered a broken neck. Both are in the hospital, but Dad should be released in a couple of days. Mom, being in traction, will be confined for a longer period. The waitresses have minor injuries, although one did bite through her tongue.

Chambermaid

Eight of us girls from Windsor and Springfield high schools work as chambermaids in Old Orchard Beach, Maine over summer vacation. Vicki and I are laid off because business is slow and we are the youngest. Relieved to return home, I find another chambermaid job at a Lake Sunapee motel.

With a driver's license and my own spending money I have greater mobility and am quite removed from my home life. My high school peer group is of greater importance to me.

Mom and Dad continue their codependent relationship, each covering for and encouraging the other to drink. Dad's responsibility for me must have kept him in balance when I was younger. As I become more independent, his drinking increases. He's never been a falling-down-slobbering or mean drunk, but he associates with other drinkers, bums in my mind. Our emotional distance is smoldering.

Mom remains solitary and secretive when imbibing alcohol. As a result, she never asks me to bring liquor to her or drink with her. I'm grateful for that.

Surrender

I've resumed a rocky relationship with the love of my life. He wants to break up with me. According to him, the relationship can't go anywhere because he's from "the wrong side of the tracks." I think he means that his future is limited.

Dad has tried to discourage me from seeing him, as have some of my teachers. I've argued that he is more respectful than other guys, but do eventually surrender to the breakup.

This is the first and only time that I briefly imagine harming myself. I might do something crazy, like drive into a tree.

Prom Queen

I'm crowned queen of the Junior Prom. As it is announced, I hear my mother shout out with pride from a seat in the auditorium. She rarely attends my school functions. I don't know how or why she happens to be here tonight.

Perhaps it's because we had enjoyed one of our epic experiences by shopping out of state for my gown. Whatever the reason, I'm pleased that she's pleased. Maybe this will stop her drinking, even if my grades have not.

My prom date is driving me to Claremont where Dad is tending bar at the Hotel Moody. I'm standing in the bar's dusky light with my brown hair coiffed in a shoulder-length flip. Surely the news, not to mention the sight of me in my pink chiffon gown and sparkling tiara, will please him.

His face exhibits no expression. He barely nods. My heart sinks. Dad, despondent and unfamiliar, is emotionally gone.

Scarlet Nails

Now that Mimi is living at the Hotel Moody, I try to see her once a week. She's in her small room as usual, only today, she's writhing in pain. Dad is downstairs, setting up the bar. I run to tell him. He follows me upstairs to see her condition and immediately calls an ambulance. I follow Mimi to the Claremont Hospital. Dad doesn't come along.

I've been sitting in the hospital waiting room for some time. Two doctors finally approach me. They explain, "We're sorry. Your grandmother has passed." I nod and look toward the door of her room, trying to absorb the news.

Having steeled myself, I step into the stillness of her room. Window blinds are partially open, allowing sharp blades of afternoon sun to enter. The light exaggerates my grandmother's death. Mimi's arms rest on a white sheet. I notice her scarlet fingernails and nicotine stains. And there's that white streak in her gray hair. I weep. What a sad and lonely goodbye ... for both of us.

Back in the waiting room, I see that Dad has arrived. I tell him Mimi has died, but he already knows. He shows no emotion. I don't know what to think about any of this.

All-Night Diner

Ruth, a new employee, is cleaning The Club while I eat lunch at the empty bar. Dad may have talked to her about me. Or perhaps she senses that I am rather lost. I can see that in photos of me. My eyes are vacant, sad.

Ruth tells me that her grandmother raised her. "There are so many things I wanted to say to her before she died, but I never did." Ruth continues, "If there are things you want to say to your father, do it while you can."

I arrive home at around one in the morning, having been out with friends. I don't have a curfew because it's usually better for me to be out of the house. Dad is sleeping on the sofa. He and Mom often sleep separately, due to some argument or other. He hears me approach and stirs. "Dad, I want to talk to you."

He springs from the sofa, throws on his clothes, and leads me out to his car. After driving and talking for about three hours, we finally stop at an all-night diner for a bite to eat.

I ask, "Why did Mom spend such a short time at the state hospital that last time, and why are you still with her?" He explains, "Patients can no longer be committed to a mental hospital without their own consent. Her mother asked for her to be released." Dad doesn't explain why he and Mom are still together.

Even though nothing is resolved, I am comforted by his eagerness to talk and our time spent together. We've become less distant, but we haven't reestablished our earlier closeness. I wonder, though, why I had to invite Dad to discuss the confusing events of our life. *He* is the adult.

French Toast

After talking with Dad, I have an urge to clean, to purge. This isn't the first time. At a younger age, my lavender bedroom called for Lestoil cleansings. I even scoured the mattress and hung my laundered bedsheets outside to dry in fresh air.

Today I've set out to vacuum and mop the floors, wash the dishes, and clean the bathroom. As I finish, Mom is crawling out of bed. Her eyes are thin slits. She makes her way to the kitchen and manages to prepare French toast. I watch as she douses it with maple syrup. Trying to steer her way to the living room, she tilts from side to side, tipping the plate. Syrup drips across the floor, forming a long sticky ribbon. I am enraged. My words pour out. "I hate you! I wish you were dead. You're disgusting. . . . I *hate* you!"

Instead of crying, I've learned to defend myself with quick, biting words, often with sarcasm. I've become skilled at lashing out. And, of course, almost anything can be said to my inebriated mother. She won't remember.

With a loud growl of disdain, I storm through the screen door, slamming it behind me. In a blind fury, I cross the parking lot and enter The Club. After marching through the dining area to the kitchen, I yank on the handle of the walk-in refrigerator door and step inside. I stand in the cooler long enough to numb my emotions.

Something stirs my attention awake. Lobsters are crawling against each other in a crate near my feet. They make a scratching sound. I look down at their protruding eyes and antennae. We connect.

I'm reminded that Dad taught me to stand lobsters upright, with tails curled beneath them. He showed me how to put them to sleep by rubbing their backs. These innocent bystanders snap me out of my tantrum.

Somber Silence

My senior year, 1963–1964, is a time of turbulence. The United States is backing a coup in Vietnam. Beatlemania infects my generation, mostly in a good way. The music of Dylan, Baez, and others is causing a rebellious stir. The women's liberation movement, the sexual revolution, and an emerging drug culture have set society into motion, like a boomerang that spins away and returns, often with unintended consequences.

It's Friday, November 22, 1963. President John F. Kennedy has been assassinated. Linda and I are at her house, watching the news unfold. A bereft Walter Cronkite explains that we humans must talk repeatedly about the tragedy, to help process our national shock, our grief.

During one of these early newscasts, I saw live footage of the accused assassin, Lee Harvey Oswald, escorted through what looked like the basement of police headquarters. Oswald glanced up and shouted, "I know you, you son of a bitch!" He was then shot by Jack Ruby, who, I understood, was also being brought into custody. That moment, which I never saw televised again, raised new questions about trust.

Tonight I'm with a date at Dartmouth College. We're watching televised commentaries and replays of the assassination on an enormous screen. We, with other young people, stand in somber silence, groping for an understanding. None of us has experienced such a singular national tragedy. We've lost our father figure. And losing a father figure resonates with me on another level. My grief is compounded.

On a happier note, my summer before college is beginning with a waitressing job at the Woodstock Inn. Several of us young people reside there. We waitresses cover all three meals but are well cared for in return. I hope to have the same job next year.

Stakeholder

High school friends and I remove surveyor stakes used to mark construction of Interstate 91. Our mild version of teen rebellion appears in this form of activism.

Removal of the highway stakes tells a greater story though. It's the story of uprooting a life, which likely strikes a chord in me.

The farm and woods where we played in earlier childhood belong to a solitary character, Romaine Tenney. He is a slightly stooped older man with a long grayish-white beard. He's reclusive, but we respect him and know that, if encountered, he will be friendly and cheerful.

His home, on the south side of Ascutney, had been in his family since 1892. The house, noteworthy for its gingerbread trim, sits opposite a barn full of cows and two teams of workhorses. The rumor is that Romaine often sleeps with his barn animals for warmth.

Now, the State of Vermont has decided to take the property by eminent domain to construct the new interstate highway. Sadly, Mr. Tenney burned his buildings and died in the fire. A shotgun was found in the rubble. People believe he committed suicide as the fire worsened. Mr. Tenney simply wanted to live out his life in the home where he was raised.

Construction is now moving ahead. Our beautiful village will forever be changed by the highway's intersection with Route 5. An interchange will replace the village green and all that it represents.

The highway may turn out to be beautiful and useful, but Mr. Tenney's home, and his place in the world, are forever lost. Mine too. On a deeper level, I know what it means to have a disrupted home.

Art Major

When younger, I had two visions for my life: to be a surgeon and to be the mother of three children. Women aren't encouraged to be physicians. Expectations are to possibly get a job, usually in typically female areas of employment, get married, and have children. Very few mothers work outside the home. After all, women achieved the right to vote only as recently as my grandmothers' generation.

I've concluded that it would be difficult to balance a medical profession with mothering. With no backup plan and feeling overwhelmed by the process, I've asked Dad to help me sort things out. He reminds me of my interest in art and home interiors. It is true. When driving at night, I enjoy the sight of different homes. Glimpses of their interiors stir my curiosity about life in the lighted rooms behind darkened windows.

Dad suggests that I study interior design at a two-year college. "If you like it, you can go on to a four-year school." (His suggestion might have stemmed from the botched sale of The Club and his loss of income, but that does not yet occur to me.)

Following his advice, I've applied to a junior college in Massachusetts. Its internship program appeals to my interest in experiential learning. I will study interior design as an art major.

Fresh Violets

I spent the summer as a waitress at Vermont's Woodstock Inn and have entered college. The Massachusetts North Shore campus flaunts its ocean setting and pleasing architecture. Boston's nearby cultural life has attracted a talented faculty, making the art department quite impressive.

Even so, I have never been this melancholy. Mom hasn't written or called. She and Dad haven't visited. And although I'm making new friends, I miss my high school friends.

So this is what it means to cut the apron strings. Even though I have already been on my own, I now feel like a helium balloon, floating aimlessly off to who knows where. When one leaves the known to face the unknown, it's like a mini death. A sense of loss settles in the pit of my stomach. And yet, most of my friends are experiencing the same thing.

I seek nourishment off campus. There's one popular coffee house, the King's Rook. My regular date and I soak up its bohemian atmosphere while sipping Darjeeling tea and enjoying musicians like Jean Redpath and Phil Ochs.

My favorite getaways are to other college campuses and art museums like the Boston Museum of Fine Arts and the Isabella Stewart Gardner Museum.

The Gardner Museum feels, to me, like sacred space. At Isabella's request, her home has been left intact. I'm astonished by the stunning works of artists like Titian and Vermeer.

There, on Sundays, a string quartet lifts my spirit. Small bouquets of fresh violets have been carefully placed on antique furnishings, adding new life to Isabella's dormant past.

Memories of my own past are also becoming dormant.

Interior Design

My internship is with a Boston firm that designs hotels and restaurants. The tasks initially assigned to me are menial, but they become more challenging. I assist others in their designs of the Prudential Center in Boston and Hotel Bonaventure in Montreal.

As a young child, I accepted life as it was. Now, I'm searching for more. This internship will bolster my résumé for the job hunt that'll follow graduation. This country girl wants to be in Vermont, as an interior designer. (And I likely need to redesign my interior self, and my idea of *home*.)

PART TWO

On the Wagon

It's August of 1966. The days are sizzling hot. I'm in Burlington, Vermont, for a string of job interviews. The city's only interior design firm is too small to hire another designer. Several architectural firms have no openings.

Charlie, a partner of Linde-Hubbard Associates, leads me on a tour of his firm. Most interesting is a large design model of Burlington's waterfront that offers greater public access. A local development company, on the first floor of the building, is planning an urban renewal project for the city. The office is abuzz with ideas.

"What is your preferred school of design?" Charlie asks. My sophomoric response is a quote from Ayn Rand's novel *The Fountainhead.* "What do you hope to earn?" he continues. I reply, "Four fifty an hour."

He agrees to hire me on a trial basis at $3.50 an hour. If I survive the trial period, my pay will increase. Health insurance, a pension plan, and paid vacations will be added. I'm thrilled.

The bold high school classmate who had found me my summer job in Maine and at Vermont's Woodstock Inn had already secured a Burlington apartment. I, with seven other young women, have agreed to share two small side-by-side units on the top floor of the Ormond apartment house on Burlington's North Winooski Avenue. Ready to move into my adult life and focus on my new job, I choose to spend as little time there as possible.

Our office occupies the second and third levels of a three-story building. Natural wood floors and brick walls define the office interior. Movable Homasote partitions provide privacy between drafting tables. Third-floor windows offer grand views of sunsets, Lake Champlain, and the Adirondack Mountains.

There are two female associates in the reception area, plus twenty-one designers and draftsmen—all of whom are men, except me. My drafting table sits between Jerry, an architect, and Clyde, a project manager.

(I cannot imagine that one will later be my husband and the other my stepfather-in-law.)

Architectural offices operate differently from most businesses. One might show up late in the morning but then work past midnight when "on charette." The term, which originated in nineteenth-century Paris, refers to a cart or wagon collecting drawings for student exhibitions. Being on charette simply refers to collaborative and intense work on a design, usually over several days.

The office is an unforgettable place to work. Italian operas or Greek serenades by Theodorakis or Nana Mouskouri play from a bulky old tape recorder. An eccentric architect and bon vivant, Peter Woodside, provides the music.

Florentine Teapot

Peter, whom we refer to as Woodside, lures coworkers to martini lunches, usually at The Lotus, a Chinese restaurant on Church Street. There are few places to eat in Burlington: Bove's, the Black Cat Café, The Park, The Lotus, and Henry's Diner.

Nearly every morning, Woodside arrives at the office later than everyone else, usually with a dramatic alibi and a "Mea culpa, mea culpa, mea culpa." One of his more memorable sagas involves a mouse whom he has dubbed Torpelina. As he reports on the poor mouse, his facial expressions range from pinched grimaces of frustration to impish grins, revealing an endearing gap between his upper front teeth.

He claims that Torpelina has made a home in his Florentine teapot. Each morning he tosses her out of the house, through the back door. She repeatedly and defiantly returns to his kitchen. He waits to scoop her up with a dustpan and whisk broom, only to toss her out again.

We, his audience, pretend not to enjoy his tales of woe, and his excuses.

Golden Thread

There is a hierarchy between designers and draftsmen. And yet general harmony exists. One exception is Fred, who barely engages with the rest of us.

I now understand his somber moods. He shared his story during a business trip. In the final stages of World War II, between January and April 1945, Germany had forced the evacuation of thousands from Poland. Fred had been only a boy. His feet were protected from wintry conditions by no more than newspaper and rags. The suffering was indescribable. I was moved by his will to survive. Fred's willingness to share that story with me was heartening. But in the office, he remained a solitary man.

Road trips have a way of opening conversations. Another survivor, Willem, also shared his story during a road trip. Captured as a boy during World War II, he chose to go with the men rather than stay with his mother. That choice led him to a concentration camp where he was tasked with hard labor. To survive, he improvised with scraps of metal and wood and proudly discovered that he could trap rats for protein. He found an uncle in the camp and later came upon his own dying father.

When I asked how he could be so positive after such a terrible experience, he replied, "My family instilled in me the belief that there is a golden thread." He laughed through a clipped Dutch accent. "Ya, I just held on to that golden thread."

Pilgrims

Several of us in the office regularly drive midweek to Montreal for the Alcan architectural film series. This same group travels to see architecture in other cities. We've seen Alvar Aalto's work in Cambridge, Massachusetts, and Richardson's Paley Park in New York City. We are now visiting Louis Kahn's First Unitarian Church of Rochester, New York.

We're poking around the sanctuary of Kahn's building. Woodside happens to peer through a slot window that's thoughtfully placed within dense concrete walls. He suddenly gives a shout of recognition. "Look, look! It's Lou Kahn!"

There, staring back at us, is Lou Kahn himself. He has come to inspect the sanctuary and its new acoustic wall hangings, meticulously designed by Jack Lenor Larsen.

We see for ourselves how the woven fibers soften sound, how colors enliven walls that would otherwise be gray.

Life Science

The Life Science Building at the University of Vermont is my first interior design assignment. Because I lack real-world design experience, Charlie has recruited Sue Sekey from the New York office of Marcel Breuer. Sue happens to be traveling regularly to Montreal to finalize design details on the Resources for Man Pavilion at Expo 67. Vermont is a convenient stopover.

Sue is a petite and spunky redhead. We are reviewing floor plans for my first tutorial. She explains that one must find a theme for the design. In this building the corridors on each of the floors surround a rectangular core of mechanical systems. She suggests that I use a theme color for the walls of each floor's core. The color might represent an aspect of life science: soil (terra cotta), water (teal blue), sun (ocher yellow).

Sue shows me how to list the finishes on the specification pages toward the back of the drawings. Finishes range from paint, flooring, and carpet to metal window frames and brick mortar.

I am finding it difficult to choose paint colors. When applied at the construction site, north versus south light, or changing times of day, radically alter the same color choice. Thankfully, the contractor is patient with my steep learning curve.

Jane Street

Sue Sekey is an expert at finding unusual furnishings and fabrics. Woodside met her during their earlier days at I. M. Pei's office. He accompanies me to New York, where I'm learning my way around the leading design houses, thanks to Sue's introductions.

We have been invited to her walk-up apartment on Jane Street in Greenwich Village. I find it difficult to believe that anyone can live in such a small space. Although Sue's pastel-blue kitchen walls, carefully placed bentwood chairs, and a painted table for two make her home remarkably charming. Still learning from her, I absorb every design detail.

Because of Sue's connection with Expo 67, many of us at Linde-Hubbard are taking regular weekend journeys to Montreal. We try to see everything, like Buckminster Fuller's geodesic dome and Moshe Safdie's housing complex that blends the architecture of cliff dwellings with that of a Greek village.

I've left home and am discovering an exciting new world, a larger world of creative people and ideas. Sue tells me with confidence, "This is when life truly begins."

Dream Attic

I'm riding with Clyde, the project manager whose drafting table is to the right of mine. We are on our way to inspect construction progress at a high school in the northeastern corner of Vermont.

Clyde stops along the way to shoot every remarkable scene. He's hoping to one day build a photography business.

Because I have a new Nikon camera, Clyde occasionally brings me to the Webb estate in Shelburne, where he and his family rent a house. If there's an unusual ice formation or sunset, he'll say, "Grab your camera!" We rush out of the office during lunch break.

Today, during one of those adventures, Clyde asks me to stay with his three daughters while he and his wife go away for the weekend. I gladly agree.

He explains, "The estate's mansion has just been opened for the summer. Mrs. Webb has invited you to bring my daughters for a tour.

She'll also give you passes to the Shelburne Museum."

Two days later, the four of us enter the front door of the mansion. We are greeted by a staff person who invites us to step into a large room. A lovely young woman in tennis whites is skipping down the main staircase. An older gentleman in a yellow V-neck sweater follows her at a slower pace. Presumably on their way to the tennis courts, they greet us with smiles. The staff person permits Clyde's daughters and me to walk through the house and take a look around.

We make our way through the second floor. I'm struck by the eclectic decorative styles that range from Colonial American to French Empire. Each bedroom has a name. Each door has a glass knob that reminds me of a seer's crystal ball.

The door to the Yellow Room is open. In one bed, closest to the door, I spot a teen's mass of curly hair. He is sound asleep with one arm dangling over the side of the bed. My thoughts are, privately, a little judgmental. It's near noon. I'm slightly bothered by this. It's like seeing my mother asleep on a perfectly sunny midday.

Another staircase appears as we walk farther along a red carpet. While taking the stairs, I notice how pleasant the elaborate wooden rail feels to my hand. At the third-floor landing, we see two more bedrooms and a bathroom. We turn right to enter a children's playroom.

With a jolt, I recognize the varnished beadboard walls, the high sloping ceilings and beams. It is the attic-like space of my childhood dream! How can it be? Although nearly forgotten, I now recognize this as the room I saw in my recurring dream. I have found it, but not in my own childhood home. A quiet sense of knowing settles in. I experience this moment of affirmation internally, at my core.

The ladder climb to the actual attic in my childhood home was more difficult than taking the stairs to this attic. The attic in my childhood home was dark, with walls of unfinished gray wood. Its only contents were a tennis racket and violin, discarded from my father's younger years.

It seems fitting that *this* room—the attic of my childhood dream—is a sunny children's playroom with beautiful toys.

(And yet, given the swirling excitement of my new life, thoughts of discovering the dream attic quickly fade ... for now.)

Radio Waves

I attend a lecture at a private school here in Vermont. Architect and philosopher Buckminster Fuller is speaking:

"When we search for and select a radio channel, we know it's there. We can't see the invisible radio waves but know they exist because we can hear the transmitted sounds. In other words, much of our reality is invisible."

Mr. Fuller speaks of the metaphysical world. His words validate my inexplicable experiences, like recurring dreams that materialize.

Total Immersion

Rachel Carson's *Silent Spring* has awakened society to conservation concerns. The United States is involved in the unpopular Vietnam War. The 1960s civil rights movement has raised questions for which there are no answers. A cultural revolution is challenging all establishment values, whether manners or morals. And a drug culture, both prescribed and illegal, is growing. If World War II produced veterans who found solace in tobacco and alcohol,

Vietnam War veterans, and college students too, have discovered everything from marijuana to psychedelics.

Meanwhile, we at the office are immersed in creativity. Ideas flow in abundance. One of our architects reflected, "This is a time when only a good idea is needed to make something exciting happen. There are very few obstacles."

Mom and Dad are continuing their dysfunctional life in Ascutney. That life is, to me, becoming a lost memory. Or the memory is temporarily hidden, buried in my subterranean conscience.

While becoming immersed in work, old wounds are hiding beneath the surface of my skin. They have not healed. My wounds open and ooze from time to time. I struggle with jealousy in my intimate relationships, mainly due to a lack of trust.

Without realizing it, work is becoming my comfort zone, an obsession. It's one way of glossing over the wounds.

My new job is to choose interior finishes and furnishings for a dormitory, a dining hall, and an auditorium at Johnson State College.

Work on the dormitory involves designing built-in furnishings and selecting items for the lounge areas. I've met with a woman named D'Ann from the Vermont Arts and Crafts Service. She's helping me find local craftspeople to make lamps, wastebaskets, and similar items. My hope is that students will treat the furnishings with greater respect if they know how, where, and by whom they were made.

The college design projects complete, I begin design work on a courtroom for a new state office building in Burlington. During a morning break, I walk to the lower floor of our office for a cup of coffee and a cigarette.

Our head designer, standing next to his drafting table, looks across the room toward me. In the presence of two or three others, including a charming engineer from Montreal, he begins a rant. "Your stupid craft ideas are kindergarten ideas. You have no business working here. It's small-minded stuff you're doing. You don't belong here. We're trying to do high-level design. You're doing arts and crafts." On he goes, addressing me at full volume.

He is bothered by my choice of handcrafted furnishings for the college dorm.

My stomach seizes. I freeze long enough to absorb what is happening. Then, well trained from childhood, I draw in a deep breath and, on the exhale, say with full force, "I am not going to stand here and take this from you. You can't speak to me this way! I have absolutely no use for you." I turn, leave the room, and quit a couple of days later.

Others report to me that when that man, known for his temper, later rummaged through my work cubicle, he confessed to having made a mistake.

I've since learned that some of my male colleagues had complex interpersonal relationships. Perhaps that bellicose colleague wanted more attention from me, or from the man I was dating. Either possibility may have caused his unseemly and devastating outburst.

Blocked Arteries

Jerry and I are dating. He's the architect whose drafting table is to the left of mine. Nine years older than me, he has my father's slender build, sports a beard, and smokes Amphora pipe tobacco.

Jerry was raised in a quiet and conservative Cincinnati home. Honest and earnest, he has a strong desire to make the world a better place by design. When making an impassioned point, he lifts his eyebrows and enlarges his pale blue eyes. His voice is soft.

We fall into a relationship. Because women usually marry after college, I am putting some pressure on him to propose. He was burned by a college sweetheart and is reluctant to commit again. So, unwed, we live together for a while.

Jerry introduces me to photography. We take an interest in planning. Sadly, Burlington's urban renewal begins with the demolition of an Italian neighborhood, documented by my camera. That moves us to get involved.

Meetings in our apartment include another architect, an attorney, and a judge to discuss the revival of Burlington's downtown. One member of our group warns, "The heart of a city is like a living heart with arteries to supply a lifeline. If those arteries are blocked, the heart dies." All of us can see how access to Burlington is plugged with sprawling suburban growth. Strip development has replaced truck gardens. The city center is dying.

We discuss the way European farmland directly borders cities and towns. The cities are connected by trains, not only by cars and trucks. Suburban strip development is discouraged. Farmers' markets connect rural lands to cities and towns. Bypassing middlemen, farmers earn a greater profit through direct sales. Urbanites purchase food at lower prices, learn how their food is grown, and gain respect for farmers. Urban and rural areas are interdependent, rather than at odds.

Jerry and I develop a "regional concept" based on these ideas. We envision reduced transportation costs, smaller units of governance, and a deeper sense of place.

Our first step is to strengthen rural areas by creating a farmers' market. The rest of our group joins others to revitalize Burlington. They hope to create a pedestrian mall and urban marketplace.

Jerry leaves Linde-Hubbard to work at another firm. In our spare time, we freelance in design work and photography. An ad agency hires us to document Vermont's rural landscape, including the encroachment of poor planning. On weekends, we explore the state's beautiful countryside.

Barns and farmhouses have their own kind of beauty. Grand farmhouses remind us of an earlier era of agricultural dignity and affluence. Today, their front porches tell the story of country life. Rocking chairs, hanging laundry, flowering vines, and tidy woodpiles are statements of simplicity.

Natural Areas

While working on the Life Science Building, I was introduced to a professor who taught me that all in the natural world is interconnected. He hires me to take photos of natural areas. We spend many hours photographing carnivorous pitcher plants in local bogs, fragile alpine flowers in the mountains, and exquisite native wildflowers in the woodlands.

Jerry converts his second bedroom into a darkroom, allowing us to develop the film. In trays of liquid chemicals, images of various plants magically emerge. I'm excited by the process, even though the tanginess of chemicals catches in my throat.

The professor also has a darkroom where more than film is developed. A relationship grows. I find warmth in the confinement. And darkness fosters the secrecy that is so familiar to me. He flatters while speaking of a future that will never be. Because he is married, boundaries are kept while he teaches me about ecosystems and natural areas.

Wedding Planners

Jerry and I decide to marry. It's July 1968. We're in Springfield, Vermont, planning our wedding with my parents and maternal relatives.

As we depart from Aunt Milly's house, Jerry and I notice that Dad, whose car is parked in front of ours, appears to be yanked backward while taking the driver's seat. His loyal German shepherd is in the car. Is the dog attacking him?

We quickly step out of our car and run to see what is happening. Jerry yells toward the house, "Somebody call an ambulance!" Dad appears to be having an epileptic seizure. His body is rigid, yet spasmodically jerking and arching. After what seems an eternity, the ambulance arrives. We follow it to Springfield's hospital.

A doctor appears in madras Bermuda shorts, clearly impatient with our interruption. Mom had been drinking and is now parading up and down the hospital corridors ranting incoherently at my father and the nurses.

Jerry goes to my father's side in the hospital room while I try to calm my mother. Emotions burn through me—fear, concern, anger, embarrassment. With my thrilling new life, I have been removed from my parents. I'm out of practice.

I turn toward Dad's room. As I enter, he abruptly springs out of bed, demanding to go home. With a leap, his body arches again. He seizes for a second time. Jerry somehow breaks Dad's violent fall toward the floor.

Against Dad's will, and in support of the doctor's need to go home or to the golf course, we have Dad transported to Mary Hitchcock Hospital in Hanover. We're told that his vitamin B levels are so depleted from drinking that he has experienced alcoholic seizures. For the first time, *his* drinking is out of control. And for the first time ever, he is truly angry with me, and unkind.

Dad is snagged by his craving. He wants only to leave the hospital and have a drink. He's infuriated with us for keeping him there. What began for him as moderate social drinking has become an addiction. His weight has dropped from one hundred seventy-five pounds to one hundred thirty.

Heartbroken and unable to reason with him, we finally return to Burlington. I send him a note:

Dear Dad,

With deepest sadness I am writing this letter to say goodbye for now. I will always love you, but it's clear that we can't be as close as we have been in the past until you can love yourself again. When that day comes, all you have to do is call, and I'll be there.

Your loving daughter,
Marilyn

Rugged Terrain

Tough love. Tough life. A dark period slowly descends upon me. It begins with fear—a palpable fear—of death. For the first and only time in my life, I am quite hooked by afternoon soap operas. A night-light is a prerequisite for sleep. Cemeteries and funeral homes haunt me.

I've constructed a belief that my death will arrive early, specifically at age twenty-six. My obsession with dying must be a sign of depression. Having traveled miles of rugged terrain, the wheels are finally coming off the wagon.

To make matters worse, Martin Luther King, Jr. and Robert F. Kennedy were recently assassinated. The entire country is shocked and bereft. No one can understand these horrific events. Justice itself is in jeopardy. A deep sense of vulnerability and mistrust falls over the nation.

Lifted Shroud

I had earlier met a stunning Black woman named Angelina. We were at a house party when she caught my attention. Though not very tall, she stood in proud posture wearing a white knit dress. Her hair was tightly drawn back into a single ebony braid that nearly reached her waist. When I asked if she worked outside of the home, she responded in a resonant voice, "Yes, I study metaphysics."

My curiosity was piqued. Angelina said she had studied Rudolf Steiner and Edgar Cayce. She was now planning pilgrimages to Egypt and India to further explore metaphysics. We decided to get together as often as her busy schedule would allow.

When Angelina spent a couple of weeks in India, she asked me to care for her two homeschooled children in their imposing Burlington home. Having established trust in that way, she has since led me in her daily meditations that include chanting. All of this is new to me. Guided by her deep, melodic voice, I am able to sink deeply into a contemplative state.

Angelina tells me that her mother read poetry to her and her sister, explaining that it would amplify their voices within a white world. It turns out that Angelina's sister is Ruby Dee, best known for her role in film and stage productions of *A Raisin in the Sun*.

In the midst of my depressive period, Angelina suggested that I read *Many Mansions* about Edgar Cayce. I believe it was in this book that I found an exercise instructing the reader to draw a triangle and label each of the three points with a personal passion. In the center of the triangle, I named an action that mobilized my three passions: nature, art, and children. The action was to work with children to instill a conservation ethic.

To reach more children, I will design courses for teachers that combine art with nature studies. Angelina, having heard my ideas, draws a parallel with Rudolf Steiner's work in education. She encourages me to investigate his work. Her words bolster my confidence.

By taking action and not ruminating on negative thoughts, my depression is beginning to lift. The shroud of depression is further lifted by reading my journal entries.

It's said that when one shines a light on a shadow, the shadow disappears. That's what is happening for me. My dark obsession with death is disappearing. The cause has been illuminated. I now see that it wasn't the trauma of witnessing Dad's seizures that caused my depression. It was that my one stable parent, my rock, had crumbled.

Holy Matrimony

Jerry and I are to be married today, on the autumnal equinox of 1968. Leading up to the wedding, I chose to spend a couple of days at Woodside's house. My friend, the professor, unexpectedly came by.

We are ending our personal relationship, but our work life will continue for a while.

I see that an affair, even an emotional one, is an escape. Escapes can become addictive. Lacking trust in others, I must have needed a back door, a way out of my closest relationships, before being abandoned. And I was likely reconstructing the triangular relationship, the drama, of my childhood.

My parents arrive. They look like hard-boiled eggs. Dad has the shakes. Mom wants to be helpful. A part of me, most of me, wishes they weren't here.

Regardless, the ceremony is lovely. My gown, a white Greek-style robe trimmed with gold ribbon, was made by two remarkable Dutch women. One was the wife of the man at Linde-Hubbard who had spoken of life's golden thread. The other was her mother. Both helped me with such sweet deftness.

A hundred or so friends and relatives gather on a natural red rock pier overlooking Lake Champlain. The only glitch is that an uncle has slipped into the lake from the pier. His new suit is destroyed. While he vents his ire, the wind section of the Vermont Symphony Orchestra plays on.

We newlyweds depart to spend one night at an inn in Saint Albans before flying from Montreal to Mexico for our honeymoon. I feel strangely hollow. There's a peculiar sadness, a loneliness, at leaving all of our guests behind.

A raging rash develops on my finger, beneath a moonstone ring borrowed from my mother.

Cloud Formations

Jerry and I arrive in Mexico City unaware that a student rebellion is taking place. We're on our way to the archaeological museum. Military soldiers line the sidewalks of Chapultepec Park. The sides of army green school buses have been cut away, allowing soldiers to more quickly descend upon the park.

A young man approaches us to explain what is happening. He urges us to leave immediately. As we run ahead, a small blast can be heard behind us.

After touring the city's open-air markets, we decide to leave the unrest and drive through an expansive landscape to Cuernavaca and to the Yucatán. Broad views of a big sky in all directions foretell the weather with dramatic cloud formations.

Cuernavaca doesn't keep us. We move on to Veracruz, where beautiful Mexican children play on the beach, scampering like young shorebirds. Brawny men haul fishnets onto the sand.

After touring Mayan ruins, our last stop is the city of Mérida. I'm happiest here, where the streets are teeming with horse-drawn carriages. Smiling children sell romantic gardenias, seemingly unaware of perfuming us.

In spite of Mérida's romantic atmosphere, I wonder what I'm supposed to be feeling. Is this love?

I leave friends and family behind to begin a new chapter of life and assume an onerous commitment for which there is no road map.

What if this road leads to an abyss? I wonder, too, about the future of my work life, my purpose.

Soil and Herbs

Three influential characters enter my life. The first is a prematurely white-haired philosopher named Mr. Brande. I happen upon him while he's presenting a slide lecture emphasizing soil fertility and the importance of composting waste materials. He speaks of a British scientist who warned that as soils are depleted or poisoned, we will see a worldwide increase in violence among humans.

Mr. Brande's photographs contrast healthy plants with diseased plants. He shows images of nutritional deficiencies in the plants, and in human jaws and teeth. I had never heard anything like this. He sparks my enthusiasm for conservation work.

The second character is more personal. I had been plagued by cystitis, a painful and persistent bladder infection. Prescribed sulfa drugs had caused a severe allergic reaction and didn't cure the problem, so I sought an alternative treatment.

An herbalist named Mrs. Carse is in the nearby town of Hinesburg. She is a tall and sturdy woman who wears her hair braided and tightly wound at the back of her head. I am drawn in by her rare smiles. Her home is a rambling farmhouse. Furnishings are sparse. A spinning wheel occupies her tidy work space.

As an anthropologist, she had studied herbalism while living with Native Americans. To request a remedy for my ailment, she writes to the National Institute of Medical Herbalists in London, England.

The response is a three-part plan that includes a tea made of dried corn silk. My cystitis is cured. Mrs. Carse invites me to learn about edible and medicinal herbalism. She is adding to the informal botanical knowledge I've been gleaning from the professor.

Mrs. Carse and I venture out to marshes and fencerows to gather herbs. We hang them to dry and mix them into concoctions. Grippe mix, a remedy for flu symptoms in adults, is made with yarrow, boneset, and mint. Children's ailments are treated with calendula flowers or raspberry and mint leaves.

She is teaching me about the dangers of mold caused by the improper drying of plants. I'm learning which plant parts are used and how long to steep the various teas. The delicate texture and scent of dried herbs pull me closer to the earth.

My friend the professor introduces me to the third character. Rather than scorning me for delving into "unscientific" herbalism, the professor invites me to audit his course in medicinal herbs, but only if I agree to complete a research paper. He wants me to see that science is involved with herbal medicine. Not surprisingly, corn silk as a remedy for cystitis is the topic of my paper.

During the course, a guest pharmacologist speaks about medicines and other products derived from plants. One lecture is titled "Newly Mown Grass." He explains that the pleasant fragrance of freshly cut grass or hay signals the presence of coumarin, used medically in making blood thinners. Coumarin is also used in the manufacture of rodenticides.

How is it possible that I had never learned about plants in school? I'm surrounded by them, living in relationship with them. Plants sustain life, whether for food, clothing, medicine, construction, or beauty. My childhood interest in nature is reawakened, enriched.

New Home

Jerry and I move from **Burlington to Shelburne in May of 1969.**
Dad had suggested that Jean, his younger sister who inherited the family home from their father, might sell it to us at a fair price. She was willing.

We buy the house and begin to gut it. Rooms are stripped down to wall studs and bare insulation. In the process, family correspondence and photographs are discovered, but I have no time to study them.

Jerry and I take turns at paid work, allowing each other the freedom to pursue creative interests. Although an art major in college, I only now resume my earlier interest in the painting of pattern, color, and landscape. Meanwhile, Jerry takes the lead as we continue to photograph the natural world and Vermont's barns.

I have ample time to garden and visit with John Tracy, the man Dad and I had seen several years earlier sipping beer in the Shelburne Country Store. Although in his late eighties, John has a large market garden next to my smaller vegetable plot. I often stroll over to rest in one of his two rusty lawn chairs. There he sits, wearing a fedora hat and double-breasted suit with a vest, tie, and pocket watch. A soft smile comes and goes beneath his gray mustache. He recommends planting silver queen corn and quotes Shakespeare. John reminisces about the days of farming, when he and his team of mules, Tom and Jerry, hauled loads of hay.

Beyond gardening, I'm learning to identify edible wild plants. Inspired by the changing seasons, new foods like dandelion soufflé, violet salad, and daylily soup appear in our kitchen. Fragrances of drying herbs, baking breads, and fermenting wines fill our home. The effervescent fuchsia of beet wine and the tawny finish of homemade tomato wine are visually exquisite.

Foods connect me to plants and the greater natural world.

Higher Elevations

Although impassioned about conservation work, I lack the proper credentials. My professor friend advises, "The way to get involved, if you don't have credentials in a field, is to volunteer."

Jerry and I reach out, seemingly with extra appendages. We've joined the Vermont chapter of the Audubon Society. He's helping with plans for a new nature center. I'm their treasurer and soon take on the role of trustee for the Vermont Natural Resources Council.

Through my association with the professor, I learn that he and his associates are researching both acid rain and Vermont's mountaintops. At above twenty-five hundred feet, mountains are extremely fragile. These scientists have observed that clouds settle on mountain summits. Needles of evergreen trees comb water droplets from the clouds, sending them down tree trunks to streams, replenishing our groundwater below.

This image somehow reminds me of the nourishment found in the water of my childhood, whether dripping into the cistern of our home or flowing into natural springs along the highway.

It's interesting that my first conservation work involves higher elevations. As a young child, I so often dreamed of getting to the top of Mount Ascutney to see the rest of the world, beyond my home.

I join The Nature Conservancy's newly formed Green Mountain Profile Committee. In a flurry of activity, our small group is helping to protect Vermont's fragile ridgelines by pressing for new legislation, and taking the information to Washington, D.C.

My marriage and conservation work mark a turning point. This is a period of inner reconstruction, while shifting attention toward healing the outer environment.

Door Knockers

With youthful audacity, Jerry and I decide to intrude upon the private Webb estate. We've heard that Mr. Webb, the owner, is exploring plans to sell off or develop outer portions of the estate. Perhaps he'll consider alternative ideas.

Even though Dad had years earlier warned against this, we knock on the front door of the Webb mansion. A lovely woman responds. She has closely cut brown hair, prominent cheekbones, and almond-shaped blue eyes. She is small and leanly muscled. Her posture is impeccable. We assume she is Mrs. Webb.

Jerry somewhat awkwardly explains, "We're new citizens of Shelburne and have heard that your property might be at risk due to high property taxes. We have information about land conservation methods. As neighbors, we'd like to offer our help." I mumble something about my work with The Nature Conservancy.

An energetic blond boy of about ten darts around our legs. The woman smiles. In a learned voice she says, "That's very kind of you. I thank you and your good wife for your offer. We'll let you know if we need help." She turns and, with the boy, enters the house, gently closing the door behind them.

Living Arts

Jerry and I become amateur bird-watchers while learning about wild flora and mushrooms. During the autumn months, he hunts ducks and upland game. While he stalks the woodlands, I follow along with my camera, mesmerized by the beauty. Sunlight slants between the tallest trees, highlighting colorful fungi and the iridescent green of mosses.

The changing seasons become my theme for living. Outdoor excursions stir my childlike sense of wonder. I find solace in nature, watching ants placing aphids on goldenrod stems for a later "milking," or finding the Fibonacci sequence of numbers in spiral growth patterns. Order can exist within chaos.

Before my marriage I volunteered for a Head Start program in Burlington. There, the schoolchildren had only pavement, without grass or trees. Many of the children lived in troubled homes, as I had.

I brought them eggs to hatch, seeds to sprout, and larvae to become monarch butterflies. A couple of extraordinary teachers dove headlong into this work. They asked the school's custodian to hang bird feeders on windowsills and remove an area of pavement to plant a tiny garden.

I think, *If more teachers are exposed to these ideas, many more children will be served! The children will learn to love the natural world. They'll find joy and solace in nature, while becoming young conservationists.*

I begin the process of designing teacher workshops, called the Living Arts program. It combines art with earth science, or nature studies. The Nature Conservancy and the Vermont Arts Council have agreed to fund the project. I now need an outdoor location.

Family Meeting

Jerry meets Mr. Derick Webb while both serve on the Shelburne planning commission. Mr. Webb mentions that rising property taxes are pressuring him to develop parts of his family's estate.

Mr. Webb had held one family meeting to prepare his children for planned changes. Jerry suggests that there might be an alternative to selling off parcels. Mr. Webb invites Jerry and a Nature Conservancy representative to a second Webb family meeting.

When Jerry comes home from the family meeting, he says, "You should meet one of the Webb sons. He shares your interest in getting children out in nature."

It is early 1971. Two or three weeks have passed since the Webb family meeting. I've returned home from a modern dance class. Jerry and two young men are sitting on the floor by the fireplace, sipping our homemade tomato wine. I join them.

Alec, who looks to be about eighteen, is the Webb son Jerry wanted me to meet. His almond-shaped blue eyes and stature match those of the woman we had met months earlier when knocking at the mansion's door. A strong neck supports his headful of long, curly hair.

The other fellow, Bill, is a classmate of Alec's oldest brother. He has dark hair and sparkling eyes. Both faces are ruddied from the chill of cross-country skiing to our house. Alec speaks not at all. Jerry had forewarned me that Alec has a speech impediment. "Not a stutter, it's more of a stammer. He doesn't say much."

Bill does the talking and, for that reason, I pay less attention to Alec. None of that matters because we spend most of the visit listening to Peterson's vinyl recording of bird sounds.

As our guests depart, I invite Alec to return, remembering that Jerry thought we had something in common. Jerry also wonders whether my teacher workshops might be located on the Webb estate. It wouldn't hurt to ask.

Laconic Vermonter

A few weeks pass. Alec appears at our front door wearing a gray down-filled vest, a maroon and white baseball shirt, jeans, and a leather backpack.

Strangers are able to communicate with monosyllables, language books, drawings, facial expressions, and body language. That's essentially how we are conversing, even though we both speak English. Alec, at various points, pulls a book from his leather bag, opens it, and points to a paragraph that conveys his thoughts.

I can't decide whether his intriguing approach is cultural, as in "the laconic Vermonter," physiological, as in speech impediment, or emotional, as in shyness. Perhaps it is all of the above. (He's fascinating enough for me to later make, from memory, a small clay sculpture, a bust that involves long, curly hair and a strong neck.)

Having described my Living Arts program, I ask Alec whether there might be a space on his family's estate to offer teacher workshops. Would he ask his father? He nods.

A Threesome

I've since learned that Alec is the fourth of six children. He attended a Massachusetts boarding school for boys beginning in the fifth grade, then went on to Groton, a secondary boarding school. A sports injury began as a setback, but turned out to be a gift. While healing, he discovered the world of literature.

Groton's dress code, daily chapel services, and the boys-only student body led to his restlessness. A school newsletter carried an interview with Alec. In his laconic "yup"/"nope" way, he assumed a leadership role in disavowing the school's rigidity.

In the middle of his senior year, Alec called his father and said, "Come and get me. I'm leaving." His father immediately complied with no questions asked. Alec's circumstance, being a senior, and the changing times, must have made his request clearly heard and unequivocal.

Because Alec spent that last semester volunteering to work with an alternative school, Groton allowed him to receive his diploma. He graduated cum laude and was accepted at Yale, but decided not to attend. Inspired by an uncle, he began the process of requesting conscientious objector status. I don't know why he returned home, but that's when I meet Alec.

Alec was away at school for the better part of eight years, including summer trips to Europe to improve his German and French. He knows few people in Shelburne and the surrounding area, other than a small social circle of family friends. By including him in our outings, Jerry and I are introducing him to the people we know.

By the time I meet him, his leather bag totes titles like *The Odyssey: A Modern Sequel* by Nikos Kazantzakis, *The Politics of Experience* by R. D. Laing, *The Hero with a Thousand Faces* by Joseph Campbell, and *The Phenomenon of Man* by Pierre Teilhard de Chardin. Without sports, literature bends him toward the philosophical, the way a plant follows the arc of sunlight.

Pasture Programs

Mr. Webb has permitted me to conduct teacher workshops in Bay View Pasture, northeast of the main entrance to the estate. Alec, with friends, had run a summer camp during the previous summer. He's decided to again operate the camp, adjacent to my teacher workshops.

Jerry and I are starting a farmers' market in Shelburne. This will demonstrate our regional concept of buying locally, connecting rural producers to urban consumers.

While I focus on my Living Arts program, Jerry takes on much of the early coordination for the farmers' market. He retains two of Alec's friends to help manage it.

I'm assisting Alec with his camp by handling the paperwork and recruiting both children and counselors. Alec's mother, younger sister, and I meet to plan food and utensils for the camp sessions. His mother is an early devotee of the natural, organic food movement. His sister will do the lion's share of providing meals for the campers.

Fledgling Nonprofit

The land where our summer programs will occur is referred to as the "outside land," the land slated for development. We naively hope to prove to Mr. Webb that public use is better than private development.

The Webb family meeting with Jerry and The Nature Conservancy results in more of the outside land being conserved for recreation. Funds have been raised to create a walking trail near Shelburne Bay.

Following several heated family meetings, Mr. Webb has reluctantly allowed Alec to negotiate with the town for lower property taxes. Alec has met with the town's select board and several neighborhood gatherings. The townspeople vote to stabilize the estate's taxes based on using the land for agriculture rather than commercial development.

Jerry suggests that a nonprofit organization be established to make fundraising possible. Alec's two older brothers, with the help of family consultants, take on that task. (In July of 1972, a fledgling nonprofit, Shelburne Farms Resources, will be incorporated. The oldest Webb brother will serve as the first president.)

Preserving the estate for conservation purposes is now a clearer vision. We are consumed by the possibilities. Ideas and plans begin to grow at a dizzying speed, even though financial success is a long way off.

I'm now spending more time with Alec. Although there's an unspoken attraction between us, it is undefined and has no future.

Sounding Reveille

What a summer this is. The weather is nearly perfect. I rise early to make bread for the teacher workshops, then bike to the camp to help serve breakfast to the children.

The teachers and I meet in a nearby location. We explore drawing and writing. I read Haiku to them. Together we read passages like "My Ninety Acres" from Louis Bromfield's book *Pleasant Valley*. The teachers contribute their own topics. In spite of modernity, there is a hunger for tying us more deeply to each other, and to the love of land.

Topics like botany and geology, consumer awareness, weather forecasting, soil health, and composting are covered by guest lecturers. Simple, healthy food is emphasized daily. We explore bogs in search of wild cranberries and carnivorous pitcher plants. We find woodland plants and alpine flora in the mountains.

An older teacher, Mrs. P., arrived this morning wearing high heels and scarlet lipstick. She intends to climb upper Mount Mansfield in these shoes. The final stretch is challenging. Several of us watch carefully for signs of a heart attack. She finally agrees to remove her shoes. With gentle coaxing and some lifting, Mrs. P. makes it to the top!

Relieved, we all take a seat on the rocky outcropping and open our lunch bags. A younger woman brings out her flute. As she plays from the summit, the rest of us lift our smiling faces toward the sun. This is pure happiness.

The children's camp has a similar story. A little girl named Anupa arrives from Montreal. She is adorable in her patent leather shoes and organdy dress. Her father scans the campsite's firepit, the crude dining table with tree stump stools, and only two tents. A shadow of concern crosses his face. The camp is truly minimalist. But in no time at all, Anupa proves her resilience. She's become a happy little tomboy, climbing trees and even mud-sliding, on the rare days that it rains.

The summer is so dry that it's possible to sleep under the stars, which I do a couple of times, without the bother of nagging mosquitos. When the morning sun first appears, squawking seagulls and cawing crows reliably sound reveille, spreading their joy to all of us.

Travelin' Girl

Perhaps because of *Heidi* and other children's books that illustrated tulips, windmills, or colorful Laplanders, I had dreamed since middle childhood of traveling. Heidi's life in the Alps touched upon my early yearnings to climb high, to the top of Mount Ascutney, and out of my home. *Heidi* was a story of healing.

I've decided to travel alone this coming fall of 1971, when the summer programs end. My mission is to see the art and architecture that I had learned about in school and from colleagues like Woodside. And getting away is not only desirable, it's necessary. Jerry's and my relationship is stagnating. We need time apart.

Off I go with a list of people, places, and things to see, on a pilgrimage of sorts. My travel goals are to see transportation alternatives to automobiles, farmers' markets, and land planning that reduces suburban sprawl. I'm equipped with a copy of *Europe on 5 Dollars a Day*; Woodside's list of things to do; and his handwritten sheets of basic words and phrases in Greek, Italian, and French.

With tickets purchased, I mention to Alec that I will be traveling. He murmurs that he wants to go to India. "Do you have a passport?" I ask out of curiosity. "Nope," he replies. I tell him, "Woodside suggests that I stay at the Plaka Hotel when in Athens."

Although I have no itinerary and have made no reservations at the hotel, it is my plan to arrive in Athens on a certain day. I give the date to Alec in the event that his travel could bring him through Greece, if he travels at all.

I don't believe that he can obtain a passport in such a short time, particularly when he is so reluctant to speak or use the phone. And traveling to India by way of Greece doesn't make sense.

I tell Jerry it is possible, although highly unlikely, that I could meet up with Alec. If concerned, Jerry doesn't let on.

First Impressions

My trip begins in London. First impressions are of sleek black cabs and domiciles of even height, all with lovely chimneys. Each small yard has a garden. There are flowers everywhere. I visit Big Ben, Parliament Square, and Buckingham Palace. At the Tate, I view extraordinary Turner paintings along with the works of Rothko, Giacometti, Moore, and others.

Woodside had instructed me to dine at London's oldest Indian restaurant. He had also advised me to see a play. On this first evening, I see *Butley*, performed by Alan Bates and directed by Harold Pinter. After taking a seat, I hear Americans speaking two or three rows behind me. The voices are familiar. I turn around to see the Snellings from Shelburne! We greet one another.

Following Woodside's advice, I order beefsteak and kidney pie at a pub. The table is shared with three others: a roof thatcher and an older Australian couple. The couple invites me to tour the Cotswolds. I am to meet them the following morning on the city's outskirts.

Because of confusion over the train schedule, I am, uncharacteristically, an hour late. There Mr. Elrington stands, still waiting. He smiles and generously says, "I knew you were a person of your word." I nearly cry with both relief and gratitude. It feels mighty good to be trusted, and not be abandoned.

The Cotswolds region is of storybook beauty. Vivid green moss accents the trees, fences, and roofs. The setting sun casts a rose-purple hue across pastures. Everything is reduced in scale. Villages are scattered on rolling landscapes. Autumn fields have been plowed or mowed in contours of mustard yellow. Streams and footpaths lace the countryside.

My new Aussie friends pull over along the way. They lower the tailgate of their station wagon and share a grand picnic of rolls, salmon, lettuce, egg pie, coffee with milk, and fruit pie.

Back in London, I find the National Institute of Medical Herbalists. Utilized by the royal family, it is located in the furrier and banking district. I am stopped at the entrance. Only herbalists certified by the institute are allowed to enter. I mention the Vermont herbalist who had written to this institute for my cystitis remedy. They open a thick directory and find Mrs. Carse listed. She is, at this time, the only American herbalist who is registered with them. I'm allowed to enter.

From here, I visit an apothecary where homeopathic chemists in lab coats are filling prescriptions. How can it be that our country lacks such resources?

Continuing on, and slightly homesick, I pause at St. Paul's Cathedral to write about my loneliness and the city's pollution.

Plaka Hotel

I depart for Athens sooner than planned. Cyprus Airways glides over bold Alpine formations. Spectacular details are visible from our low altitude. I silently marvel at the beauty, but also at our ability to fly. As we prepare to land, a double rainbow arcs across the blue sky. The sun is shining! My spirits are already lifting.

Upon landing, I find a tourist information booth and request a cab to the Plaka Hotel. When the Greek gentleman who tends the booth hears that I have no reservation, he telephones ahead to the hotel. With a dejected look, he hangs up and reports that the Plaka is unfortunately full. He suggests another place for me to stay. I ask, "Is it as close to the Acropolis as the Plaka Hotel?" He reassuringly responds, "Oh yes, yes. Is very good place. You will like." He then summons a cab, and off I go.

The driver stops at a monolithic marble building. He escorts me to a side door. A small bronze plaque provides the only signage. Oddly in English, it reads: *Imports, Exports, and Tariffs*. We enter a cavernous room with a high ceiling, a sprawling black and white marble floor and a wrought iron, spiral staircase. There is no furniture, or receptionist. He leads me to the center of the room and up the staircase to the second floor.

There, I am introduced to a Greek man who appears to be in his thirties. He explains that he speaks English, "because he served in the navy." He shows me to my room and quotes the price which, according to my travel guidebook, seems too high. He then strongly encourages me to take a tour, which he will lead the next day. "Meet me at eight in morning," he firmly instructs.

I close the door to my room, set down my bag, and open a louvered window. There, in an alley below, are starving cats, mewling and prowling around open garbage cans. I am nowhere near the Acropolis or the center of Athens.

My first reaction is to sit on the bed and sob. In moments, I stop crying long enough to discover the purpose of anger: survival. I am convinced that the man at the airport had feigned his call to the Plaka. There probably *is* an available room at the Plaka Hotel.

Determined to find another place to stay, I leave the room and go to a small coffee shop across the street. With my very few words from Woodside's list of useful phrases, I engage with an older Greek woman. With hand gestures and monosyllabic questions, she asks where I am staying. I point to the building across the street. She frowns and says, "No good. No good," shaking her head emphatically. I write how much I am paying for the room and she repeats, "No. No. No good," still shaking her head.

The kind woman teaches me how to use Greek currency and how to make Turkish coffee. We then say our goodbyes. With map in hand, I walk a long way to the Plaka Hotel and ask for a room. It is confirmed that no rooms are available. They will, however, reserve a room for me on the next day.

Deflated, I take a cab back to my accommodations. The so-called lobby is eerily empty. Wary of the suave landlord, I push a heavy table, dresser, and chair against my bedroom door for protection. Even though I have a key, he likely has a copy.

At this time, there are general travel warnings about young women being kidnapped for prostitution. I can't sleep. At around 4:00 a.m., I leave my key along with enough Greek currency to fairly cover the cost of my room. I sneak out of the building, having seen no one.

I wait in the Plaka Hotel's cramped reception area for about three hours until my room is available. Following a nap and late breakfast, I have the pleasure of touring the Parthenon temple. It was originally built on the hill of the Acropolis in dedication to Athena, the Greek goddess of wisdom and war. Wisdom and war together seem an odd combination.

Easy Target

Late in the afternoon, a handsome Greek man approaches me on the street. I must look baffled. He offers his assistance in English. Wearing a gray V-neck sweater over a pressed blue shirt, he looks clean-cut and seems very much a gentleman. I respond with, "A friend told me I must see the Plaka district. Could you please tell me how to get there?" He offers to lead me.

We're completing our walk through the Plaka as daylight is ending. While descending a steep, dimly lit street, he takes my hand, which

I interpret and welcome as protective. We are chattering away. He suddenly pulls my hand sideways toward his exposed penis. I yank my hand away and run down the street as fast as my legs can carry me, eventually arriving at my hotel, safely alone.

I've since been told that American women are considered easy targets because of the way we are often portrayed in our movies. Whatever the reason, I have to find a better way of touring the city.

Greek Hospitality

I'm attending an event at the Athens Center of Ekistics. Doxiadis, a Greek architect, had written *Architecture in Transition* in 1963. The book conveys his ideas about building neighborhoods and communities. He bemoans the way that machines have dominated our world, and our society.

Doxiadis's ideal solutions were focused on basic human needs, such as housing, and protection of the natural world. His work is supportive of the regional concept Jerry and I are developing at home.

At the National Archaeological Museum, overlapping timelines of ancient world cultures, now with the added influence of mythology, piques my curiosity. I wonder how much more engaging it would be to learn world history, not only through the study of wars, but also through art, architecture, and archeology.

At the American embassy, many tourists are seated at outdoor tables. Among them are two fresh-faced young Swiss men. I introduce myself and ask whether they would escort me into the Plaka district this evening. They are willing.

The Plaka, a historical hillside neighborhood, slants away from the Acropolis. After exploring the winding streets, we find a place to sit overlooking the city. Ouzo is served on a wooden tray with a full glass of water and a side of pistachios. Traditional Greek music is our backdrop. This setting is what I had hoped for.

From there, we come upon a diminutive Greek Orthodox chapel nestled within narrow streets. We step inside. A single family occupies nearly all the seats. After the service, the head of the family introduces himself. Michael invites the three of us into his nearby home. Clean and simple, cave-like, the home is dug out of a hillside, into white-painted rock.

The kitchen is spare, with only a table, marble sink, cupboard, and two-plate gas burner. Seated at the green wooden table, we wait while our host prepares food for us. Our shared languages are Swiss German, French, English, and Greek. We manage beautifully.

Michael offers wine and a savory soup of shrimp, onion, tomatoes, and greens. He then, in broken English, reads my fortune from espresso grounds, predicting that I will have a big surprise during my time in Greece. I pass his prediction off with a laugh.

Altered Schedule

My young escorts and I had decided to meet on the following morning. We're now heading toward Piraeus, a port city southwest of Athens. After lunch, I bid a grateful farewell to my Swiss friends and catch a ferry to the island of Hydra.

Arriving in Athens earlier than planned, and now leaving sooner, my timeline changes completely. Perhaps foolishly, I leave an impersonal note with the hotel desk manager. Barely legible, it reads

"Gone to Hydra, then Delphi. Marilyn."

I don't think Alec will ever see my message. Without a passport or tickets, he had given no indication of travel plans, other than saying he wanted to go to India. But having said that I'd be at the Plaka Hotel on a certain date, it seemed rude not to leave a note.

An Omelet

Hydra, a jewel of the Aegean Sea, becomes visible as our ferry approaches. Vaulted buildings cluster around the seaside harbor and creep up a steep hillside. After docking, I walk along a stone street in search of a guesthouse. Along the way, I pass a bakery with an enormous oven that is shared by the local women. A windmill stands in the distance.

Fortunately, the first guesthouse that I come upon has an available room. I'm pleased with its simplicity, its green louvered windows.

Strolling back to the village center for dinner, I learn that no one will serve me. Because four hundred Americans had arrived on cruise ships, all seats are reserved. Disappointed, I walk the narrow back streets and eventually find a modest establishment. A benevolent cook kindly prepares an omelet for me.

Random Ferry

The rising sun slowly **brightens the village. Roosters crow. Donkeys bray. A horse's hooves echo on stucco and stone. As exquisite as this island is, I'm choosing to leave sooner than planned. I'll take the first ferry of the day.

A young Canadian woman boards with me, probably because she, too, is hungry. We introduce ourselves, and spontaneously decide to stop at another island. Closer to Athens, Poros, we're told, is a favorite getaway for Greeks.

On Poros, we enjoy an early lunch, explore the harbor area, then follow paths that lead us along a ridgeline behind and above the town. We notice that the painted trim on houses matches the color of the island's lichens. Lovely!

A black dog follows us. We wander through autumn wildflowers along the hilltop, awed by the sky's immensity, the sunlight's clarity. It's no wonder that Greece has produced such philosophers as Socrates and Plato.

From this elevation, we spot in the distance, and randomly decide to catch, an approaching ferry. It will take us to Athens before nightfall. We hurry down the hillside, back to town.

Big Surprise

Stepping onto the ferry, I hear a timid utterance: "Marilyn?" There, just below deck, is Alec, sitting on a bench! With feet propped, his knees are bent toward his chest. A journal rests against his knees. He is poised to continue writing with pen in hand. In a state of surrender, his forlorn shoulders droop inside a maroon sweater.

I am speechless. Moments pass as I try to understand what I'm seeing. "Alec?" Michael, the Greek man in the Plaka, had foretold a surprise when reading the espresso grounds. I had dismissed his prediction.

Stunned, I find comfort in seeing a familiar face, but wonder what this means. As with most of my emotions, I move forward not knowing what the next steps might bring.

Alec had reached the Plaka Hotel only to read my impersonal note of departure. He had found the guesthouse on Hydra. The owner said that I had been there, but had left the island. Alec, in that moment, resigned himself to head for who knows where.

As we leave the ferry, I spot an older woman. She is about sixty and has a *National Geographic* face, finely lined like a contour map of her life's story. "Alec, look at that beautiful woman. We should offer to carry her bags." She is with another woman, so we offer to help both of them.

As we say goodbye, she hands us a business card: MASHA RABINOVICH, ISRAEL'S DIRECTOR OF THE SCHOOL OF INDOCTRINATION FOR THIRD-WORLD COUNTRIES. She says, "If you're ever in Israel, just show this card."

Simple Beauty

Alec and I are enjoying views of bare red hillsides, some brushed with hues of tan or black, against a blue, blue sky. We are traveling northwest of Athens by bus. A Linde-Hubbard friend, Tom, and his wife, Kelly, had told me of a charming and basic guesthouse near the bus stop in Delphi.

Masonry steps lined with cobalt blue pots lead us to the guesthouse.

A donkey leans over a half wall to greet us. Lush vines flaunt grapes above our heads. Plump pomegranates, red symbols of fertility, grow along the stairwell.

The owner, a middle-aged Greek woman, shows us to our room. There are two metal-framed single beds, like army cots, which suit us. Although Alec is single, I am not. We feel a discreet timidity, even with a growing physical attraction. More intrigued by each other's minds, most of our time is spent philosophizing.

For breakfast, we walk down two flights of narrow stairs, below grade, to a tiny kitchen. On the way, we each pick a handful of grapes. Our breakfast consists of the green grapes, hot water with a lime wedge, and bread that our hostess had baked early that morning in the community oven. Honey from the woman's own beehives adds golden flavor to the warm bread.

Touring the town and surrounds, we learn that Delphi was known by Greeks as the center of the world and as the seat of Pythia, the high priestess of the Temple of Apollo. Pythia, one of the most prestigious women of the classical era, was also known as the Oracle of Delphi. Two of her ancient and wise precepts, still useful today, are inscribed at the temple: "Know thyself" and "Nothing to excess."

We set out to climb a small mountain behind Delphi. Mount Parnassus is visible to the east. A vast valley of patterns stretches to the sea below us. The midday sun is hotter than we had anticipated. Lacking adequate water, we begin to worry about dehydration. As we near the summit, a faint jingle of bells can be heard. In moments, we are walking within a melody of sheep.

Ahead, we spot a much-needed freshwater spring and a young shepherd. Wearing blue work pants and wide leather shoes with hand-knitted socks, he is combing his black hair while listening to a portable radio. We offer to share our lunch of retsina, pears, and cheese pastry. The shepherd gladly accepts. He joins us in a most basic form of communication.

The young man then leads us, sheep and all, to the road back to Delphi. Coming off the mountain at sunset, amid fragrances of goodness and earth, we are surrounded by the tinkling of sheep bells, the voices of donkeys and dogs.

From Delphi, by bus and ferry, Alec and I make our way to Corfu and hitchhike to the quiet village of Kassiopi, also recommended by Tom and Kelly. Olive growers, fishermen, and herders live there. Women work looms outside their homes, next to the turquoise sea. Their exquisite rugs match the color and texture of their white-and-black porous stone-scape. Pastel towels hung near blue walls accent the simple beauty of this place.

Below our louvered windows, villagers pass in the moonlight. We hear the sea at night, roosters in the morning. And whether walking the shoreline or the hillsides, we meet beautiful Greek people.

Last night we celebrated with a free-spirited group of dancing souls. Now, as we leave Kassiopi at five in the morning, we stop by the community oven. Bread dough, dropped into a vat of hot, freshly harvested olive oil, is our seasonal farewell treat.

Lonely Whistle

Alec and I spend two days in Bari, Italy, awaiting a ferry to Dubrovnik and the Dalmatian coast of then Yugoslavia. Last night in Bari, I had a dream about a market table full of persimmons. This morning, we venture out into the streets and come upon an outdoor market. Here we see urns of olives, brass scales, flowered balconies, and a table stacked with a pyramid of persimmons!

The overnight ferry ride to Dubrovnik takes us through stormy seas. Waves, concealed by darkness, thrust us twenty feet high, or more. By sunrise, it's evident that our ashen crew had been swabbing the decks, ad nauseam. We are never told, but sense how fortunate we are to arrive at our destination.

We rent a room from a sweet older Dubrovnik couple. The man, who is in charge of business dealings, appears professorial in his soft shoes, well-pressed shirt, and cardigan sweater. On the wall of their modest living room is a painted black tapestry of John F. Kennedy.

Woodside had recommended that I see Dubrovnik as an example of a pedestrian city. The city is a complex chiseled sculpture of incomparable beauty. Surrounded by protective walls, its red-roofed buildings of stone appear to be carved in relief. We walk a maze of thoroughfares, patinaed by years and years of human footsteps.

Woodside also recommended that I visit a friend of his. Because of his description of her grand home, Alec and I anticipate high ceilings and frescoed walls. Upon arrival, we take a seat at her invitation. All three of us squeeze together like peas in a pod. Our chairs abut the gas range in her miniature kitchen. Inches apart, our knees nearly touch.

There we sit face-to-face, awkwardly unable to communicate. The kind woman seemingly awaits an explanation. Alec and I attempt to suppress a smile, but that causes us to laugh uncontrollably. Tears run down our cheeks.

Our hostess remains calm throughout our unintended rudeness. She graciously smiles on. We catch our breath, apologize, thank her, and depart as quickly as possible, never knowing what mistake we might have made.

In preparing to leave the walled city, we discover that our landlord has stolen money from our luggage. We're told that under communist rule, a general melancholy, a dark cloud, has enveloped this lovely city. The landlord's actions simply reflect that dark cloud.

We make our way to the train station. Alec is having doubts about going to India. I suggest that he instead find Masha Rabinovich. He is noncommittal.

Again, following Woodside's travel advice, we order two glasses of slivovitz, a damson plum brandy. The train's lonely whistle announces its arrival. We say our goodbyes, to Dubrovnik, and to each other, without a future plan.

It is fun to explore with Alec, but I am on a personal journey, and after all, I *am* married. Now is the time to part, with a few tears and a blurred kiss.

(Alec did travel on to Israel, found Masha Rabinovich, and discovered that she was able to open many doors for him.)

Morning Prayer

On the train ride north to Zagreb, I stand for six hours on the train's exterior deck. Sulfurous black smoke spews each time we pass through a tunnel.

Having safely arrived, my impressions of Zagreb are of sycamore trees, yellow park benches, and church bells. I visit a farmers' market at dawn, before my departure. Displays of figs, bay leaves, violets, and fresh greens are lovely in this early morning light. I purchase a gray hand-knitted wool sweater.

En route to Venice, still by train, the mountainous landscape is breathtaking. Feeling hungry and cold, I accept a man's offer to go to the dining car for a hot drink. We return to again stand on the exterior train deck. Another man joins us and stands at my other side. Both appear to be businessmen who know each other, although they haven't acknowledged that possibility. Given our language barrier, my senses are keenly alert. In rudimentary English, the first man offers me the chance to visit his hometown, our next train stop. I politely decline.

A conductor passes us, purposefully carrying a brass lantern and leather pouch. Ah, my heart skips a beat when I glance toward the sky. The moon has risen! Her warm familiarity tethers me to the rest of the world, especially to those at home. Until that moment, I had forgotten that we, on this planet, are linked by the same moon, though sometimes miles and hours apart.

The train slows to a stop, the hometown of these two men. Turning to exit, they attempt to move me along with them by tightly squeezing me between their respective sides. As we step from the deck to the aisle, I reach down for my bag. An older woman is sitting alone in a private compartment. In a split second, I cross the aisle and duck into her compartment.

Using hand and eye gestures, I ask for permission to stay with her. The kind woman protectively insists that I remain with her until we reach Venice, our destination, her home. The disgruntled men depart, like two hyenas that have lost their prey.

Venice is the perfect place to stay for a couple of days. Though still unsettled, and wanting to stay for a while, I need time and a place to recover from the turmoil that is fermenting within me. The city is a visual collage of flower pots, enclosed squares without benches, stylish shoes, mosaics, gondolas, and umbrellas.

Busy canals work cooperatively with pedestrian streets. The architecture of Palladio, and, of course, Piazza San Marco, are all that I had wildly imagined. Sometimes the man-made is as beautiful and inspiring as the all-encompassing natural world.

In the predawn, I venture down a narrow street and cross an

intimate square. A children's choir sings from somewhere above. Lyrical Italian sounds, a cappella voices, melodically echo within stucco walls. The sun rises, revealing a black waterway. Black gondolas glide through wet reflections of mauve and ocher facades. All of it is, to me, a sweet morning prayer.

A Promise Kept

I move on to Grindelwald, a Swiss village and a doorway to the Jungfrau. In Switzerland, everyone, young and old, seems to walk, just for pleasure. I plan to walk to a youth hostel suggested by Woodside.

Snow begins to fall, so I purchase a wool coat and leather tie shoes before going higher into the mountains. Boots would have been a wiser choice, but too heavy to carry when I leave the mountains. I set out on the climb toward the hostel.

By the time I arrive, there are about four inches of snow on the ground and it is nightfall. I'm greeted at the door with "Do you have bedding or a sleeping bag?"

"No. I'm sorry. I didn't know..."

The greeter tells me that there is no room, but there is a small guesthouse about three houses down the path that I had climbed. I turn to look in the direction of his pointing finger.

A short, very broad man with a black beard and fur coat is standing behind me. Though only in his thirties, he reminds me of the British actor Sebastian Cabot. I look past him. The few chalets look like glimmering lanterns in the falling snow.

The man behind me is also turned away from the hostel and follows me down the mountainside. We don't speak.

I knock on the guesthouse door. A middle-aged woman responds.

She speaks almost no English and I speak no German. Vertically extending her index finger, she implies that there is one room only. She then asks, with a hand gesture, whether the man and I are together. I emphatically shake my head no. The man begins to converse with her in German. I think, *Ha! Coercion is taking place. He will get the room and I'll be left here in an alpine snowstorm.*

He then speaks to me, explaining that we have no choice at this hour, and in this snowstorm. We have to share a room. I mention that I am married and can't share a room with him. Ironic, I know. He persists.

The woman is harrumphing with impatience. Our negotiation continues. "Would you *promise* to be good?" I ask. He gives me the assurance I need, and says, slightly amused, "Yes, *promise.*" My security rests in knowing the woman is living here, in this chalet.

Thankfully, there are twin beds. My roommate respectfully leaves the room while I change into sleepwear and slip under the covers. He returns and undresses. Out of the corner of my eye, from beneath the covers, I see red Speedo-type briefs and a hairy back climbing into the other bed.

We talk for hours, well into the next morning. He is intelligent, soft-spoken. As it turns out, this stranger is a lawyer and violinist, a Marxist exiled from Brazil, now selling diamonds through Europe's underground market. At this point, I question my safety, just a bit.

He voices strong resentments against the United States, claiming that while briefly imprisoned in Brazil for his political beliefs, he had heard members of the CIA ordering a firing squad in the prison yard. He speaks about American imperialism in Greece, France, South America, and beyond. Referring to Marx's lectures, he talks about wages, profit, and capitalism. He believes, though, that capitalism was "fundamentally correct, until the monopolies of today." His interest is keenly focused on how language affects minds and governments. I had never heard anything like this.

He approaches my bed twice during the night. I, both times, remind him of his promise. Thankfully, he is a man of his word. He retreats.

We awaken after very little sleep. As a seasoned traveler, my roommate is prepared. He shares a breakfast of milk, cheese, chestnuts, a pear, and yogurt. We walk through snow back to town, where he takes me to my train. I board and, while waiting for departure, hand my journal through the train window, asking for his name. "Dino," he replies, but writes Alcedino Bittencourt Pereira.

He quickly runs off to purchase a yogurt for me. The train whistle signals departure. I roll away to Basel, Switzerland, without saying goodbye.

Looming Confusion

Exhausted, I want a homey place to rest. In Basel, my cozy hotel room feels like a whisper, or a child's lullaby. "Hush, little baby, don't say a word. . . ." The bed is gift wrapped in a hand-embroidered coverlet and feather comforter. A small table, draped in delicate cloth, holds a charming pincushion and porcelain tray. A framed woodcut hangs on the wall above an easy chair. And an umbrella has been thoughtfully placed in a stand by the door.

There, on that welcoming bed, I collapse into a fetal position and fall deeply asleep.

My mission in Basel is twofold. Seeing the art collection of the Kunstmuseum is a must. And my friend Angelina had urged me to visit a Rudolf Steiner Waldorf school. I spend a day observing the teachers' interactions with children and with each other. They incorporate the arts and sciences, revere the natural world, honor a child's developmental stages, and integrate classical learning.

The Waldorf teachers urge me to visit their philosophical center, the Goetheanum. I travel on to the town of Dornach. Designed by Steiner, the Goetheanum's architecture and setting are unusual. The scale is overwhelming and the design unappealing from my point of view. And yet Steiner's integration of education, medicine, agriculture, art, science, and architecture strikes a chord in me. His philosophy supports the interdisciplinary, hands-on education that I, in a much smaller way, have begun to explore.

Most memorable is meeting Mrs. Simons, who was originally from America and is now the lead instructor of eurythmy, a performance art based on movement, language, and sound.

While I am at her home, a tall, gray-haired man named Mr. Macbeth drops by. I learn that he lives in Hard Scrabble, Vermont, where my grandparents had lived and farmed! Evidently, he was born in California, where he practiced law until he was diagnosed with bladder cancer.

As Mr. Macbeth faced treatment options and wanted to avoid surgery, he remembered that, in his boyhood, his mother had read Goethe to him. He recalled Goethe's belief that the body knows how to heal itself. Having researched facilities that embraced this notion, he found the medical center of the Goetheanum. There, with treatment, he had avoided surgery, healed, and now, twenty or more years later, is a member of the Goetheanum's board of trustees.

As I travel on toward France, moments of confusion about my life and marriage loom within my not-so-lofty animal self. I begin to obsess over the meaning of relationship. I am learning that being in relationship is a mirroring process, a way of understanding myself. Ah, the Oracle of Delphi. Know thyself. Self-knowledge is, theoretically, essential to spiritual growth, even with mistakes along the way.

A Chapel

As I arrive near Ronchamp, France, the closest accommodation to my bus stop is a miserable "hotel" with bedrooms above a saloon-like bar. I hear rats in the walls of my room. People seem crude and unfriendly. Of course, four years of high school French is barely adequate for making friends in rural France.

Early morning, I walk uphill along a lonely road to see Le Corbusier's chapel, called Notre-Dame du Haut. The road itself is quite beautiful. Its pavement, blackened and glistened by morning rain, is imprinted with fallen leaves of yellow and tan. At the top of the hill, billowing autumn clouds part like theater curtains. The rising sun turns a spotlight on the chapel as I catch my first glimpse. Extraordinary! The form is daring, a perfect blend of the traditional and the avant-garde, the spiritual and the irreverent.

Molded wooden pews supported by concrete are shaped for kneeling, praying, and sitting. Some glass windows are stained green and yellow, while other glass is clear, framing views of sacred trees. Here, in this place, I experience both a tender stillness and an ode to joy.

Finishing Touches

On to Paris. Train travel provides an opportunity to meet people, to see the changing landscape. There is time to generally ponder: First class, second class ... the importance of education in providing greater equality ... materialism, industry, greed, and pollution ... I think, *Everyone is trying to be someone and already is.*

Near the Fischbacher book shop, I meet a man from Wisconsin. He suggests that we dine in the Latin Quarter, on the left bank of the Seine. Here, strangers are seated with strangers. The place is abuzz, the opposite of stuffy. Some customers lift the ruffled skirts of waitresses who scurry with cancan-style fanfare. Others raise their glasses with a "Salut!"

I'm struck by the way pink salmon is simply and elegantly presented, alone, on a black plate. Sides of crisp leafy lettuce, crusty French bread, Epoisses cheese, and wine, are the finishing touches.

Venturing southwest of Paris, I visit Notre-Dame de Chartres. So much time, labor, and reverence were required to build such a structure. The cathedral is teeming with workers, worshippers, tourists, and beggars. I am intrigued by the mandalas, as well as the apparently handmade brooms. Everyone seems to be sweeping.

Although not prone to crying, I am sobbing on my last night in Paris. Stories of the great impressionists and their lively café conversations pass through my mind. I gaze at the dirty Seine River while loudly spewing autos overtake the streets. Paris, I fear, is stimulated by the newness of machines. . . . My heart aches. I see the depths and darkness of the role we humans play in all of this, and I cry for our loss of awareness. And yet, the sun is still shining.

Perhaps I am also reminded of the pollution of my childhood.

Tired Mind

My final stop is Amsterdam. I feel poorly, as I did in London. The weather is cool and gray. Inhospitable.

I'm surprised to find such unhappiness in me. I long for home. Disturbing dreams of my parents interrupted my already restless sleep during the last two nights. Travel has been a distraction, but now, returning home, I struggle with the triangle I've re-created in my personal life. The dreamed appearance of my parents is a reminder of dysfunction, theirs and mine.

Perhaps Jerry will have thoughts and will help to resolve this. *Dear God, I do not want to put pain in his eyes. . . . Perhaps there are alternatives not yet considered.* Then I think, *How perfect this triangle is in some ways.* I'm smiling. *Absurd! This is serious,* I admonish myself. What am I thinking? Am I re-creating the chaos of my childhood? Is my conservation and environmental work a way of bringing order to my personal chaos and pollution, to fix my own inner environment? Oh, but I don't mean to trivialize my work.

Having been away for thirty-eight days, I have no more patience, strength, or desire to travel. But where do I want to be? What had been the full, comfortable moments in my life? Did I leave home too abruptly? Could my marriage become a place of fullness? Have I failed? Such enormous questions for such a tired mind.

I realize that there hadn't been a true home, a golden thread. I'm torn between working on my marriage and fleeing.

The odor of a foot is covered by a polished shoe, I muse.

Hatching Plans

Roughly three weeks pass before Alec and I reconnect in Shelburne, which makes sense. He rarely uses a phone, and we haven't spoken of a future relationship. Our conversations have usually focused on ideas. We've made many lists, diagrams, and outlines.

I tell Jerry that Alec and I did meet in Greece, after all. It is not something for me to be proud of. Nonetheless, a dynamic team effort begins. Inspired by my recent travel and the successful summer programs, I'm eager to expand upon Jerry's and my regional concept, using the European model. We think we can help support local agriculture, preserve a rural landscape, conserve natural resources, and, theoretically, reduce suburban sprawl.

I hatch a plan with my new friend D'Ann to train unemployed women to make rag rugs out of recycled fabrics. That idea is viewed as competition by the Vermont Weavers Guild, so we opt for a less viable plan that supports sheep farming and spinning wool for knitwear. My tasks are to apply for nonprofit status and raise early funds.

Alec asks his father for permission to use the Annex, a vacant building on his family's estate. The Shelburne Spinners begins in 1972. (In spite of hiring Victoria, a dynamic director, and receiving national publicity, the project ends in 1979, but with many positive results.)

Jerry's task is to move next summer's farmers' market to Burlington. He procures a location on the corner of College and St. Paul Streets.

Alec's brother Marshall and his wife, Emily, with another couple, have taken responsibility for the children's summer camp. In a new location, where the Webb estate's old greenhouses had been, they'll operate the camp and raise vegetables for the farmers' market.

Historically, the mansion's furnace had been scrapped for

ammunition during World War II, and the Marble Dining Room was opened for the fabrication of bandages during World War I. I've seen a touching photograph of Red Cross workers milling about like gentle white doves.

Mr. and Mrs. Derick Webb had previously offered tours of the dairy farm and held American Field Service gatherings on the estate, but ongoing public programs had never been offered.

The private estate is now becoming a public resource, albeit slowly.

Turning Point

So here we are, a loosely knit group, naively trying to convince Mr. Webb that public programs would be a higher use of his agricultural estate than commercial development. Many emotional family meetings that I, too, attend, have begun to take place.

All six Webb children sign an agreement to confirm their desire for public use of the property rather than having the property bequeathed to them. Their generous commitment marks a significant turning point.

The Webb children's unanimous agreement is unusual. I believe that it stems, in part, from their close relationship, shared purpose, and general sense of goodness. The adults in their lives have influenced their values. Their father has devoted himself to his Brown Swiss dairy farm. Their mother was surrounded by small farm animals as a child. She now has a passion for healthy food and the outdoors.

Furthermore, the children's great-grandparents, William Seward and Lila Vanderbilt Webb, had created a model farm of historic value and unfading natural beauty. They provided a rare opportunity for this generation.

Repeating History

Swept up in youthful idealism, we are influenced by a counter-cultural movement. An energy crisis sparks a back-to-the-land, anti-establishment sentiment. There's growing concern for the health of our environment. A cooperative theme emerges. Food-buying co-ops are expanding and communes are appearing around the state. Nonprofit organizations are multiplying.

D'Ann and I are working at the state level to promote the regional concept. An interagency council is formed to encourage the use of local resources.

Alec applies for conscientious objector status. His alternative service is to be fulfilled at the Vermont Arts and Crafts Service, under D'Ann's direction. He will join D'Ann and me as we travel the state to encourage craft cooperatives.

(I later learn that Alec's grandmother, Aileen, had, years earlier, founded the American Craft Council in order to provide work for women and men who were left unemployed by the Great Depression.)

Separation

Jerry and I have separated. We are less than four years into our marriage. I'm not surprised. We were slow to arrive at the idea of marriage. It was my idea, not Jerry's. And the subject of having a family was never raised.

Leading into our marriage, my relationship with the professor provided an escape, a way out. Childhood imprints must have caused me to conflate commitment with abandonment. Although that was not a conscious thought.

Have I learned this on-again, off-again behavior from my mother, who moved in and out of sobriety? When Mom was sober, she and I engaged. She taught me basic bookkeeping and how to ride a tricycle. She took me clothes shopping. Mom was my biggest fan.

I believe that she loved me, but in an awkwardly blocked way. I cannot recall physical contact, like being held or hugged. My most intimate memory is of us sometimes lying in bed and making "om"-like sounds with our out-breath. I loved the way we laughed at that.

But following our brief moments of closeness, I braced myself for her regular return to alcohol and then, most often, I detached emotionally and became an observer, on the sidelines. I must have believed that opening my heart would cause her love to disappear. I would move on with my life, until she and I next connected. Dad was the constant, the stabilizing third side of our family triangle.

Now, I am again repeating the pattern of avoiding abandonment, with Alec as my escape. This is not to trivialize my intimate relationships. I have truly cared about the other. My point is that I have re-created the triangular relationship with my parents, and the chaos, once again.

I only vaguely experience Jerry's and my separation. As a child I had learned to numb my emotions. Perhaps my feelings are now frozen in guilt. I feel fleeting moments of sadness and regret, but move on. Expressing vulnerability would be healthier than showing strength, but I seem to be blocked.

Jerry and I had been doing freelance design work for a woman client named Norrie. She has become a friend. As a result of my whimpering, Norrie has kindly invited me to temporarily live with her and her young son.

Drooping Ears

I'm spending my birthday at the summer camp. Although Marshall and Emily are in charge, Alec and I are showing children how to winnow and grind wheat to make flatbread on an open fire. Hand-winnowing wheat yields such a minuscule amount of grain that it's comical. We are determined, though, as part of our educational plans, to teach children about their dependence on natural resources like soil, air, and water. Food is the perfect teaching tool.

Urban children seldom see soil or sky. Many children don't know that milk comes from cows, or that blue jeans come from a cotton plant. We believe we can change that. Meanwhile, Mr. Webb must be trying to imagine how we are going to save the farm, let alone the planet.

To me, it is quite pitiable that my birthday has not been acknowledged. Even though I have brought this situation on to myself, I feel invisible, the way the child of an alcoholic parent often feels. Birthdays are important to me. Mom had ignored most special celebrations, but not my birthdays.

Feeling like Eeyore with drooping ears, I return to Norrie's, my new home. As I enter, she and her adorable son are singing "Happy Birthday." He holds a handmade teapot filled with Queen Anne's lace. She extends a warm apple pie. Both gifts are meant for me.

Alec and I return to the camp. Some of the children are from the Head Start program where I previously volunteered. A mini fair is underway. The counselors have designed an array of contests. Campers can't wait to show their parents the vegetables they've proudly grown and also won as prizes.

As the day winds down, Mrs. Webb brings a birthday cake and ice cream for her daughter-in-law Emily. I again feel self-pity. But what can I expect? I'm a married woman, soon to be divorced, six years older than Alec, and not a blue blood. Neither am I officially part of the family, or ever expecting to be.

(Mrs. Webb has since acknowledged, on more than one occasion, that she and Mr. Webb were not welcoming toward me. She apologized for that, but I do understand their concerns.)

Wisdom Teeth

And yet, I recall a day from the previous summer. All four of my wisdom teeth had been extracted. I sat in a wicker chair on the South Porch of the mansion, waiting for Alec to arrive. It was a lovely spot, with terra-cotta tiles and brick. An expanse of green lawn stretched toward the lake, framing views of the Adirondack Mountains.

Mrs. Webb stepped through a screen door and onto the porch. She was carrying chamomile tea and yogurt-like clabber milk, intended for me. Both were served in oversize Quimper pottery bowls. I was touched by her soothing motherliness.

Alec then appeared from the direction of the lake, wearing his football undershorts and carrying his leather bag of books. Although it was one of my earliest meetings with him, I had a strong premonition that I would one day have to protect him from the public. That seemed incongruous, given that I barely knew him. And Alec was painfully shy. I couldn't have imagined him in a public role.

Coming to Pass

Alec's parents and siblings are having dinner in the mansion, which they refer to as the Big House. They're seated at a round table in the kitchen. I'm presenting a diagram showing how the regional concept might influence plans for Shelburne Farms, their family estate.

Mr. Webb promptly dismisses me, "Okay, I don't think we need to hear any more of this." Marshall's wife, Emily, daringly speaks up. "No. Let her finish, Derick." He concedes and politely listens to my awkward presentation from renderings, drawn by Woodside and paid for by Alec. Ideas of urban-rural interdependence are tolerated, but not welcomed. I feel their consternation, yet plow ahead.

(I later learned that they wondered, *Who is this person and where is she from?*)

Alec and I had asked Woodside to create a bird's-eye view of Shelburne Farms as it might look in the future. We are envisioning walking trails, a meditation site on Lone Tree Hill, incubator businesses in the Farm Barn, and children exploring the outdoors. Now, in the summer of 1972, our vision seems highly improbable, yet we hope it will come to pass.

Movable Carrot

Although the Big House is the family's summer home, Mr. Webb gives me permission to hold a two-day meeting there in a few weeks. The meeting's purpose is to discuss the regional concept.

All invited government officials and university professors arrive. It is immediately evident that, as we had imagined, the history and grandeur of Shelburne Farms *can* attract people and ideas. I see the property through their eyes:

William Seward and Lila Vanderbilt Webb, with the help of notable characters like Robert H. Robertson, Frederick Law Olmsted, and Gifford Pinchot, had created their dream agricultural estate. At the entrance, redstone gates open to an allée of graceful trees. Roads wind through vistas of farm fields and woodlands. Spectacular views of Lake Champlain and the Adirondack Mountains appear in the distance. Grand structures punctuate the landscape, yet somehow blend.

Their dream was great enough to inspire the dreams of others, including mine. The beauty and magnetism of the estate calls for higher human values.

My personal focus is less on the trappings of the estate than on a mission. I'm like a workhorse with blinders, plowing ahead.

I assume the role of president for the Shelburne Spinners and the Burlington Farmers' Market. The Jupiter Building, prime retail space on Burlington's Church Street, awaits reconstruction for the city's urban renewal project and a pedestrian mall. We are given temporary use of the space for our third season of the farmers' market.

The new farmers' market location proves to be successful. It will remain open through the winter holiday season. (At least two of the city's current businesses grow out of that success.)

Yet we do not have enough momentum to convince Mr. Webb that we can succeed with ideas for his estate. He is continuing to pursue his plan to sell portions of the estate. Family meetings with him become increasingly painful. Some end in tears.

We of the younger generation feel that his goals keep changing, like a movable carrot. Stabilizing property taxes is not going to be enough. We are frustrated, and so is he.

At roughly this point, Mr. Webb's lawyer and his accountant call us young people to a meeting. We take our seats around a large conference table. The two men ask us to stand down. "Derick wants the freedom to spend and do as he wishes."

I don't know what gives me the audacity to speak up. I'm not a family member, but choose to intervene as the oldest. "How can you, as his advisors, encourage him to spend his way into deeper debt?"

A third-party voice is sometimes needed in family situations, particularly when there's an unusual level of reticence. In this moment, we take another step forward.

Taxing Burdens

I should step back and explain more about Mr. Derick Webb. He had lost sight in one eye as a Yale undergraduate. With concern that he might lose the sight in his other eye, his parents suggested that he move to Vermont and operate Shelburne Farms. He took the unconventional step of converting the estate's nine-hole golf course to agricultural use and established a herd of Brown Swiss cows.

Derick hired an architect to design a more modern barn. Rather than using traditional dairy stanchions, he allows the cows to freely move about from an open loafing area to a mechanized milking parlor. He shares these modern practices with other farmers who can't afford to experiment.

Although Derick dabbles in politics, his time and finances are focused on the dairy operations, and a new charter airplane business. Meanwhile, other parts of the property, like the Farm Barn, Coach Barn, and Big House (mansion), are neglected.

Mrs. Elizabeth Webb tells me that she saw the weight lifted from the shoulders of Derick's late father, Van, when Derick assumed responsibility for managing the property.

Elizabeth speaks highly of her father-in-law's quiet demeanor, keen intellect, and dry humor. She feels that Alec inherited many of Van's traits.

By the early 1970s, when I first became involved, the Farm Barn housed livestock. Structural sills and columns were decaying from manure and roof leaks. The grand courtyard had a concrete trench for the storage of silage. A long dilapidated shed ran along one of the stone walls.

I'm seeking funds for structural repairs of the Farm Barn. (The first grant will be generously donated by Norrie, the friend I earlier mentioned.)

The mansion, or Big House, is used only as a summer home, primarily to continue the tradition for Van's widow, Aileen Osborn Webb, called Gigi by her grandchildren. Aileen arrives annually from her apartment in New York City or from her country home in Garrison, New York.

Aileen walks with a cane and her speckled dog, Turtle. She resides in a summer cottage, near the Big House and next to a pottery studio. Her afternoon naps are taken in a net-covered hammock.

Although Elizabeth runs the Big House, Aileen oversees the

formal gardens, maintained by a local landscaping company. A small network of friends, like Maria Von Trapp or prominent craftsmen, socialize with her, but most often, Aileen dines in the evenings with her family.

Culture Shift

Jerry's and my divorce is finalizing. Four years of marriage is ending without much drama. There is no blame. I'm skilled at numbing my emotions, compartmentalizing. I most often put my head down and, with blinders firmly in place, move forward.

I select a few items that we owned together, such as Claire Van Vliet and David Bumbeck prints, Benedictine pottery, a fondue pot, and Fella, our beautiful black Labrador.

We own a small camp on Shelburne Pond that I'll donate to The Nature Conservancy. Jerry and I will split the proceeds from the sale of our house, which will be around eighty-five hundred dollars each, or less, given that there's a mortgage to pay off.

I rent an apartment in the nearby town of Charlotte. To cover living expenses, I take a part-time consulting position with Garden Way. A local businessman, Lyman Wood, is promoting his company's rototillers and gardening. He's starting a community garden program similar to the victory gardens that supported the war effort during the 1940s. There are a few test plots on Shelburne Farms land and at one site in Burlington.

My first assignment is to procure local food and craft products for the Living Center, Garden Way's new retail store.

Lyman also wants me to create a Vermont's Own label for local producers. I ask the Vermont agricultural department to certify the labels so I can sell ads to food and craft producers. Ninety-six postage-stamp-size ads are needed to fill one page in each issue of the local newspaper. Lyman writes an accompanying editorial that addresses energy shortages, conservation, and the need for buying local products.

His words dovetail with the regional concept, Shelburne Spinners, and Burlington Farmers' Market. Because Lyman has many employees and promotes the philosophy of "producing a lot more of what we consume and consuming more of what we produce," the culture begins to shift, at least in our corner of Vermont.

Lyman hosts weekly lunch meetings in his log cabin. A series of guest speakers, like Robert Rodale, a leader in the field of organic farming and gardening, enhance a back-to-the-land movement. Lyman revives the World War II conservation motto: "Use it up, wear it out; make it do or do without."

Ideas overflow at these meetings. Standards change. And it's proven that a successful business *can* benefit the community. I'm thrilled to be a part of this venture.

Cathartic Laughter

My Charlotte apartment has a water shortage and flea infestation, so I move to a new apartment in Burlington.

Mom called today to say that she and Dad are separating. Dad has evidently moved in with a woman, is drinking heavily, and is living a derelict lifestyle, "preparing his meals on a hot plate." Mom asks to move in with me. Life doesn't get much crazier than this.

Typical of a codependent child of an alcoholic, I simply accept her arrival. And my Russian Orthodox Church roots have undoubtedly reminded me to "honor thy father and mother."

She arrives as her sober, clear, mature, and charming self. I truly enjoy the sight of her. We easily work out our living arrangements. Privately, though, I worry that Dad might drunkenly drive into a telephone pole, as Mom had, or harm a roadside pedestrian.

I don't know why Mom is resting in bed. She *is* sober. Alec has come by for a visit. He and I are sitting in chairs at the foot of her bed. While conversing, something comical is said. Alec exhales a snicker through his nose. Cake crumbs scatter from the plate that he's holding on splayed fingers, next to his face.

Mom begins to chuckle, which causes us to chuckle. As her belly laugh intensifies, Alec and I are afflicted with spasms of laughter. Tears streak our faces. This is a good moment.

Seed Planting

I'm lying in bed unable to walk due to stress-induced back pain. I hear a knock at the door and call out, "Who is it?" "It's your father. May I come in? Please?" And then, "I'm asking for one more chance."

Mom is out, having taken a job at an office supplies store. I leap out of bed and run to open the door. My father looks broken, as broken as a man can be. He's gaunt, miserable. Not surprisingly, my back pain disappears.

Dad moves in with Mom. I will move out. We are discussing possible work for Dad. At age fifty-six, and having been self-employed, he is struggling to find new work that is fulfilling. Alec again drops by. He suggests that Dad make a proposal to Lyman Wood to expand the community garden program. What a good idea! If accepted, it will combine gardening with Dad's love of people and the outdoors.

Lyman accepts his proposal. Dad, as director of Gardens for All, sets out to establish 1,200 plots for 3,500 gardeners. His life is turning around.

House Design

Alec and I move into Marshall and Emily's home while they are away for a six-month trip. By now, Alec and I have a more intimate relationship, but my insecurity and his shyness keep us from freely expressing our affection. We love each other's thoughts. Our passion for implementing ideas makes us more like business partners.

Now that Marshall and Emily have returned, Alec and I have temporarily moved to a wood-heated room in the Farm Barn. Driven by ideas related to the environmental movement, Alec and I are becoming ardent workaholics. We joke that our very different backgrounds make us alike in this way. I'm driven by an infusion of immigrant work ethic and he is driven by guilt, particularly during these countercultural, anti-establishment years.

One of Alec's great-uncles, having no heirs, has kindly provided modest trust funds for his grandnieces and nephews. When Alec and I talk about building a house, without talk of marriage, he chooses to liquidate that fund to cover construction costs. Derick agrees to provide a house site on the northern end of the estate. We begin to select spruce and pine for the construction.

Although Woodside wants us to use his house design, which includes an "essential terrace for martinis," we are more interested in having a windmill and composting toilet. Woodside is disappointed. He calls us Maoists, which probably isn't far from the truth.

Alec and I are auditing a Chinese language course and have applied to visit China. We are curious about how human waste can be composted and used as farm fertilizer.

Chinese officials ever so politely decline our request.

Family Dinners

I now address Mr. and Mrs. Webb as Derick and Elizabeth, and am often invited to dinners at their winter Orchard House, or their summer Big House. Twelve or more family members may dine at the Big House. A typical menu includes poached salmon; zucchini and cheese casserole; a vegetable salad garnished with pepitas and grated beets; freshly baked bread; and raw milk from a refrigerated dispenser. The kitchen is always supplied with homemade yogurt and crackers, along with many sweet treats, especially ice cream.

Two yellow labs, Radar and Flyer, are always present, often asleep on an oversize sofa in the Main Hall. Alec's youngest brother, Robert, has a pet crow that sometimes flies across the Big House dining room to perch on an upholstered high-back chair.

Alec's pet pig, Porky, seems to smile as he tiptoes on four small hooves to greet guests at the Orchard House. When he follows Alec on long walks, they sometimes pause to nap in the sun. Porky's head rests on Alec's chest.

Family dinners at the Orchard House generally seat eight or ten people. The mood is strained. Derick usually leads conversation from the head of the table. His very short haircut gives the impression of a stern military officer. There is a stiff awkwardness about him. He might offer a point of discussion, such as the Vietnam War.

Derick, with two of his Republican friends, traveled to Vietnam to see for themselves whether the war is warranted. He believes it is. The children vehemently disagree. As a curious observer, I don't engage in these family disagreements.

Regal Posture

During family dinners, Derick is accused, through innuendo, of being overly scheduled and strict. His wariness of organic food is another "foible." Also implied is that he doesn't understand the children, especially when they are in trouble.

Elizabeth is quite humble, sometimes defiant, but in no way haughty. Highly invested in good health, she often quotes two Adirondack mountain gentlemen. One was to have said, "Breathe your deepest every day." The other, when asked how he stays in such good shape, replies, "I'm exercising now," while standing with perfect posture. Though short in stature, Elizabeth holds herself in perfect, almost regal posture.

This brings me to a lesson in noblesse oblige. I once asked Elizabeth for permission to cut from the magnificent lilac bushes that line the Big House driveway. "I'd be happy to cut the lilacs for you," she replied. In this manner, she hadn't refused me, but I would never ask again.

A nanny had helped Elizabeth raise the children in their earlier years. By this time, a nanny is seldom needed. Mrs. Denton does the house cleaning. Mrs. St. Peter and her daughter run the kitchen. Elizabeth manages the staff, allowing her to volunteer, oversee food quality, and enjoy outdoor adventures.

Mr. Boisvert keeps things running like clockwork. He does whatever is needed, from managing the water system to delivering mail and making minor repairs. His wife, Armande, an excellent gardener and seamstress, helps the Webb family by turning collars of shirts or darning the heels of socks. I admire her ability to extend the life of clothing. Her mending is beautiful to the eye.

Scaffolding

Meanwhile, Dad, with so many gardens underway, asks to move his Gardens for All office to the Farm Barn. Space is available because Derick's property manager is no longer needed. Dad wants to support our effort to create rent-paying, mission-related enterprises in the Farm Barn.

Gardens for All adds a community canning center, thanks to Lyman's sponsorship. This Gardens for All era is marked by a comical photo of Alec on a tractor. Rows of potatoes, planted in front of the Farm Barn, are ready for harvest. Lyman's son-in-law lurches behind the tractor with legs spread apart, struggling to maneuver a handheld potato digger.

Although we are working in earnest to prove success, Derick must view our efforts as child's play.

The farmers' market has to move from the Jupiter Building to a new Burlington location. To satisfy safety requirements and save money, Alec and I agree to drywall the ceiling. In our youthful idealism, atop scaffolding, with no experience whatsoever, we miserably attempt to tape Sheetrock.

Dad moves his Gardens for All operation from Shelburne Farms to the new farmers' market location in Burlington. This helps cover the market's rent, especially in the off-season, and frees office space in the Farm Barn for us to expand.

(The farmers' market goes on to have many iterations, led by others. Markets have since sprung up in towns throughout Vermont, including Shelburne, once again.)

Unsurprisingly

The strained mood at the Orchard House dinners can now be explained. Elizabeth leaves her marriage in the spring of 1974, following a candid conversation with Alec. Clyde, who had worked next to me at Linde-Hubbard, and resided on Shelburne Farms for about eleven years, leaves with her.

They marry and move across the lake to a village near the Adirondack Mountains. I am not surprised, nor are the children.

Departures

I should explain the whereabouts of the other Webb children following Elizabeth's departure.

Only Derick and his youngest children, Lisa and Robert, live in the Big House during the summer of 1974. Perhaps because the mansion's future is in question, a Mr. Kaplan requests permission for two harpsichordists to play in the Marble Dining Room.

This leads to hosting the Vermont Mozart Festival during the summer of 1975. Hosting means providing for concert lawn performances and housing musicians during three weeks of the summer. (Marshall and Emily moved into the Big House to assume that task for four summers, until they separated in 1978.)

While living in the Big House, Emily comes upon the diaries of Lila Vanderbilt Webb. She studied historic preservation at the University of Vermont. Given her background, and Derick's approval, she's having them temporarily stored, along with other important documents, at the university's Special Collections. (They are later archived at Shelburne Farms.)

Emily also begins the process of requesting that the estate's three major structures be added to the National Register of Historic Places.

Meanwhile, Marshall is using personal funds to paint the exterior trim of the Big House and Coach Barn. He's also working with the county forester to develop a plan for the estate's woodlands. (His work later earns the Vermont Tree Farmer of the Year award.)

Marshall becomes manager of the estate's buildings, grounds, and forests. His photography documents the beauty of the landscape that he's helping to maintain.

The remaining siblings and in-laws have varying levels of involvement during these early years of Shelburne Farms Resources. I had met

Alec's oldest brother, Derry, in early 1967, when Clyde brought him to Jerry's Burlington apartment for a visit. He was a quiet, wholesome young man with curly hair and a lightly freckled face. Sadly, while serving in Vietnam, Derry developed serious health issues. He was briefly married, worked at Shelburne Farms as crops manager, and later worked as president of SFR. He then spent less time on the estate. Along the way, Derry changed his name to Quentyn. He remarried and has one son.

Alec's older sister, Mary, and her husband moved to the estate in 1973. With one cow and seven sheep, they began their own small farm. Alec and I were recruited for the butchering of their sheep and chickens, and for planting an orchard of fruit trees on the northern edge of the estate. Mary and her husband organized a sheep-shearing event in the Farm Barn, tying in nicely with the Shelburne Spinners. They had a son and a daughter before moving away. (Mary eventually remarried.)

Alec's younger sister, Lisa, studied nursing in those early years. She married a bright young British agriculturalist who had originally come to intern on the estate. Derick quickly hired him as dairy manager. (Lisa and her husband later left to operate their own Vermont dairy farm. They raised a family of three daughters and one son.)

The youngest Webb son, Robert, was still in school during much of this early period of SFR's development. He was the young boy with Elizabeth when Jerry and I knocked on the door of the mansion. (Robert later left home in pursuit of his passion for the mountains and outdoor adventure.)

(By the end of 1978, only Alec, Marshall, and I, of the sibling-in-law group, were living on the estate. Marshall soon met and married Juliet. He later married another fine woman named Kate.)

Second Marriage

I'm evidently a marrying kind of girl. Alec and I marry on March 1, 1975. Alec had never been married. He is regarded as young and innocent. I am viewed as an outsider and an intruder. Both sets of parents are our awkward witnesses. One set was recently divorced. The other set could have been.

Alec's youngest brother, Robert, sweetly insists on accompanying the six of us. We receive no congratulatory words, cards, or gifts, other than a thousand dollars from my parents. The seven of us drive from Shelburne's Episcopal Church to "our" new house. We solemnly digest refreshments, as well as the wedding itself, which is quite pitiable.

At the time of our marriage, I know nothing of prenuptial agreements. It is, in retrospect, surprising that I wasn't asked to sign one. However, I have a verbal understanding with Alec that the house will remain within "family bloodlines." This seems perfectly reasonable to me.

My work with Garden Way is providing our primary income. SFR doesn't have enough income to compensate us for our work. We budget with cash kept in small manila envelopes, each designated for various needs, like food or entertainment.

With signed contracts that I find annoying, my parents agree to loan us a thousand dollars on two separate occasions, to help move our work forward.

A Getaway

Travel is inexpensive. We are frugal. Alec and I are on our way to France. We had read in *The New York Times* that the French village of Bardou once supplied the farmers' markets of Paris with chestnuts. Two Americans recently restored its buildings to create an artists' colony. We hope they'll have ideas for our work at Shelburne Farms.

Having hiked up a forested hillside, we arrive at a cluster of medieval stone buildings. Although their interiors are dark and damp, one is welcoming. We step inside. Flames from a fireplace cast warm light across a stone floor where two dog dishes sit. Founders of the colony greet us and willingly answer our questions. The village is charming and interesting, but not particularly useful for our planning purposes. We make our way back down the mountainside.

Driving south through the Pyrenees, we pass lush little farms tenderly cared for by their owners. As we enter Spain, the weather turns gray and rainy, but the pastel blossoms of fruit trees lift our spirits. Having miserable head colds, we stop only briefly along the coast. From here we head for Barcelona, then southward to Seville in search of the sun, making stops in cities along the way.

Holy Week is underway in Seville. We are relieved to settle here for a while. Alec and I tour farmers' markets, where produce is artfully presented. One pyramid of lemons is arranged with rose-tinted garlic and bouquets of bay leaves.

Woodside had recommended that we see the annual procession of pasos, or floats, depicting Christ's story from Palm Sunday to Easter Sunday. Bent beneath unbearable weight, behind shrouds, penitents lug the pasos on their backs. Onlookers reach through the shrouds to offer the suffering men sips of water and drags on cigarettes.

Following a brief visit to the Costa del Sol, we travel on to Lisbon and the Portuguese fishing village of Nazaré. On the way, we notice groups of women carrying rudimentary hand tools as they head to work on communal fields. The land is parched and sterile. I'm disheartened by the contrast between this scene and the vibrant family farmland of the Pyrenees.

In Nazaré, we stay in what had once been a captain's home. Its charming interior stairway will soon be replicated in the house we are about to build on Shelburne Farms.

Louvered windows open to the Atlantic shoreline. Local women play with their children on a broad tan beach. Men haul generous nets laden with fish, soon to be peddled at a nearby market.

Earthy Home

Since working at Linde-Hubbard, I have kept a clipping from the Sunday *New York Times*. It features the studio-home of sculptor Alexander Calder and his wife. Nestled into a contour of the French countryside, their earthy stucco home has an arched entrance with exterior potted plants. The aging Calders are shown romantically picnicking in a field. I borrow their design ideas for our house.

Bruce, a high school friend of mine, finds a builder who knows plaster and stucco construction. Both of them will build our house. Two of Bruce's friends will build an adjacent barn.

Alec and I want to be as ecological and self-sufficient as possible. Our house is built into a hillside, leaving land for vegetable gardens and fruit trees. The hilltop is designated for a windmill. Our basement will have rudimentary root and wine cellars. Day by day, the buildings are taking form. We'll soon have a traditional barn raising.

My jobs are to seal the foundation walls with tar and help find recycled windows, doors, and old-world tiles for the construction. I'm gathering furnishings, reglazing the windows, and sealing pine floors with a well-researched concoction of linseed oil and turpentine.

Working at the house on clear mornings, with classical music and a thermos of coffee, is like sipping summer nectar.

On one of these mornings, Alec's mother, Elizabeth, comes from across the lake for a visit. Members of the construction crew are introduced to her. She is so gracious and lovely that a hush falls over them. When she departs, they exhale with a *whoosh* and mumble, "It was like meeting a queen."

Research and Development

Alec and I are busy with our gardens, beehives, windmill, and Clivus Multrum composting toilet. Lyman Wood agrees to hire us as part-time consultants so that our solar home, and lifestyle, can be used for Garden Way's marketing purposes. In truth, by supporting us, Lyman is indirectly supporting our work for SFR.

Alec and I take several small trips in search of ideas and financial support. Some are to meet with Derick's sister and two brothers. We also meet with Derick's mother, Aileen, at her New York City apartment and, on two or three occasions, at her country home in Garrison, New York.

Derick is with us on this particular trip to Garrison. Aileen's generation is one of comforting routines and rituals. The three of us are invited to a family Sunday brunch held at her brother's home, Castle Rock. The imposing "castle" is like something out of a fairy tale. And yet, it has telltale signs of the same financial pressure that many estates, like the Webb estate, are experiencing. To economize on heat, whole portions are closed off with sheets of plastic. The family can appreciate our challenges in Shelburne, but they have their own challenges.

In Aileen's home, afternoon tea with pâté, crackers, and sherry is served daily by Lightbody. As a butler, or personal assistant, Lightbody exudes both loyalty and efficiency. One of his tasks is beekeeping.

I love that he, rather uniquely, cuts comb honey into one-inch cubes and tidily places them in small plastic boxes. The honey is placed at each person's breakfast setting. A toaster sits so close to the table that our toast is warm enough to melt a luscious spread of butter and honey.

Thinking Big

Alec and I make several visits to the Farm & Wilderness Camps in Plymouth, Vermont, gathering ideas for children's programs.

The director, Kenneth Webb (no relation), reprimands us for arriving twenty or so minutes late. He says, "The one way in which we are all equal is that we have the same number of hours in a day." That reverberates with Lyman's words: "When you're late, you're stealing other people's time." I take both reprimands to heart.

Because of my interest in local, seasonal foods, Alec and I visit the American Culinary Institute. We're exploring the idea of having a cooking school in the Big House.

Although we decide not to pursue a cooking school per se, local, seasonal food will become a principal element of our programs. I've planned a summer cooking course, to be taught in the Big House by

Vermont Life's food editor.

My workshops for teachers continued to be offered in these early years of SFR. Various program ideas are being suggested by others. Alec's grandmother, Aileen, has written a proposal suggesting that we "think big" and incorporate craft industries into the Farm Barn.

Marshall said early on that he saw the estate as "a school without walls." He wants to see more done with renewable energy. A Buddhist teacher from California's Tassajara Zen Mountain Center visited with an entourage, including Stewart Brand of the *Whole Earth Catalog*. Having noticed the Farm Barn's dragon weathervane, the group believed the property should become a spiritual center.

I'm in the process of creating a brochure for SFR. Writing the mission statement, a group endeavor, isn't easy. The estate is a richly woven tapestry of historical characters, noteworthy architecture, and a natural-agricultural landscape. The public is curious about the history of the wealthy Vanderbilt-Webb team that created Shelburne Farms, but our intention is to change the image and purpose from a private estate to a public resource.

We, with Alec's siblings, want to instill a sense of stewardship. Education programs will provide an appreciation and understanding of natural ecosystems. And we'll use the farm to demonstrate conservation practices.

The beauty and spirit of the place are certainly powerful enough to attract people. We hope the public will support our efforts, but there is one obstacle in attracting financial support: The property is owned by the Webb family. We hear again and again, "Why should anyone give money to the Webbs?"

We answer with: "The Webbs are land rich, cash poor. The goal is to conserve the land for education and public use. To accomplish that, we need public support."

Shifting Sentiments

It's 1976. Derick has donated the three primary estate buildings—the Farm Barn, Big House, and Coach Barn—to the nonprofit corporation, SFR. I've been elected president of SFR.

Derick had remarried in the previous year. Enter Helen, Rusty to us, a tall and strikingly attractive redhead. She is a fun-loving, adventurous woman who adores Derick. His silver hair now grows a bit longer. He laughs more. He practices "Stormy Weather" on the piano, in case he loses sight in his other eye. They travel for pleasure and winter in Captiva, Florida.

Rusty is the big sister I never had. Thanks to her endorsement, Derick begins to accept me. With his transfer of the buildings, I am largely responsible for making them accessible to the public. That means inventorying, preserving, or auctioning their contents.

Now that it's time to empty the Big House safe of its china and silverware, Derick relinquishes the secret combination to me. His sentiments have surely shifted.

Heavy Baggage

I am expecting our first child while assuming my new role as president. Pregnancy is marked by the tear-stained pages of my journal. I deeply hope that my baby will not carry my own burdensome story into his or her life. Perhaps I am afraid to be a mother. Will I know what to do? Will I be like my mother?

Even though I know how to feel better, I am unable to act. I sometimes sit and stare at dust particles, wanting to remove them but feeling immobilized.

I choose to blame my depressive state on the loneliness I feel. It's not only that our house is in the middle of nowhere; I don't belong here in this new community. And living in an enclave with in-laws, employees, and "customers" is unusual, not easy.

Of course, since childhood, I've been carrying my own heavy baggage for this journey. Packed in my bags are distrust and a fear of abandonment, both of which I somehow manage to keep fresh.

Fluttering Moths

Because I'm not able to see my feet during the final weeks of pregnancy, sleeping upstairs without a bathroom is challenging. A chamber pot kept under the bed fulfills the need and prevents a fall down the stairs. We have a small Jotul woodstove on the main floor, but our idealism also means that a wood-fired cookstove has to be stoked late at night. In the cold of winter, that is challenging.

The "digester" of our Clivus Multrum composting toilet fills most of the basement. It looks like an inverted fiberglass boat and works on the principle of mixing carbonaceous with nitrogenous material. This means kitchen waste has to mix with toilet waste for the digester to work. Therefore, when we tossed discards from Fella's dog dish down the kitchen chute, we unknowingly introduced meal moths to the system. Yes, we, and our guests, experience the shock of fluttering moth wings when using the toilet.

One hundred and twenty-four batteries in our basement rarely store enough power generated by the windmill. The windmill either generates too little energy or nearly implodes during high windstorms. We always have enough power for lights, but rarely enough for the water pump. Our stove, refrigerator, and hot water heater are gas operated.

The director of our local chapter of The Nature Conservancy comes to dinner one evening. Finding great humor in our living situation, he sidles up to a window. Gaining a glimpse of the windmill, he jokes, "It's like a *New Yorker* cartoon. 'Honey, do we have enough wind to invite a guest for dinner?'" He then chortles a throaty "Heh, heh, heh."

Sweet Baby Scent

Our exquisite daughter is born in October of 1976. "The times they are a-changin'." Fathers are now allowed in the labor and delivery rooms, even though newborns are rarely allowed to stay with their mothers.

As I'm taken to the labor room, the nurse promptly sizes up the situation. "If this is your first, you've got at least another twelve hours." I hear other women moaning or screaming in neighboring rooms.

Alec is told that he can join me. Seeing my distress, he pulls out of his shirt pocket a folded sheet of notes from our Lamaze classes. Glancing at his tiny handwriting, and following a brief assessment, he calmly says, "I think you're already in transition labor." Screams and groans continue to emanate from the other rooms. Needless to say, the nurses are too busy to help us. Alec coaches me through the breathing, as we had been taught.

A nurse finally arrives. She is appropriately alarmed at the speed of my progress. I am dying to push. In fact, it seems as though I could push a mountain. But no, my instructions are "Just keep breathing. Don't push yet." En route to the delivery room, I remind the nurses that I want no IV, and I want to breastfeed my baby. This is to be an all-natural event, as encouraged by my mother-in-law, Elizabeth.

In just over four hours, and with one cathartic push, a baby girl is born. She's placed on my chest and, with encoded wisdom, immediately begins to suckle. In a matter of moments, I pass from agony to ecstasy, from misery to love.

We name our child Anna. Having been snatched away for tests, Anna is quickly returned to me, swaddled in a pink blanket. The nurse whispers, "Here's your little munchkin." Corny perhaps, but I melt. "Could she please stay here in the room with me?" The answer is "Yes."

Motherhood is like joining an archetypal sisterhood. Rusty so loves babies that she is the perfect mentor. She has arrived at the hospital with a bountiful basket of fresh fruit and a smile.

Moments earlier, my mother had refused to purchase a nursing bra for me. That was a surprise. I thought Mom would enjoy this moment as much as she had claimed to enjoy my birth. Evidently not. I was disappointed, but accustomed to it. I just gulped, swallowed the sadness, and looked ahead. Rusty now lifts my spirits.

Anna, my firstborn, is the most beautiful and miraculous thing I've ever seen. Although a stranger, really, this angelic infant gazes at me with wise, knowing eyes. Her tiny fingers grip my thumb as she nurses. Platinum wisps of hair form a spiral vortex at the crown of her head. Like a wild animal, I am drawn to her sweet baby scent.

In these moments, following the darkness of the birth canal, Anna's arrival brightens and forever changes my life. Becoming a mother is a continuation of caring for others, but I love having a baby. When she naps, I often stand over her, gazing in wonder at the profound existence of her small being.

Log Pile

I'm grateful for the chance to redefine motherhood. It is a process of healing. Even so, I'm seeking support from a psychological therapist. She asks what my living situation is like. After hearing about moths and stoking the woodstove for night feedings, she says, "You might want to make a few changes to your living environment."

She adds, "Try to lower your high moods and raise your low moods, to find greater balance." She means, *Pay attention to your hormones.* When up, I love the world and take on too many commitments. When down, I want to isolate myself and lack patience. It's a question of learning how to work with my biological cycles.

As our visits progress, my therapist asks whether Alec and I might not want to try an open marriage. I must have complained that he didn't express much affection. Apparently she and her husband are experimenting with this new fad that has spread from California to Vermont.

One day, while Alec and I are stacking firewood, an adult mouse appears out of a large, disorganized pile of logs. Then a second adult mouse leaps from the pile. We lift a log and see a nest of hairless, pink baby mice. I say, "Ohhhh," meaning "how adorable." Soon, a third adult mouse appears. In his droll way that I love, Alec remarks, "Cal-i-for-nia."

Women's Movement

At age thirty, I begin dual roles as a new mother and the president of SFR. My first task is fundraising. With Anna nearby, I sit on the second floor of our house with a Smith Corona electric typewriter.

Two small grant proposals, if successful, will hire a gatekeeper to welcome visitors and an office assistant.

Next, roughly three hundred letters are sent to potential donors. This is an appeal for general support. I assume that Webb family relatives and friends will surely be delighted to see the younger generation working to save the property.

Sadly, the largest gift is one hundred dollars from Alec's great-uncle. The letter raises a total of about three thousand dollars. We clearly need a more compelling story.

I'm disappointed, but shouldn't be. Until the three major buildings were donated by Derick, SFR's only assets were a roll of linoleum and an old farm tractor.

We have encouraging news. Two small foundations award historic preservation grants. This validates our effort. I now dare to request funds from Vermont's governor, the same man who sat behind me at the theater in London and one of the two men who visited Vietnam with Derick.

At our meeting, he responds with "See this?" Pointing at a stack of papers on his desk, he continues, "Projects like yours are a dime a dozen. I don't have time for things like this."

I leave with my tail between my legs but determined to show the governor how many jobs we will create *when* successful.

Predominantly male business leaders do not give women executives much latitude. The women's movement is underway. I host a women's group and Equal Rights Amendment meetings in our home. A strong woman is called bitchy, so I'm taking an assertiveness training course. Although, it's okay to be called bitchy once in a while, when seeking excellence.

Balancing Act

Neither Alec nor I have had financial training, other than the basic bookkeeping taught to me by my mother. That is of some help with basic budgeting, but not with accounting or financial management.

Alec is keeping the legal and accounting records. He's asked the estate's accountant to train him. Cloistered in a small room with an adding machine, he's learning about debits and credits, assets and liabilities.

Both of us are going to Montreal for a course in Financial Accounting for the Non-Financial Executive.

During these couple of years, the property is finally named to the National Register of Historic Places. My tasks are to create a more formal board of directors, fine-tune contracts for special events, begin a school field trip program, and continue with budgeting and fundraising.

Balancing work with mothering isn't easy for me, or for anyone. Luckily, Anna is resilient. If I have an unexpected meeting and can't prearrange childcare, she attends the meeting, crawls under a table, and sleeps. Typically though, a caregiver comes to the house, or Alec can sometimes cover for me.

We finally bring electric power to our house. My parents give us a washing machine, which helps, particularly with laundering diapers. From an environmental point of view, we had wanted to use cloth diapers, but quickly learned that hand-washed, line-dried diapers can cause terrible rashes.

Life has greatly improved since another new mother told me she uses disposable diapers. She feels no guilt whatsoever. Now that I've converted to disposables, the rashes have disappeared, and Alec is pleased to help. I feel relieved, and somewhat guilty.

Economic Logic

We are seeking the advice of business leaders who care about conserving natural resources. It seems ironic that such leaders are rare. After all, the words "economic" and "ecologic" share the same root meaning home, or place to live. "Economic" refers to managing the home, and "ecologic" refers to understanding the home.

Natural resources support life and fulfill our basic needs. Goods and jobs depend upon them. But if we can't clean or replenish our resources, we will lose the land, air, and water that we, and all beings, depend upon for our health and well-being. There must be a way of balancing economy with ecology. We must first have a relationship with the natural world, one that is built upon wisdom and gratitude, rather than exploitation and greed.

Sinking Ship

The dairy and Derick's new charter flight business are carrying about one million dollars of debt. The dairy has invested in Harvestore silos. Corn crops have been paltry. It has been too wet to harvest the fields, thus the silos aren't full enough to cover their cost. Supplemental grain has to be purchased at additional cost. Dairy calves are mysteriously dying. We're trying to stay afloat to save the farm with idealistic public programs, while the dairy is sinking the ship.

Alec and I are attending a two-weekend conference in Tarrytown, New York. It is called Entrepreneurship for the New Age and is being led by a Mr. Schwartz. His primary message is on the importance of networking.

Each participant is asked to make a trial pitch for financial support. Alec requests capital to manufacture wooden tool kits.

My pitch is made to a panel of individuals posing as foundation trustees. When we present a slideshow of Shelburne Farms, everyone bursts into laughter. Our audience had anticipated a Vermont hillside farm with a stanchion barn and silo, not a sprawling Vanderbilt estate.

(We've since learned that one member of the panel does serve as a foundation trustee.)

Months pass before I contact Mr. Schwartz. "I'm organizing a conference on agriculture and the environment. Do you know of someone who could be a keynote speaker?" Without hesitation he suggests Paul Hawken, a pioneer who had started Erewhon, a natural foods store, and subsequently founded a well-known gardening company. Paul's a businessperson who is trying to balance economy with ecology. His name will attract others to attend.

When I call Paul in California, he initially declines the invitation. With persuasion, he agrees to be our keynote.

Paul's stay at the Big House was evidently memorable. He was given the Rose Room. Because he had arrived after dark, he had no sense of place. In his paraphrased words, "I awoke the next morning in a canopy bed. When I lifted my head, there were stunning views of a lake and mountains in the distance. On the bottom shelf of a nearby bookcase, I saw a 1956 issue of *Life* magazine. I stepped out of bed, turned a crystal glass knob, and opened a heavy door. In both directions, as far as I could see, was a red carpeted hallway. It was as though I was in a time warp."

(Paul later joined the Shelburne Farms board of trustees.)

A Simple Song

Elizabeth is settling into her new life across the lake. We see her only twice during Anna's first two years. I feel somewhat miffed by that, but understand the awkwardness of her coming to the property.

Alec and I are pleased that she and Clyde have invited us to join them, and two other couples, on a whitewater canoe and camping trip in northern Maine. This is an opportunity to wean little Anna, whom we have never left overnight. Rusty willingly agrees to care for her.

Clyde's photography business has grown. He is documenting this Allagash River trip for *Country Journal* magazine. Photographs of us peacefully cooking over wilderness campfires conceal my fear of taking the rapids.

We have no choice but to trust that Clyde, and the canoe, know what to do. We follow Clyde's commands shouted from the shore or ahead of us on the river. Our canoe seems to have a mind of its own. We are amazed by the way it knowingly maneuvers through the whitewater.

Although it was good for us to get away, we couldn't wait to see Anna. She's now riding on the back of my bicycle. Out of the blue, our two-year-old is singing, "Mommy's milk is all gone. Mommy's milk is all gone." She's resolving her loss with a sweet and simple song.

Warm Spirit

Elizabeth and Clyde had been on an earlier trip to Alaska. Elizabeth calls to say that, on the trip, she had met a young woman named Eileen. Eileen is moving to Shelburne and would be contacting me about renting space for a weaving studio.

Eileen comes by for a meeting and we immediately connect over our mutual love of the natural world. I find her to have a warm and outgoing spirit. She asks to create a weaving studio in the Farm Barn and offers to work as a volunteer for SFR.

Eileen and another volunteer meet with me weekly to develop a seasonal calendar and oversee our school field trips. Eileen becomes a part-time communications director. She's assisting with fundraising by opening many doors for us and our work.

As a result, Eileen and I are planning a visit to Dartington Hall, a fourteenth-century estate near Totnes, England. We're told that Dorothy and Leonard Elmhirst restored and converted the estate in the 1920s. Like SFR, their estate offers agricultural, cultural, and educational programs.

I learn that the Elmhirsts were influenced by Rabindranath Tagore, a Bengali Nobel laureate. He espoused the importance of physical work, a close relationship to the natural world, and social justice. Having come across a book about Tagore in the Big House library, I now wonder whether William Seward and Lila had also been influenced by him.

Eileen and I leave Dartington Hall surprised by the parallels with Shelburne Farms. I've gleaned ideas for an improved staffing and management structure. We travel by train to Florence and are staying in the pensione where Woodside resided as a young man. The chinaware is identical to that used by Woodside in Vermont, a reminder of the little mouse, Torpelina, and her home in his Florentine teapot.

We continue on to Italy's northern village of Bellagio. A driver meets us at the station and takes us north along Lago di Como to a point of land. Our first impression is one of towering mountains. Their green jaggedness is slightly softened by mist as they plunge into dark blue waters below.

Eileen has a personal connection with the Bellagio Center, a residency program for writers sponsored by the Rockefeller Foundation. We assume this visit can provide ideas for Shelburne Farms.

Narrow cobbled streets and chiseled buildings wind their way up to the center, a hilltop villa. Along the way we are greeted by the glorious aroma of baking bread, the sounds of crowing roosters, and church bells. The villa is surrounded by terraces of cypress, olive, and fruit trees. Colorful houses are painted terra cotta, ocher, and mauve.

Our guest rooms are simply and elegantly appointed. A tall louvered window opens onto the panoramic view of lakes and mountains. Dinner is brought to us on this first evening. We enjoy cold meats, artichoke hearts, sliced tomatoes, beans with vinaigrette, wine, bread, and fruit.

Every element of the villa is treated with utmost care. To prevent wilting, freshly cut flowers, cosmos, I think, are moved from our bed stands to the hallway. When safe from the afternoon sun, the flowers are returned.

Eileen and I, as welcome guests, are soon referred to as lamplighters, possibly because we enliven the sober retreat setting.

(Due to an introduction made in Bellagio, I am appointed by President Reagan to serve on a USDA advisory board. This involves interesting travel to various parts of our country four or five times a year over two years. The assignment is to appraise the president's agricultural budget and report citizen recommendations for American agricultural research.)

Spicy Stew

Alec and I briefly separate. It's the summer of 1979, our fourth year of marriage. Both of us are living on the property, but in separate houses. We work well together, and love each other, but somehow have not learned how to show our affection.

Whenever I believe that I'm unlovable, doubts pile up. Then my list of Alec's missteps begins to grow. He retreats and becomes more shut down. I, more convinced of being unlovable, lash out. He further retreats. What a racket this is. Showing vulnerability, or simply requesting what I need, would be a wiser, more loving approach.

Bodily changes from childbirth have added some spice to my stew of self-doubt. Loathsome self-images sometimes ensnare my thoughts, like cobwebs catching bugs. There are days when I am startled by my reflection in a mirror. My imagined self is a bedeviled hag. Yet my reflection looks incongruously welcoming, like an old friend.

Snagged by historical patterns learned in childhood, I continue to avoid rejection, or abandonment, by keeping an escape, a way out. I have a fling with a guy who works on the estate. Alec, not surprisingly, finds his own escapes.

Mothers' Wings

With our separation and his greater involvement with the dairy, Alec travels to Kansas for a course at the Graham School for Cattlemen.

When I stop by the dairy, I see that Alec has returned. He exudes attractive confidence as he maneuvers an enormous tractor in the yard. I feel a heavy sense of loss. *We must be able to work this out*, I think.

I've been tending bull calves kept in the barn next to our house. Chickens live on the other side, opposite the calves. Sadly, raccoons have sometimes slain our chickens despite so-called foolproof latches.

This morning, though, as I enter the barn and approach the chickens, I hear a chorus of high-pitched peeps. I peer into the coop. At first glance, the hens appear to be normal, but something is changed. Fluffy chicks are chirping away, hidden safely under their mothers' wings. Feeling emboldened, they peek their tiny yellow heads out at me. In that sweet moment, I smile.

Finding Safety

Alec and I are in the midst of our two-month separation. Derick and Rusty invite me for dinner at the Café Shelburne. As the dinner concludes, Derick says, "However this turns out, I want you to know that we will always love you." I can't believe this is the same man who had worn the militaristic haircut and seemingly found discomfort with intimacy. Rusty may have coached him, softened him. But the words are his own. He is sincere.

If Derick and Rusty had been judgmental or mean-spirited, Alec and I might not have reconciled. I would have run like a wounded dog, as far away as possible. Instead, we're back together. We begin marriage counseling twice a week. (Counseling continues for eight years.)

We have two counselors, a man and a woman. They are encouraging us to "check things out" before reacting. Today, as I leave work, Alec arrives at the Farm Barn. We meet on the stairs. He barely acknowledges me. I stop him and say, "Just then, from your expression, I felt like you were repulsed by me." Stunned, he says, "Oh no. I was just lost in thought."

What a relief for both of us. He had been at the dairy and was pondering whatever had taken place there. He was completely withdrawn, lost in his head. I was projecting my own insecurity onto him, internalizing my childhood abandonment as repulsion.

Normally, I would have accumulated a list of transgressions and then created an argument. This time, I "checked it out," and was reassured. We are making progress.

Cheddar Cheese

Since Alec has taken more responsibility for managing the dairy, he often carries Anna in a backpack during the morning milking. He also does the milking during holidays, to give employees time off. In hay season, both of us have the pleasure of bringing sandwiches and beer to those working late in the fields.

After milking, I arrive at the barn to do calf chores with Anna. We're met by the sweet smell of grain and milk as we fill the feeding bottles. Having been a nursing mother, I worry about the calves being removed from their mothers to live alone in small huts. But with some relief, we discover that egrets and other critters, like skunks, keep the calves company. I suggest that calves be given at least enough time with their mothers to ingest colostrum. Rich in antibodies, the colostrum might help prevent the calf deaths that were occurring.

We are hiring a new dairy manager. We've also met with two successful dairy farmers to learn practices that might make the herd healthier, more productive, and profitable. One suggested the individual calf huts. He advised us to depend more on grass silage than corn and to avoid spoilage by storing the silage with greater care. (This will lead to the removal of the costly blue Harvestore silos.)

Eileen obtains a grant for an economic study of the dairy and the mansion. Recommendations are to increase the size of the dairy and convert the mansion to a private membership club.

We don't want the mansion to serve only a private elite group. And I strongly believe it is better to keep the dairy small, to instead create value-added products that increase profitability. Alec agrees, as does one of our trustees who is Vermont's commissioner of agriculture. We had already been thinking that the estate should develop a specialty product.

The first product is raw milk, but that is soon discontinued. Cheddar cheese is next. Our first cheese maker, assisted by Marshall and one of Alec's classmates, begins production.

A logo is being created with the help of two designers, Lynda and Joe. I've asked them to express agriculture and nature with a Swiss motif. Thinking "Brown Swiss" and "upscale," we want the cheese to be packaged in a dark brown wax. The color red is supposed to be good for marketing, so the designers have opted for a maroon label.

Our design group, including the dairy manager, chuckles over trite lines like "udderly delicious." Despite our meandering meetings, the two designers somehow create attractive packaging and an enduring logo.

Sofas and Cradles

At this point, Marshall briefly remarries. Juliet, called Pearl by her friends, is a musician and singer who brings more music into our lives, literally and figuratively. During the summers, Marshall creates sculptural "sofas" out of beach stones. All of us sit around a bonfire and roast food. Some have guitars. Marshall and Juliet lead us in songs she had written.

Their daughter is born while Alec and I are expecting our second child. This is a happy time for me. Rusty, Juliet, and I are close. We laugh a lot. Rusty loves babies. She loves us. We love her. I am cradled by that.

Kindled Warmth

It's December of 1981. We were at Derick's and Rusty's holiday party last evening. A major snowstorm was underway. Because I was extremely pregnant, one of Rusty's friends spoke from experience: "You have to stay in Burlington tonight. You may be delivering at home if this baby comes and you can't get out of here."

We followed her advice and stayed at my parents' home, about four blocks from Burlington's hospital. Mom and Dad were pleased to have us there.

Labor begins before dawn. We rush to the hospital. As we get out of the car, wintry air seems to oxygenate my labor. I nearly give birth in the elevator. A custodian appears as the door slides open. I call out, "Help me. I'm having this baby!"

There is no time to practice breathing as instructed. Our baby crowns before the doctor gets there. When he arrives and sees the situation, he grumbles, "Goddammit." A pretty infant with lots of dark hair is born.

Heidi comes into the world with a bang. A willful, affectionate child, she already kindles warmth in just about everyone she meets.

To prepare for Heidi's birth, we had modified our house to make life a bit easier. We removed a wall and added a stone fireplace. I spend many predawn hours nursing by the fireside. How I cherish these sacred times with my beloved new infant.

Perhaps hormones are at play, but these hours by the fire spark a dream of women banding together to stop war. Why wouldn't we protect the lives of our precious children? Hormones make that dream seem possible.

Mother's Day

All of life is either giving birth or being born. It's so fitting that this is Mother's Day, the first following Heidi's birth. White shadbush and golden marsh marigolds dance in the greenness of spring. A soft warm rain falls over the land.

We light a fire in the stone fireplace. Recorded mandolins play as our sleepy infant rests in my arms. Life is full.

Kermit Mayo, an old beekeeper, comes to the door. His face reflects the recent harsh winter he speaks of. He leans toward the warm fire. Upon his departure, we sense that he is, sadly, among the last of his kind.

As Alec and Heidi nap, Anna and I walk through our garden in the rain. We're thrilled to see miniature green plants, the first sign of what will soon be our salads. The asparagus is up. All the fruit trees are blooming: cherry, apricot, plum, and apple. Our new Gravenstein blushes pink. Daffodils are browning. Tulips are unfolding.

There is a feeling of wholeness as we walk out on the hill and down to the pond. North Pasture looks sensual in the distance. Fresh greens blend with naked contours of flesh-colored fields, newly seeded and smooth.

The pond is like a song. There's a graceful rhythm of swallows circling the water's surface. A muskrat skims his way to a hideout. A duck couple swims away from us in hopes that we won't find their nest. We do not.

Oh, how I love this day!

Home Companions

Although tensions and marriage counseling continue, Alec, Anna, Heidi, our dog, Fella, and I are a close little family. During dark winter evenings, we watch National Geographic documentaries, or light the dinner candles while tuning in to *A Prairie Home Companion*.

On warm summer weekends, we work in the garden or picnic on a pebbled beach. Friends and family usually join with guitars and song as we roast ears of corn and legs of lamb.

Whenever guitars appear, Alec reveals a more animated self. He's less reserved. With persuasion, he charms everyone, especially me, with Loudon Wainwright III's "Dead Skunk in the Middle of the Road," or the more sacrilegious "I Am the Way."

Generational Electricity

During this busy phase of balancing family life with our workaholism, my parents give us two rabbits. I'm not joking.

They certainly are skilled at adding burdens to my life. But this is their way of connecting, like Dad bringing home surprise raccoons and woodchucks when I was a child.

Awakened by a raging summer storm, and worried about the rabbits, I stumble out of bed and down two flights of stairs to make my way outdoors. Alec and I find each other on the stairway, unaware that the other had left the bed. He stands holding a flashlight, having checked the windmill–the high winds needed to generate electricity regularly caused damage.

Here he is, in a rain slicker. Water droplets trickle from his hood, onto his face, and down his nose. We wordlessly look at each other, register the absurdity, and laugh.

Going with the Grain

We have little to show in the way of financial success, even though SFR's programs have grown. Two board members rightfully criticize me, saying that more professional agendas and budgets are needed. A couple of advisors chastise me with "You've got to get something more tangible going on here."

A few days pass. Alec and I are in nearby Burlington. We spot two bakers crossing the street. They are the Conways. We have enjoyed their pastries at a bakery in Central Vermont. I call out to them. We explain our goal of attracting incubator businesses, like a bakery, to show how humans depend on natural resources. They happen to be looking for a new location. We invite them to come and see the Farm Barn.

The Conways move their bakery into the space that the Garden Way Canning Center recently vacated. They are experienced artisanal bakers developing a line of organic sourdough breads. For them, bread is more than a product. "It's a living thing that responds to changing grains and seasons."

Growing Pains

We hire David to be the education program director. He'll manage school field trips, train teachers, and organize public tours. Meanwhile, summer courses and conferences, musical concerts, structural repairs, guest weekends at the Big House, and the cheddar cheese business are underway.

Two board members strongly believe that we need a free public event to change the image of Shelburne Farms as a private estate. A harvest festival is suggested. I say, "Good idea, but who's going to run it?" At this point, our poorly paid, often unpaid, skeleton staff is overwhelmed. We are both surprised and grateful when Judy, a local citizen, generously volunteers to oversee the annual festival.

Meanwhile, Derick plans to sell five hundred acres. In exchange, he will, at our request, donate much of the remaining property to a land trust to conserve the land in perpetuity. These transactions require much of Alec's and my time.

While growing pains increase, one gnarly internal event occurs. Marshall had produced a marketable calendar using historical photos of Shelburne Farms. Now, months after the calendar was announced, Alec receives a letter from a Webb family elder who is claiming ownership and control of all historical photographs.

The Webb elder writes, "Marilyn is known in the community of Shelburne as an 'electrified bulldozer' . . . If Marilyn wants to play the role at Shelburne Farms of Queen Elizabeth I of England or Catherine the Great of Russia, believe me she has 'met her match' if she wants to tango or tangle with me!" He suggests the possibility of taking legal action, even though we've never met.

Our attorney verifies that the photos are in our ownership and there are no grounds for a lawsuit. My response to the Webb elder, Mr. J. Watson Webb Jr., or Watson, politely states as much.

As I see it, his bulldozer metaphor is likely accurate, but only with the intention of forward movement, not overrunning him, or others.

Healing the Wounds

Derick and I have a falling-out over Watson's accusation. I believe he should defend me. Now, while visiting him and Rusty in Captiva, we are exchanging words about it. He finds humor in the situation. I do not. He says, "You're too compartmentalized," which may be true, but that doesn't make me feel better. I'm annoyed with Alec too, for retreating and not supporting me.

This afternoon, Derick and I are taking a leisurely stroll on Bowman's Beach. We wade over bars of sand left by a receding tide. An occasional conch shell appears. Their stunning interiors match the coral pink sky. Our attention alternates between conversation and beauty.

Still quite amused by my earlier overreaction, he places his arm across my shoulders, pulls me toward him, and resolves, "You know, I love you the way I love my own daughters." Reparenting is taking place. I melt right here and now into my love for him.

To further heal the wounds, Derick and Rusty are hosting a summer lunch now that they've returned to Shelburne. Watson is invited. We get on nicely.

I receive an olive branch from Watson. The book *Tyrone Power: The Last Idol* arrives with passages highlighted in neon yellow. Salacious lines involve Watson and his life in Hollywood. This, incidentally, is the same Tyrone Power that my Dad is thought to resemble.

Catching Cold

Alec, Anna, Eileen, and I had, before Heidi's birth, visited the Colonial Williamsburg museum, created by Eileen's grandparents, John D. Jr. and Abby Aldrich Rockefeller.

Eileen and I return to meet with Colonial Williamsburg's president, Mr. Humelsine, to learn more about managing tour groups. He rolls out the red carpet out of respect for Eileen and Van Webb. Van had been a trustee and legal advisor in creating Colonial Williamsburg.

One of his suggestions is to make tours more profitable by offering samples after showing the cheese-making process. On his advice, we open a small shop in the Farm Barn, but know that a larger and more welcoming center for visitors will be needed.

I am now leading the board of trustees more professionally, with proper agendas, reports, and financial accounting.

We create a separate taxable corporation under the umbrella of the tax-deductible SFR. Operations like the new cheese business are taxed. Profits, after taxes, are plowed back into SFR. This provides a fair and innovative way of supporting the nonprofit education programs.

The days leading up to a board meeting are the most stressful of all. Board meetings are equally stressful for Alec, who, with our accountant and board treasurer, creates the financial reports. We usually catch a cold.

Teaching Tool

Following Aileen's death, and given the departures of Elizabeth and Emily, converting the Big House from private to public use is a challenge. Lynda, one of our logo designers, is our part-time director during this first summer of transition.

(Three other nonfamily women later serve as Big House directors: Sansea, Del, and Marnie. Although the mansion looks quite tattered, each director brings a distinctive style that carries over to food service. Sansea brings a creative air of abundance and revival to the house and gardens, in spite of previous neglect. Del brings a refined style to the house and begins restoration of the mansion's gardens. Marnie's organizational and aesthetic sensibilities ready the mansion for increased public use.)

Meanwhile, the market garden, where the estate's greenhouses had been, is revived by the Miskells, an organic farming couple that has arrived from Europe. We can now offer cheddar cheese, the Miskells' produce, and the Conways' breads.

Producing local, seasonal food is an extension of my earlier work with the Vermont's Own label, the farmers' market, and the cooking school idea. Food production illustrates our dependence on natural resources like sun, air, water, and soil. Food is becoming a teaching tool for our education programs.

Cool Cheese

Alec and I arrive in New York City to market the cheese. We're proud of our product and its packaging. With the dark brown wax, eye-catching maroon label, and Shelburne Farms logo, we can't go wrong.

Ken, a friend of Shelburne Farms, provided a list of shops that are not to be missed: the Cheese Board, Zabar's, Dean & DeLuca, and Balducci's. As neophytes, we have no idea that August is the worst possible month for marketing cheese. It's quickly apparent that summer heat causes the cheese to sweat. We intermittently return to our hotel room to chill cheese samples on the air conditioner.

Our first stop is The Cheese Board. We enter a narrow shop with newspaper clippings on one wall and a refrigerated display case along the opposite wall. The clippings verify the shop's popularity. We're excited about the prospect of showcasing the cheese here.

A man gruffly calls out from behind the counter, "Can I help you?" "We have Vermont cheese made from a single herd of Brown Swiss cows—" He cuts us off by shouting "Get the hell out of here! I've heard it all before. The Amish tried to sell me their cheese. Oh, their precious cheese. I know all about it. I don't wanna hear it. Get the hell outta my store right now, goddammit!"

We take a deep breath, rechill our samples, and venture on to Zabar's. A man reaches over the counter to grab a sample from us. "How much?" We tell him the price per pound. He says, "Too much," and walks away, shaking his head in disgust.

At Dean & DeLuca, a man reaches over the display case to take a sample from us. He cuts into it and tastes the cheese. While savoring the cheese, he gazes into the distance, nods. "Yeah. I'll place an order."

We've broken through! Balducci's also places an order. We now have credibility. Our trustees and other marketing outlets need to hear this. The cheese idea is going to work.

Cross-Pollination

The growing momentum is influenced by the passion and cross-pollination of nearly everyone involved. A woodshop opens in the Farm Barn. Two fine furniture makers, Bruce and Jeff, are committed to using local wood. Their lyrical designs respond to the wood's natural character.

Those involved with the formal and market gardens are devoted to soil health and the cultivation of plants. Alec, with his Graham School training, can deliver a calf or supply calcium to a cow whose muscles have weakened from birthing. Marshall is passionate about trees and takes great pride in producing lumber from the property's woodlands. We, a small group, are feeding on each other's imaginations.

In roughly 1982, the public is as protective of the property as we are. At a summer concert on the Big House lawn, a lower tree branch obstructs the view of the orchestra. I ask Marshall, the woodlands manager, to remove the small branch. When he does, members of the audience instantly react by harshly scolding him. "Hey! You can't do that! What do you think you're doing?" Marshall's daughter, Molly, begins to cry out of concern for her father.

This signifies a turning point. Visitors are protective. Volunteers are deeply committed. Donors are giving generously. Impassioned people are encouraging Shelburne Farms to be all that it can be.

Overcoming

Momentum grows, and yet we have ongoing obstacles to overcome. Groups with similar land conservation aims are sometimes the least cooperative; historic preservation officials had long delayed approval of our application to the National Register of Historic Places. When asked whether funding is available for restoration of the buildings, a scholarly leader in the preservation field responds with "We have no interest in those white elephants. We're more interested in urban structures like train stations."

There is also resistance within our board of trustees and the community. What we are doing is quite radical for financial conservatives, although politics per se are rarely discussed. We're making every effort to be apolitical in order to build broad community support.

To sway the board and donors, I use examples like Central Park in New York. Historic renderings of the park reveal that it was originally surrounded by open farmland. Who would have guessed that it would become the urban oasis that it is today? Given that Central Park and Shelburne Farms were designed by Frederick Law Olmsted, a parallel is easily drawn. For future generations, we have to be forward-thinking.

To convince trustees that we should expand our education programs to other countries, I present *National Geographic* images of children who had tragically lost limbs owing to chemically polluted rivers in Asia. Our education programs are needed, both here and abroad.

I see parallel threads between my work and my childhood. Protecting the environment literally leads to survival. And my interest in children likely stems from concern for the child that I once was. *Perhaps my work is helping me heal.*

Food, nature, and art comforted me in my early years. Our education programs might heal inner lives while healing the outer environment.

As a child, I found strength in my community. Now the Shelburne Farms community is not only growing, it includes the larger public, "the village," so to speak.

These thoughts are new to me.

Empty Shoes

Mom and Dad become more engaged with Anna and Heidi now that the girls are past infancy. They help with childcare. Dad called last evening to suggest a television program that they might enjoy.

Evidently, he had stopped at the Elks Club for a drink or two and had come home for an early dinner. Mom said he'd eaten a hearty meal. He was in a jovial, even flirtatious, mood. When she decided to go to bed, he said, "You go ahead, hon. I'll be there in a few minutes." Too much time passed. Mom went downstairs to check on him. Dad had died in his easy chair, most likely painlessly. Although EMTs arrived quickly, they couldn't revive him. It's March 1983.

Alec and I are at the hospital, unprepared for what is to come. We're offered a chance to view Dad. He's behind curtains, laid out on a gurney. The top of his head faces us. We step around closer to see his face. He looks grotesque. His mouth is agape with teeth bared, like a wild horse reined in. We stumble out immediately, almost in shock. I can't bear the sight of him.

If only I didn't recoil. I wanted to be fully present and at ease in this moment. Perhaps if I had been told what to expect. Or if he had been less starkly presented.

I'm bidding Dad a final goodbye. Alec is waiting in the car with Anna. I enter the funeral home. There's no thought of protocol. I grieve deeply, from my bowels. I declare my love, cannot say goodbye. I wail, I kneel, dropping away from consciousness into a separate dark place.

With closed eyes, I stand again and somehow find my mother. I hold her and she holds me. Gasping into her coat, I'm startled by the inhalation of fur. Then Uncle Joe holds me until I can return to the moment at hand. Like a small child, I find Alec and Anna, two anchors, waiting in the car. Heidi is too young to attend.

Everyone proceeds to the cathedral. Anna and I are hand in hand throughout. After the service, we continue on to the cemetery. There is an unfriendly chill in the air. Alec has no coat. The fatherly bishop spreads open his robe like a colossal black bird. He takes Alec underwing. This is what I remember.

Losing a parent isn't easy, regardless of the circumstances. I had not wholeheartedly invited Dad into my life during his later years, even though he generously supported Alec and me. My guess is that he desperately wanted to matter to me. He did try. And he had done so much to protect me as a child. Yet I had become ashamed and quietly judgmental of his drinking and smoking, especially in light of Anna's and Heidi's well-being. *How can I be judgmental? I, too, am imperfect.*

But now, in a moment of grace, I regard Dad as perfectly human, made of both strengths and weaknesses, two halves of a whole.

I'm helping Mom organize Dad's belongings. While gathering his empty shoes into my arms, I feel the shock of his absence pass through me. His shoes are here but he is not. His being, his presence, now intangible, has dispersed into fathomless ether. My father is gone. He is elsewhere.

I'll add that Dad's physician said he had been a textbook case. Having recently been diagnosed with angina, he was medically examined the day of his death and had checked out well. It was the first day of his retirement. The autopsy report said his heart muscle had weakened from excessive alcohol, typical of veterans of his generation. But I wonder whether being put out to pasture, coaxed to retire, had broken his heart.

Dad had received a national award and was asked to speak about the virtues of community gardening throughout this country and abroad.

I was proudest of the work he did in Antigua, where land for food production had been converted to coffee plantations. Dad provided seeds and plotted gardens for the islanders. Before retirement, he was told not to spend more money on Antigua. Dad returned to the island using his own financial resources.

I do believe my parents loved each other. The last ten years of their lives were their happiest. They'd purchased their first pleasant home. Age had tamed them and their drinking. Although Dad continued to drink socially and Mom continued to binge alone, only occasionally, but enough to lose her job.

As far as I know, Mom's drinking has stopped since Dad's death. She is now treating the four of us to an autumn vacation in Switzerland and Bellagio, Italy. Here in Switzerland, amid the grandeur of the Alps, people of all ages walk for both purpose and pleasure. We visitors walk from village to village, inn to inn, soothed by healthy breakfast buffets and divine featherbeds.

Sacred Place

On the land near my home, walking has become an act of love. As an outsider, in terms of bloodlines, I think of the Indigenous people who once inhabited the land, and the farm families who followed. I sometimes wonder how anyone can actually *own* land.

The dirt road that leads to our house crosses a narrow stream of marsh marigolds in early May. A maple tree stands beyond, like a sentinel. It will announce each new season as it changes from bare buds to blossoms, green leaves to red. Honeybees from my hives will hum and dip into spring's tree blossoms, summer's clover, and autumn's goldenrod.

Brown Swiss cows meander through the greening pastures, blinking, chewing, and swishing their tails. They wander over to the fence for a closer look. I pause to gaze into their eyes, and admire their moist noses.

Beyond the fields and lake, ancient Adirondack Mountains rise in all their glory. On this side of the lake, flat gray stones of shale ring the shoreline. The smooth stones, marked with white stripes of calcite, were formed more than four hundred million years ago! When these stones are sealed in ice by high winds and wintry temperatures, a visual treasure trove of diamonds and pearls appears.

Fencerows teem with birds and wildlife. These creatures prefer the edges, where they're protected, but can venture out to feed in open fields. Birds and small mammals dwell in decrepit trees, often leafless and limbless. I once saw such a tree struck by lightning. Like a massive torch, it caught fire, burned through the night, and smoldered for days. I was struck by the force of nature, and also by this metaphor for my inner life.

Best-Laid Plans

It's November of 1983. Alec and I receive a letter from Derick that explains his reluctance to sign the property over to a land trust. He is concerned about tax liability. And, more so, does not want to relinquish all control until the public programs are truly sustainable.

I would therefore, for the time being at least, feel more comfortable if my will stated that any shares of SF Inc. owned by me at the time of my death were bequeathed to you, Alec, rather than to Ottauquechee (land trust) as suggested in the current draft agreement. This could be easily changed, of course, if everything was worked out satisfactorily in the next few months. . . . I guess I'm trying to answer the question, which I have actually been asked a number of times by interested people, of what happens to the place if it fails in a year or two and has been pledged to OLT in its entirety.

We are disappointed, but I am thirty-seven and Alec is thirty-one. Derick is seventy. Perspectives change with age. Death is more believable, inevitable. And, over a lifetime, one has seen best-laid plans go awry. (I begin writing this memoir at age seventy.)

Bad Omen

Three months pass. Alec, the girls, and I are spending February vacation in Captiva with Derick and Rusty. They have built a modern home on the bay side of the island. An almost life-size portrait of Rusty hangs over a white brick fireplace in the living-dining area. Cathedral ceilings and a south-facing wall of windows create an airy sunlit space. A pass-through connects this larger room to a galley kitchen and breakfast nook.

During the evening cocktail hour, Rusty expresses concern that her two daughters, who were so close to Derick, had not been included in his will. His demeanor and quiet comments indicated that, given the tradition of keeping property within bloodlines, to do so would be too unconventional, too uncomfortable for him.

Now, this morning, Derick, Rusty, Alec, and I are in the breakfast nook playing Boggle. Anna and Heidi are in the living room, entertaining themselves with pastel coquina shells they've found on the beach.

Derick is planning to revise his will when he returns to Vermont in about three weeks. He restates his concerns about signing his property over to the land trust. "Traditionally, Quentyn, as the eldest son, should be the heir. And yet his health problems have kept him less involved in the farm's operations. Marshall is a hard worker, such a hard worker. I admire that, but he hasn't been involved with the business or legal end of the property. I'd feel more comfortable leaving the property to you, Alec."

I immediately intervene. "The estate taxes would devour the remaining property, and besides, Alec's siblings would never speak to him again." Alec agrees.

Our discussion somehow leads to Derick's wishes upon his eventual death. Because he rarely shares such personal thoughts, I'm surprised when he says, "I'd like to have my pilot friend, James Pyle, spread my ashes over—" Rusty abruptly finishes his sentence with "—Shelburne Farms. I knew you were going to say that," revealing her wish that Florida had become *their* new home.

During the previous summer, Rusty had organized Derick's seventieth birthday celebration. Old and new acquaintances attended. Perhaps that event had renewed his fondness for friends from years past and explains why James Pyle now so quickly comes to mind.

I suddenly notice that a lapis lazuli stone is missing from the ring I'm wearing. The ring had been bequeathed to Anna by Derick's mother, Aileen. Each great-granddaughter born by the time of Aileen's death had received one or two pieces of jewelry from her estate. Because the ring is quite large, I wear it on my middle finger until it will one day be resized for Anna. Being superstitious, especially about rings, I think, *Uh oh. This is a bad omen.*

Rusty and I drop to our hands and knees to search the floor. We sweep the floor, then search for the stone in the garbage compactor. With extra persistence, we take the compactor bag downstairs and dump its contents onto a concrete slab. Amid coffee grounds and other debris, we find the stone!

The phone rings. Rusty's young brother has died in a hang gliding accident. Perhaps the lost ring signaled this tragedy, but that doesn't seem right. *The omen should have related more directly to Derick, or his family.* They immediately depart for Georgia on the first flight out. Derick says, "I'll see you soon in Shelburne."

We tidy the house before leaving for Vermont. Upon our arrival the next day, Derick calls to confirm that we have safely returned home. "We're fine but have found quite a surprise," I groan. "Mice, or worse, have carried sunflower seeds two stories up to our bedrooms."

Varmints had found birdseed in a large storage crock kept in the basement. "They've stashed one black seed pile, five or six inches in diameter, between the sheets of each of our three beds!"

Derick is so entertained by my report that he's still chortling when we say goodbye.

Whip-poor-will

A friend and relative, Bill Webb, calls from Florida. He asks to speak with Alec. I hear Alec say something like, "Oh, no. Okay, okay. Yup. All right. Thank you. Thank you, Bill. Yup. Okay. Bye."

Derick died of a massive heart attack while golfing with friends on March 13, 1984. *Another parent lost. He seemed so vital when we were with him only three weeks earlier.* We learn that he had, similar to my father, been diagnosed with angina shortly before his death. I think, *The ominous lapis ring.*

Alec and I weep. Unprepared for this shock, we try to sort our shattered emotions, to make sense of the news. Anna disappears upstairs.

In her quiet way, she returns with a drawing of a shamrock. After all, St. Patrick's Day is just around the corner. She has drawn a tear-filled little face in the middle of the three-leaf shamrock. Above the face are her grandfather's initials, D. W., with a rainbow and a heart. The drawing resembles a crucifix with two outstretched leaves, or arms. Anna's image is one of love, suffering, and open-armed surrender. No words are needed.

Alec and Marshall fly to Captiva to support Rusty and sort through Derick's files. I stay behind to plan the Vermont memorial service and reception. While writing the obituary, it occurs to me that, in lieu of flowers, we might request funds to build walking trails on the property. That will be a more lasting memorial, and might encourage the idea of walking for pleasure and health, as we experienced in Europe. I call Captiva to run the idea by Rusty, Alec, and Marshall. They all agree.

Marshall, his crew, and David, the education director, create the trails. It takes a while for walking to catch on, but it eventually becomes more popular. We hire a wonderful mason to build a redstone memorial on Lone Tree Hill, the promontory behind the Farm Barn. Half of Derick's ashes are buried at the memorial. The other half are spread from a plane piloted by his Groton classmate James Pyle.

We learn that Derick bequeathed his property, and his full faith, to our unproven nonprofit organization, SFR! The contents of his will had been unknown to us, and had not yet been altered by his planned trip to Shelburne. Derick's will was left largely as he wished.

He honored the wishes of his children to keep the land as undeveloped as possible for public education and enjoyment. I see how much he must have loved his children, including an in-law like me, to do so.

Early this spring evening, I hear the call of a whip-poor-will outside Heidi's bedroom window. It's a sound we heard when visiting Derick at his winter home in Florida, but I had never heard one in Vermont.

Stewardship

Saddened and rattled by Derick's unexpected death, we're somehow wading through the aftermath, one day at a time. It's simply a matter of putting one foot in front of the other.

Everything has changed. We are even more determined to make SFR sustainable, in honor of Derick and his faith in us. His ownership no longer obstructs our fundraising efforts. We begin to plan for a capital campaign. Our board treasurer, Ray, says, "It's easy. You just create a budget and a brochure and go out to solicit."

We set out to raise two and a half million dollars with our first capital campaign. I want a better name, something new for our larger donors, and come up with Steward. Our attorney thinks it sounds like a waiter on a train or airplane, but we're going ahead with it, to instill the concept of stewardship.

A fundraising consultant is hired, but lasts only a short while. I'll direct the campaign with support from Karen, our exceptional office manager. The trustees and a part-time grant writer assist us.

In the early years of SFR, we had turned to Quentyn's Groton School classmate Hunter. Accomplished in the financial world, his first words to us were "You've got to stop the hemorrhaging." Our first budget cuts were in the buildings and grounds division.

None of us family members received compensation during those early years. Our time was volunteered. Alec and I were still supported by Garden Way fees and from the sale of Jerry's and my house. My parents were able to help us with a couple of loans. They had received payment for the second sale of The Club, had received an inheritance from Mom's parents, and had earnings from their recent employment.

We youngsters aren't thinking of our own security or retirement. We want to dispel any appearance of using the nonprofit organization for our personal advantage. Furthermore, our priority is to compensate Derick's longtime employees: the St. Georges, Boisverts, Bessettes, and Dentons, and a revolving dairy staff. They are like loyal family.

Ellen St. George, for example, plays an important role in welcoming each new Webb infant. She prepares antique fabric for the family bassinet by deftly mending, washing, and pressing the fragile gossamer. With each new birth, like Anna's and Heidi's, Webb sisters or aunts prepare the traditional bassinet with delicate fabric restored by Ellen.

When I first met Ellen, she told me she had cared for my great-grandmother Thompson in her waning years. I'll surely visit Ellen in her waning years.

Since Derick's death, fundraising and the various operations have increased SFR's income. We can finally, barely, afford to hire more employees and modestly pay ourselves. (I, for one, am paid from $15,000 to $20,000 per year, without benefits, during my last four years as president.)

Imaginary Friends

Before we fully embark on the capital campaign, my mother is again treating Alec, Anna, Heidi, and me, to a vacation. We're paying a brief visit to my Aunt Ede and Uncle Harold on Nantucket Island.

When we arrive at their door, they don't invite us into their home. Ede is standing behind a screen door, communicating less with words and more with tears. Harold is seated behind her on a sofa. They seem unwell, sorrowful. I don't understand, but sense that alcohol is involved. Sadly, we won't see them again. I had imagined a much warmer reunion.

Our spirits are lifted by Heidi and her imaginary friend, Ginny. Anna had previously adopted two imaginary friends, Sees and Saws. I, too, had a dreamlike imaginary friend named Judy. In my case, I identified for my parents a particular house where Judy lived, and would ask if she could have dinner with us. Oddly, I knew that my fantasy wasn't quite true, yet believed it.

Judy's house burned, allowing me to let go of my imagined friend. Now, we honor Heidi and her colorful fantasy by stopping here and there so that she can "visit" Ginny.

Stormy weather makes for a turbulent ferry ride back to the mainland. The girls and I have to lie down. Alec is green, but my mother is sitting upright, nonchalantly eating a pastry and a pear. She seems unaware that the deck hands are dutifully mopping vomitus.

Mission Impossible

The capital campaign is well underway as we approach the end of 1984. We name it the Centennial Campaign, intended to culminate in 1986, one hundred years after William Seward and Lila Vanderbilt Webb began Shelburne Farms. We mark the date by listing the SFR phone number as ending in 8686.

I present the trustees with three possible uses of the Big House: a conference center, a tour destination, or an inn and restaurant. One trustee, Paul, definitively states, "An inn and restaurant." Looking at me, he finishes with "And you have to do it." A strong current of impossibility passes through me.

The campaign quadruples our workload. A five-year business plan is needed. It must include construction and operating estimates. We have no experience with this, but will have to do it. If successful, income from an inn and restaurant will support the costly education programs.

I'm responsible for educational and public programs, budgeting, fundraising, publicity, and strategic planning. My added tasks are to coordinate trustee meetings and lead division managers' meetings. Alec and I share work on the cheese catalog. The SFR newsletter is under my purview.

Alec takes on the role of general manager with a focus on the dairy and cheese operation. Because of the "stay within bloodlines" precept, he works in liaison with family members during this period of transition. He is responsible for overseeing legal contracts and financial accounting. We are fortunate to have found a certified public accountant who is knowledgeable about nonprofit corporations. He is my mother's brother, Uncle Joe.

Alec's and my work relationship is easy. We numb our childhood wounds by working in excess.

At Peace

My work schedule is arranged around Anna and Heidi. I usually leave work in the afternoon when Anna comes home from school. Heidi has been with cheerful Obbie, her part-time caregiver. I take them to lessons like piano, ballet, horseback riding, skiing, or gymnastics. Since Dad's death, we check on Mom before returning home for dinner.

Today when we stop at Mom's house, she's complaining of a severe headache. Her expression is clear and pensive. I assume it's because she's been missing Dad even more as time has passed. We've recently talked about her selling the house, and moving into an apartment building where she would be less lonely.

Out of concern I say, "Mom, I'll take Anna and Heidi down to the Oasis Diner for a quick bite. We'll come back and watch the evening news with you." She responds with "Okay. I'll make some pudding for the girls."

We quickly return, but the front door is locked. Mom doesn't respond to the doorbell. The three of us walk to the rear of the house. I find a key that lets us into the kitchen. Lights are on. The stove burner is red-hot. There, behind a cooktop island, Mom has collapsed. She is lying facedown. Her glasses have been crushed by the fall.

I flash back to Florence falling and breaking her glasses at our Lake Sunapee camp. My mind races to understand what has happened. *Has Mom so quickly become inebriated? Or could this be diabetic shock? She does have adult-onset diabetes.*

"Mom, what happened? Have you been drinking?" She nods slightly and attempts to speak. The only utterance is a gurgling sound. I've seen her this way, falling-down drunk, so many times. But this time, she is breathing heavily. Her face is flushed.

Little Heidi goes to her, eases Mom's glasses off, and hands her blankie to Grammy. Heidi is just over three years old. I, useless in medical emergencies, especially related to my mother, take half a dozen steps toward the phone to call Alec. He is in downtown Burlington at a karate lesson. He tells me to call 911, which I do.

Being so close to the hospital, EMTs arrive quickly, but seem clumsy and confused in their actions. Alec also arrives. I follow the ambulance to the hospital. Anna and Heidi go home with Alec.

Everything is a blur. A doctor finds me in the hospital waiting room. He explains that my mother has suffered a severe cerebral hemorrhage. "If she survives, she will most likely be in a vegetative state. Do you want us to put her on life support?"

How can this decision be my responsibility? I can't choose to take my mother's life!

Struggling for clarity, I remember, with great relief, that Mom had shown me her living will. I know what she wants. "No. She did not want to be on life support." The doctor nods. He assures me that she will be kept as comfortable as possible.

Alec and I are at the hospital on the following morning. We are closeted in a windowless waiting room. I can hear Mom groan as they administer CPR. Her organs are failing. This does me in. I can do nothing to save my mother, the woman who gave me life. I kneel on the floor of that awful little room and sob into its dismal carpet. Poor Alec. He calmly tries to console me.

I walk to Mom's room. She is in a coma, but still might hear me say "It's all right for you to go, Mom. I know you don't want Alec and me to go through this again, but it really is okay for you to leave. If you want to stay, I'll be here for you. I'll be with you. But if you want to go, we'll be fine. You really can go now, but only if you want to."

Alec returns home to be with Anna and Heidi. My uncles Walt, Joe, and Eugene arrive. Like caricatures of three big birds, they surround me next to my mother's bed. I feel deeply touched. My broad-shouldered uncles, who have always been so loving and supportive, are here with me.

Uncles Walt and Joe say their goodbyes and depart. Eugene stays on. I go home to check on the girls and freshen up before the next vigil. It occurs to me that Mom, who smoked only in the bathroom and rarely drank publicly, is a private person. Perhaps she wants to die alone, privately.

As I arrive at home, the phone is ringing. A kind nurse calls to tell me that Mom passed on. "Your uncle had left the hospital," her nurturing voice continues. "I washed your mother's face and brushed her hair. You should know she was very much at peace." It is March 1985. One parent had died during three consecutive years, each in the month of March.

Alec's sister Mary, who had been a Waldorf School teacher, soon calls. I describe how Mom groaned, as though she was giving birth while dying. Mary says, "Yes, she was being born to the next plane." This sounds right to me, even though no one knows for sure.

(Mary sends me a book that explains death in a way that works for me.)

With Mom's death, it is little Heidi who beautifully expresses her loss with a drawing. The death of yet another grandparent may be causing our young daughters to feel somewhat abandoned.

As an only child, with both parents now gone, I feel like an orphan, even though I have my own nuclear family. The major stars of my life's constellation have, in a blink, lost their light. I am disoriented, but at the same time, free from constant worry.

Balanced by the love and support of friends and family, it's as though I've been handed a silver tray of grain. Some is ripe and fresh, some is moldy, but all is grist for the mill of my life. The death of both parents comes with forgiveness and grace. I finally see them as whole. Wholly human. It's no wonder that the words whole and holy stem from the same root.

Nesting Toys

I perceived my mother as a painting of light and dark tones. She was sometimes my greatest supporter and at other times my greatest nemesis, but she was always my teacher.

Mom was angry whenever I tried to talk to her about her drinking. Only once, toward the end of her life, did she admit to her alcoholism.

I never understood why anyone would choose to live in such an empty place. She missed out on so much. I've tried to understand. In fact, trying to understand "Why?" has constituted much of my life's journey... the work toward my own wholeness.

Mom and I were like Russian matryoshka dolls, nesting toys. She came from her mother as I came from mine, and as my children came from me. *Yes, I came from my mother, but I am not her.*

Sadly, when I found Mom collapsed and dying, I misinterpreted her cerebral hemorrhage for drunkenness. I was initially alarmed, and then felt both confused and accusing. I didn't give her the benefit of the doubt. And yet, in my defense, her drunkenness had been confirmed so many times before.

Mom played an enormous part in giving me my life and in shaping me, for better or for worse. I am deeply grateful for that. She shared with me her dark and private world where no other was allowed to go. There, I experienced the stinking, frightening underbelly of life, sometimes teeming with snakes or droning on with songs of sorrow.

Yet just as one coin has two sides, I encountered laughter, and the rare, glistening beauty of a mother's spirit. Her mothering appeared, though, in the form of praise, not coddling, or cuddling.

Another Attic

Although it is soon after Mom's death, we are attending a family reunion that was planned months earlier by my mother-in-law, Elizabeth. Alec, our daughters, other family members, and I are here in her birthplace, Charleston, South Carolina. We're visiting an attractive brick home owned by Elizabeth's aunt and uncle, and located in the lovely historic district.

Elizabeth quietly leads me to a renovated attic space on the third floor of the brick house. It is spare, with little room to move about. I scan the floral wallpaper, a low ceiling, and a dormer window that overlooks the street below. She and her mother had resided here.

When Elizabeth was born, her father was in his seventies. He predeceased his much younger wife. Although a New York attorney, he evidently did not provide for his wife and children. Their lifestyle was greatly diminished after his death.

Elizabeth, the youngest child, and her mother were beholden to family for this humble accommodation in the attic. Elizabeth points through the dormer window. "From here, I saw them take my mother away. I knew she was very ill. I never saw her again."

It's no wonder that Elizabeth had dreamed of becoming a doctor. Like me, she likely wanted to save her mother. She was told, though, that women can't be doctors.

Elizabeth wasn't allowed to cry at her mother's funeral. At age eleven, she was sent to live with her older sister, a newlywed. She arrived at the door with whooping cough. Although Elizabeth was close to her sister, she could feel that her arrival was understandably disruptive.

Elizabeth had watched while her mother was taken away, just as I had. She and I had become ill when our mothers were taken away, she with whooping cough, I with pneumonia. We'd both dreamed of becoming doctors, to find a cure, but never did.

Elizabeth, too, had stuffed her emotions while being shuttled around, perhaps feeling like an outsider. She and her mother had briefly landed in an insecure financial situation, as my parents and Dad's mother had. Elizabeth's mother received no inheritance, as my father and his mother did not. What interesting parallels. And how steeped Alec and I are in our family patterns.

Welcoming Footpaths

This fall, Alec, our children, and I are traveling in England. We visit the Lake District, the Cotswolds, a cheddar cheese region, and London. We enjoy welcoming footpaths in the north, where we visit the home of Beatrix Potter. She donated profits from her Peter Rabbit stories to protect the landscape there. That is now a pipe dream of mine. I'll write children's stories in my spare time. The proceeds will help protect the land at Shelburne Farms.

The Beatrix Potter visitor center, where the décor and merchandise reflect her mission, is my model for the new visitor center we're planning at Shelburne Farms.

Project Seasoning

We return home. Fundraising is proceeding at a frustratingly slow pace. Our trustees are wondering whether we can meet campaign goals. During this low point, I receive a surprise phone call.

It's a woman whom Alec and I had met at the entrepreneurship conference in Tarrytown, New York. Having since learned that the woman is a trustee for the Rockefeller Foundation, I applied for funding, but was shown little interest. The surprise call is to offer a $100,000 grant to our campaign! My knees feel like jelly.

Someone from New York, a well-known philanthropist, will donate the largest gift yet. Our trustees now feel a bit more confident. We are gaining momentum, but still have a long way to go.

Our mission is at the forefront. Education director David and I meet weekly to review material for a seasonal curriculum based on agriculture and the environment. The staff is growing. Programs emphasize our dependence on nature. We want to show how all things are interconnected, beginning with such essentials as soil, and the lowly earthworm.

Project Seasons, our first teacher's manual, is published in 1986. David's foreword quotes Anna Comstock (1923):

"For what is agriculture save a diversion of natural forces for the benefit of man.... Nature study is the alphabet of agriculture, and no word in that great vocation can be spelled without it."

Rejection Overturned

Our school programs are supported by the community. We receive donations to purchase children's snowshoes for winter tracking and to build a maple sugar house. IBM has annually supported the education center located in the Coach Barn. We request a $100,000 grant from IBM to support the new capital campaign.

I am stunned to discover that someone sent a letter to IBM's executives and to sixty or so other Vermont leaders to discourage them from supporting us. The scathing letter was sent by the director of a neighboring nonprofit organization that is competing with us for IBM funds.

Written in cahoots with a mail-order businessman, the letter refers to me as Marie Antoinette, ascribing to me a "let them eat cake attitude, saving an estate while other Vermonters live in trailer parks." I can't understand how converting a private estate to public use fits that accusation, but our grant proposal to IBM is rejected.

Having learned about the loss of the IBM grant, the Lintilhac Foundation has provided a $50,000 grant to repair the roof of the mansion. The foundation also pledges a $1,000,000 grant, to be paid over five years.

Having such a generous pledge as collateral, we are able to borrow from a local bank to begin construction. The donors, and the banker, clearly want to help launch our project.

Ribbon Cutting

There's growing public interest in tours of the estate. For the tours to work, we must enhance the training of our volunteer tour guides. And a new visitor center is needed to welcome individuals and bus tour groups. Cheese and other products could be sampled and sold there, to help support SFR's mission. The gatehouse at the entrance of the property will become the new visitor center. This is the first goal of our capital campaign.

I ask the Vermont Division for Historic Preservation to provide a list of architects who will be sensitive to the historic fabric of the structure. We select Martin Tierney, partly because he serves on Vermont's historic preservation advisory council. We soon discover that he is not only skilled, he's also pleasant and cooperative, fun to work with.

Martin's designs are thoughtful. While he's adapting the structure for public use, Rusty, her friend Puddy, and I travel to the New York Gift Show. Puddy is to be the manager of the visitor center.

We three enjoy the search for farm and nature-themed products. The new visitor center is to feel "natural, woodsy and clean," in keeping with our mission.

To help interpret the past and future of the estate, I'm working with staff and consultants to create a slideshow for visitors. We've also been supporting two authors who are writing historical books about Shelburne Farms.

On this July day of 1986, there's cause for celebration! We're having a ribbon-cutting ceremony for the new visitor center.

Inn Team

Our next goal is to open an inn and restaurant in one year. We are busy with budgeting and fundraising for what we now call: Shelburne House, the Inn at Shelburne Farms, not the Big House. Shelburne Farms Resources, or SFR, is now simply referred to as "Shelburne Farms."

I discover, midsummer, that something is seriously wrong with my digestive system. I must not be managing my stress well. All the tightness I feel when "staying strong" is finally causing a problem.

Medical tests reveal nothing, so Alec and I sign up for a series of evening meditation classes.

I find that going into meditation is like entering a safe harbor or sanctuary. My symptoms are quickly disappearing, but I'll continue to practice this ancient tradition.

Martin, our architect, has begun to design details for the inn. Marnie, the current director of the mansion, will operate the new inn. She'd been a restaurant chef and had worked at another country inn, making her an essential member of the team. Three other members of the inn's team are Remo, a trustee; Linda, our interior designer; and

Rosalyn, our staff publicist.

We had hired a contractor to develop construction estimates for the inn. He wasn't a good fit. Our board treasurer, Ray, suggests that we replace him with a construction manager rather than a general contractor. He recommends Mark Neagley, who is working on his house.

We interview Mark, who had previously worked on the Shelburne House South Porch as an employee of Moose Creek Restoration, although I had not met him then.

We hire Mark, but the situation is tenuous. There is no certainty that construction can move forward because we haven't raised all of the necessary funds. Yet we urgently need his construction estimates in order to raise the funds and create a work schedule.

Mark is completing a job on Nantucket Island. Due to fog and canceled ferries, he sometimes misses our meetings. Worried that he isn't all in, I'm uncertain about working with him. The pressure is on. Time is of the essence. I am frustrated, but, in fairness to him, he doesn't yet have a guaranteed contract.

Martin coincidentally shares office space with Mark. I call Martin. "Can Mark do this job?" After a long, thoughtful pause, Martin says, "Yes. I think he can."

Mark enters my office only moments later. Knowing that both of us are frustrated, he announces, "I quit." He continues, "For the first time in my life, I've just seen a therapist. I have five female clients and they're all making me crazy."

I ask, "What did the therapist say?"

"She said I might learn something from doing this job."

"What do you need for this to work?"

"I need to feel appreciated."

"Well, I need trust and dependability. Should we try once more, and see if it can work?"

We decide to give it one more try. Mark is the final member of our inn team.

Wild Ride

Construction begins during the frigid month of January. We intend to open the inn in six months. The mansion is unheated. Temporary heat is inadequately blasted through long and wide plastic tunnels into the hallways. Mark is often seen eating an entire bag of pecan sandies to, theoretically, raise his body temperature. Conditions are miserable.

As construction begins, we learn that there is asbestos in the basement. The estimate for removal is $120,000, which is not in our already tight budget. A friend of Remo's has come to the rescue.

The septic field is another challenge. We find an engineer who can design an innovative system. I invite two dynamic women from state government to learn about and hopefully support the plan. Alec works with the engineer to complete permitting for the system.

The work pace accelerates. Alec's and my duties are divided. We intersect at the Farm Barn office and during meetings, but our orbits are separate until we meet over dinner at home.

This is the beginning of a wild ride.

Dream Attic

Martin and his wife, Linda, had introduced us to the island of Vieques, Puerto Rico. Alec and I will go there with our daughters during February school vacation.

Before leaving, I give Alec his first tour of the now-gutted mansion. Flooring has been removed to make way for new plumbing and fire safety. Plaster is being repaired. Some furnishings have been moved to the Marble Dining Room for safekeeping. Other furnishings are being repaired or reupholstered elsewhere. Bathrooms will be renovated, if not newly created. Demolition is taking place in the East Conference and Dutch rooms. Preparations are underway for wallpapering or painting. The work is both daunting and exciting. Alec seems quietly pleased.

Here I am, involved with gutting another home. But gutting this house means inviting the public in, as though retrieving the comforting village of my childhood.

And it was in *this* home, that I had come upon my beautiful dream attic.

Now, on the island of Vieques, we are soothed by soft, easygoing sea breezes. Paso Fino, fine-gaited horses, roam the island unfettered, free. Tree frogs sing. Orange butterflies float among wild hibiscus blossoms. The temperature of the air and our skin are one and the same. Time seemingly stands still, until our return.

Linchpin

New obstacles arise. Another trustee has a change of heart. He believes it makes more sense to endow the land rather than "sink funds into the buildings." I worry that we will not succeed if we halt construction, given our tight time frame.

One trustee, Selma, sways the vote. "Nothing ventured, nothing gained. Sometimes you have to take a risk. Income from the inn is the linchpin for supporting the education programs," she says.

I breathe a sigh of relief. With only four months to go, there are too many moving parts to put our plans on hold.

But then a third trustee requests a second pause. She wants us to study the idea of making the inn a year-round venture. I instinctively believe the slow months and costly winter conditions will drain all profits gained over the more clement seasons.

We complete the study. Its findings confirm my instincts. Our business plan does not have to be revised. The inn will be seasonal, as planned.

If the inn is to open on time, we have to create a reservation system, hire and train the staff, design a kitchen, and purchase all supplies. What if we have no guests? National publicity is beginning to appear, but that is not a guarantee. And we are still raising the necessary funds for construction.

We also need an outstanding chef. Del, who had previously operated the mansion, and her husband, suggest David, a chef from Scotland's luxurious Royal Scotsman train.

Though Scottish, much of David's culinary experience had been acquired in Italy. We're told that he's a fine chef who prefers locally grown ingredients and charmingly engages with customers.

We plod through immigration procedures. David is temporarily admitted, due to his unique skills in crafting local, seasonal cuisine.

Historic Fabric

Martin, our architect, creates a set of measured drawings. Engineering is his next hurdle. Fire safety has to meet state requirements while preserving the historic fabric of the house. Having come up with sensitive designs, he coordinates with state officials and engineers to accomplish that aim. They, too, are essential to the process.

Much of the original electrical system is accepted because it is state of the art. To conserve funds, detailed plans and specifications are not needed. Mark and his crew are able to implement design details through Martin's verbal descriptions.

Linda, the interior designer, and her colleague complete a study of the mansion's history in order to recommend upholstery, paint colors, and wall coverings. Marnie and I work with them while addressing furniture repairs, bathroom décor, bed linens, and room amenities while redesigning the kitchen.

She and I are also deciding on staff uniforms and wine lists. We plan an afternoon tea service, as well as a breakfast buffet similar to one my family had experienced in Switzerland. Informal floral linens are being fabricated for morning meals. Evening meals call for more formal table settings.

How should we serve water, juice, champagne, beer, wine, and cocktails with a limited budget for glassware? How should bread and butter be presented? Will we have candles and flowers? Marnie and I turn to other inns for ideas.

We fly to Boston to select glassware and linens. Here, Marnie finds white Italian bed covers that appear to be identical to those in historic photographs of the mansion! It may sound silly, but a simple surprise like this keeps us going.

Work is overwhelming and exhausting, yet feels quite natural. As a child, I had experienced renovations of The Club and had filled salt and pepper shakers for customers. I'd shopped for food and liquor with Dad and prepared bank deposits with Mom.

The dairy farm of my grandparents and my neighbors in Ascutney make the dairy here in Shelburne seem familiar. Even my love of nature and pleasant school experiences are tied to the education programs we are creating.

And pouring myself into work provides an adventurous escape.

Chain of Events

We, of course, have never managed an inn. Some trustees are suggesting that a hotel chain should assume management. Although the concern is valid, we and some trustees feel the family connection is important. Marnie's and David's skills give us confidence.

As mentioned, I again find myself living between a hospitality business and a dairy farm. The content may be different, but the process is similar to that of my childhood. Children learn by osmosis, from their parents and other natural teachers. And my work during my teen years as a chambermaid and waitress is now useful experience. This gives me confidence.

Meanwhile the dairy operation and education programs are ongoing. The dairy staff feels neglected and disgruntled. One reason is that the inn is the new center of attention. And Alec, for good reasons, has changed milking procedures. The changes have been met with resistance. He and I hold special meetings at the dairy to improve communications.

Paul Webb, no relation, works in the milking parlor. He is also a musician. When the inn opens, we'll hire him to play in the library on a donated grand piano.

Footprints

Fundraising continues. There are days when I sign as many as a hundred thank-you letters. We haven't yet reached our goal, even though individuals, foundations, and companies are supporting the campaign. Villeroy & Boch, Oneida silver, and Old Deerfield Fabrics will donate dinnerware, flatware, and wall coverings, respectively.

Old Deerfield is reproducing several of the historic wall coverings. The company will provide most of our wall coverings in exchange for creating a Shelburne House line. As the mansion is becoming more attractive, we realize that we can't get away with bypassing certain renovations. The kitchen is an example. We thought we could make simple improvements but now realize a complete upgrade is needed.

The president of Blodgett Ovens offers to reach out to other corporate executives to request donations of kitchen equipment.

Well-known Vermont restaurant owners and innkeepers are extending their help, rather than feeling threatened by us as competitors. They assist with reservation systems, ratios of staff to guests, kitchen design, customer surveys, occupancy rates, and even furnishings. One resort has donated an oak bedroom set for the Oak Room, which had suffered major damage from an earlier roof leak.

These businesspeople may be amused by our inexperience, but they are genuinely supportive. They are surely leaving their mark. We are deeply moved by their profound generosity.

One capital campaign donor, Harriet, reminds us to show

appreciation toward those executing the work. With that advice, Marnie provides muffins or chili and cornbread for the construction crew on Fridays.

We invite the entire crew to a reception and a viewing of the slideshow at the new visitor center. With a shared mission, there is a growing sense of family, and pride, among the many who are involved.

Harriet also advises us to leave footprints of earlier construction whenever possible. Two historic elements have been uncovered. One is in the Dutch Room, where the removal of a dropped ceiling has revealed the original beams.

The other is a previously concealed fireplace in what had been the family's modern kitchen, now being restored as a conference and dining room. When it was uncovered, we were surprised to find brass andirons and wall sconces carefully stored in the fireplace.

The old mansion, a retired dowager, had been waiting to reappear in style.

Old Kitchen

Chef David Taylor has arrived at Burlington's bus terminal. I'm looking forward to meeting him there. We had mailed him a copy of the new Shelburne House book to give him a preconceived image of the estate.

As David and I drive south along Route 7, he is aghast at the suburban strip development. I fear that he might refuse our job offer. Given the beauty of his own country, Vermont is not what he had anticipated. He breathes a sigh of relief as we enter Shelburne Farms.

David's arrival means housing him. We hadn't included an apartment in the construction budget. The original kitchen of Shelburne House, referred to as the Old Kitchen, is attached to the rear of the building. The kitchen extends to a long wing that had once been the mansion's servants' quarters. The wing is now in extreme disrepair, with areas of collapsed ceilings and floors. Our plans called for demolishing the servants' quarters to create access for guest parking and service vehicles. We can create an apartment for David above the Old Kitchen.

The Division of Historic Preservation steps in to appeal the demolition. This is the most challenging obstacle that we've encountered. In my mind, halting the demolition will sabotage the entire project because of added cost, impaired access, and an already tight timeline. To pay off our bank loan, we must open the inn on time.

We can't ask guests to walk in darkness, or in foul weather, from another parking lot. And the inn, with only twenty-three bedrooms, is not large enough to afford a twenty-four-hour shuttle service for guests.

The controversy is growing. Someone from the preservation community asked the local newspaper to write an exposé. A reporter has asked to tour the wing. I say it is possible, but only if a waiver of liability is signed, given the collapsing floors and ceilings. The reporter hasn't appeared.

The Division for Historic Preservation is holding a meeting at the mansion. Martin has recused himself from the discussion because he chairs its advisory board. The division is deciding to oppose the demolition.

Martin pulls the director aside and explains that he fears their decision will terminate the entire project. He judiciously suggests that the Old Kitchen be kept and properly capped where it joins the servants' quarters. He also recommends leaving foundation stones as a historic footprint of the servants' quarters.

To our great relief, the division reluctantly accepts our plan. I now have to present the plan to Vermont's Act 250 district office for final approval.

Demolition of the servants' quarters reveals that the Old Kitchen was previously capped and defined. The quarters must have been added at a later date.

Martin sketches a design and we squeeze money out of the budget to renovate a space above the Old Kitchen. Mark and his crew, as a last gasp, will create a modest apartment for Chef David.

The Old Kitchen and the South Porch are my two favorite parts of the mansion. All of us had wanted to keep the Old Kitchen. Its marble and tile surfaces are beautiful.

Now, while clearing the kitchen for construction, Marnie finds an antique handheld fan. When it is unfolded, she sees that individual men's names are written on each wooden slat. She spots the name William Seward Webb.

Coincidentally, a volunteer named Shirley has been studying Lila Vanderbilt Webb's diaries. In one of the diaries, Lila mentions adding the name of a suitor, William Seward Webb, to her fan.

Such synchronicity! We joke that Lila is making an appearance, perhaps for the sake of keeping the Old Kitchen.

In Trust

Budgets keep me awake at night. All of the numbers are somehow in my head. As each new, often unplanned expense arises, we must cut items or raise additional funds. During the last several weeks of construction, stress is at an all-time high. On most mornings, I quietly get out of bed at around two. Careful not to awaken Alec, I rework the numbers and make to-do lists.

Pauses in nocturnal sleep can be like a meditation. Without diurnal distractions, I'm able to more vividly see what is happening. My thoughts and emotions are tamed by making the lists. I then return to a more peaceful sleep.

The inn will open in a month. I'm leading a large group of people through the mansion, to see the work in progress. Nearly everyone, including construction experts, warns that we will not be ready for opening day. And yet inn guests have reserved dates for their arrival. We cannot cancel their reservations, assuming we intend to meet our financial goals.

A few days pass. Mark and Martin are walking me through the mansion. We just concluded our weekly team meeting. The painting crew that was chosen, insisted upon, by the interior designer is lagging far behind. I begin to chastise the lead painter.

Mark stops me. He takes charge. "You hired Martin and me to do this work. Now let us do our job."

Trust does not come easily to me, but I have no choice.

Opening day is near. The staff has been hired. An Austrian maître d', loaned to us by another inn, is training the dining room staff with precision. Seventy or more construction crew members are completing their tasks.

Another seventy or so volunteers arrive to polish furniture and rehang prints and paintings. I'm sitting in what is called the Tea Room doling out cleaning supplies and directions. The new housekeeping staff is simultaneously cleaning bathrooms, making beds, washing windows, vacuuming, and mopping floors.

I experience a pleasant sense of unity, fluidity. All of us are fueled by commitment, and a dose of adrenaline.

Grand Metamorphosis

A celebration will take place this evening, before public guests check in tomorrow. To show appreciation for our trustees, we've invited them to sleep overnight following the celebration. They'll test the hospitality, as well as the plumbing.

It's four o'clock. I'm taking a final walk through the house to be sure everything is in place. In one bedroom, an electrician had hung a wall sconce. A small pile of sawdust lay on the carpet beneath it. His electric drill is lying on one of the white Italian bedspreads. My blood pressure is rising.

Then, as I peer into the bathroom of the William Seward Webb bedroom, I notice something amiss in the skylight. Dirt? No. Artists who had been hired to paint wall designs had painted a large spider and web in the highest area of the ceiling. A play on "Webb"? I'm not amused but must accept it. We are out of time.

Downstairs, Mark and three others are carrying an ornate mirror to hang in the Marble Dining Room. I glance around the room. The silk damask wall covering was too expensive to replace, but we did have the marble floor and plaster ceiling professionally cleaned. New tables have been added. Chairs have been repaired and reupholstered, the light fixtures restored.

Indoor palms, like those in historic photos of the house, have not yet been delivered. My only choice is to trust, or hope, that they will arrive.

Now on autopilot, my thoughts are blurred. I'm going home to change clothes. Guests will arrive in an hour.

When I return, everything is in place, including the potted palms! The house smells fresh and clean, renewed. Gardens are at their peak. Trained staff bring savory appetizers from the new kitchen. The liquor bar is in order. Eye-catching flowers are artfully arranged. Guests are beginning to stream in. There is new life, thanks to a magnificent team of many.

Staff, construction crew, volunteers, donors, and trustees had aimed for a nearly unattainable goal. How I wish I could name each person who helped. Everyone has pulled together and trusted one another. Both we, and the old mansion, have experienced a grand metamorphosis.

Marnie, Mark, Martin, and I sink into an oversize maroon sofa in the Main Hall. The beauty of it all is indescribable. Dumbstruck, we sigh with joyous relief, and awe. Even though far greater things have been accomplished in the world, this is one of my most satisfying and exhilarating moments.

Start-up Girl

At the inn's opening celebration, I speak of the significance of the Webb family's historical stature and the family's ongoing love of nature, farming, and Shelburne Farms. And, I add, "More significant is the growing extended family that is now keeping the place alive."

New demands arise with the opening of the inn. Summer guests write ahead of their arrival asking me to meet them. The dining room manager strongly encourages me to visit during the dinner hour "to create a buzz." I often go to the inn after tucking my children into bed. "The buzz" seems odd because I'm simply the girl from Ascutney, as I was before assuming this role.

The opening of the inn is a new milestone. Shelburne Farms now has seventy employees, including seasonal staff. The inn is meeting its financial goals. Fundraising is solid.

Even so, I'm in transition, needing either a rest or a change. Administrative duties are all-consuming, and I am more of a start-up kind of girl than an administrator.

Obsessive work seems to have parched my spirit. During a recent Florida vacation, I expressed to Alec that in the future, I hope to take a step back. "You can be president and I can help with programs and fundraising." He didn't see that as a viable option. Although more self-assured, he is shy, and likely lacks confidence in assuming the role of president.

I sorely miss personal time for nature, reflection, and the arts. And as my daughters grow older, they need more parental support, not less. While Heidi is about to enter first grade, industrious Anna, five years older, has found her way into the work world.

Anna helps in the inn's laundry room during this first season by folding bedsheets that greatly out-size her. Next year, she plans to offer childcare for guests. All of her providers will be CPR trained. Perhaps my daughters need a less driven mother.

Toasting Success

Near the end of the inn's first season, I invite J. Watson Webb Jr. to see the newly outfitted Shelburne House. He arrives with Hollywood actors Robert Wagner and Jill St. John. Glowing with appreciation and overflowing with information about the house, Watson has clearly forgiven us for using photos that he had believed were his.

The other operations at the farm continue. Martin, Mark, and I have met to plan for a new education center that will be located in the Farm Barn. By now, we are friends, not only colleagues or teammates. Alec and I spend social time with them and their spouses, Linda and Sandra, respectively.

Linda helps me plan an end-of-season dinner for David, Marnie, and Mark. Eighteen of us gather. A Scottish piper plays in David's honor. Next to a roaring fire in the Marble Dining Room, a seemingly medieval feast of turkey, stuffing, salads, and chocolate cake is enjoyed by all.

From there, we join the entire staff at the Coach Barn to dance for hours. A few of us gather in the Shelburne House library, to toast the inn's successful first season.

Russian Roots

November's bare trees expose contours of the land. The air is seasoned with the spice of fallen leaves. Fencerows wear the woven tweeds of earth tones. Apple trees are line drawings, painted with fermented fruits of red, yellow, or brown. Sunlight bursts through ink-blue clouds to spotlight a field here, a hillside there.

My Russian roots, love of earth, and curiosity toward the unknown are stirred, as always, by the moodiness, and the beauty, of November.

Peace Movement

A Shelburne Farms attorney invites me to the Soviet Union as a Vermont peace delegate. Because Gorbachev is signaling a more open government, Bridges for Peace has organized a women's exchange. I'm taking language classes and reviewing Russian history.

In preparation for departure, our delegation is attending a contentious seminar on conflict resolution at the John F. Kennedy School of Government. Our Soviet counterparts are scornful toward Americans. This doesn't bode well for the peace exchange that's about to occur.

Ten New England women are making the journey, beginning in Helsinki, Finland, where we'll spend the night. I enjoy meeting the unusual members of our group. One is a senior partner in a Boston law firm. Another is assistant dean of Harvard's medical school. All have unique backgrounds and talents.

I'm feeling tired and a bit lonely. Alec, and Marshall's wife, Juliet, had written loving notes for my departure. Their words embrace me with both softness and strength. I plan to arise early tomorrow morning to take a refreshing sauna and swim.

We depart for Moscow on an overnight train. Stowed away in confining cabins with one bunk bed per person, we roll along, absorbing the train's steady rumble. I peer into darkness through my cabin window. Etched by our train lights, barbed wire fencing eerily appears through falling snow. The fencing continues for miles and miles.

Upon our arrival in Moscow, we are taken to the Hotel Ukraina. I am immediately comforted by a sense of familiarity. The hotel, with its prim floral-patterned carpet, sectional sofas, and floor lamps, reminds me of my grandparents' home. How can this be? They were so young when they came to America and never returned to their native land. And yet, they brought this style with them.

I find the Russian manner of speech to be emotional, emphatic, and sometimes tinted with exaggeration, much like mine. This, too, is familiar, and comforting.

Invisible Glue

Our first day begins with an earthy breakfast of cooked vegetables: cabbages, beets, and potatoes.

I, with half of our group, opt to take a side trip to Yerevan, Armenia. The other half goes to Minsk, the region of my grandparents' roots. Here, in Armenia, we tour the impressive museum of ancient manuscripts, a textile factory, and an artist's studio. We also visit a nursery, hospital, and children's museum. One family invites us to dine in their home. We see how difficult life is, and yet we all enjoy music and dancing.

We Americans are now having a face-to-face exchange. Ten of us are seated on one side of a gloomy room. A similar size group of Armenian women, most of them dressed in black, enter and sit opposite us, about eight feet away. All of us depend upon the interpreter. I gaze at olive-skinned faces. The women's dark eyes penetrate our American self-confidence with kindness, and forgiveness.

I retain few of the translated words, but will not forget these women. All of life has been held in their rugged and calloused hands. They've delivered babies, raised children, nourished families, healed the sick, and buried the dead. They are, unwittingly, like glue in the binding of a book, the invisible glue that humbly holds their society together.

Bambi Story

Back in Moscow, we and the Soviet women are meeting in an enormous conference center. Amid a sea of red chairs, chandeliers, cameras, and microphones, each member of our delegation has been asked to address a certain topic. I speak about the connection between nature studies and the pursuit of peace.

We learn that the Soviet women are concerned about the environment, but little action is being taken. One woman admits, "We teach about nature only by reading the Bambi story to children." The magazine *Soviet Women* asks to run a story about our education programs at Shelburne Farms.

Jewel Box

Before returning home, we want to visit the Orthodox Church of Saint Nicholas in Moscow. The day is cold and dreary. As we step from a gray streetscape into the church, we are met by the blended scents of burning wax and incense. The sanctuary's floor-to-ceiling walls of polished brass shimmer in soft candlelight. Chanted Russian words rise to a place high above.

One old man looks like Tolstoy, with his long white beard, cane, and heavy black coat. Women stand here and there. With their babushka-hooded heads bent in reverence, they look like matryoshka dolls. With greater freedom to worship, there is hope, if not faith.

Like a musical jewel box, this church glows with human spirit, now that the lid has been lifted.

Messaging

During a meeting with our Soviet counterparts, we suggest sending a telegram to the leaders of our two countries. Everyone agrees. Our message will encourage peaceful negotiations. We trust that it will be sent to President Ronald Reagan and Chairman Mikhail Gorbachev in advance of an upcoming summit to be held at the United Nations in New York.

Ten days later, on December 7, 1988, Gorbachev concludes a lengthy speech with these words: "I would like to believe that our hopes will be matched by our joint effort to put an end to an era of wars, confrontation and regional conflicts, to aggressions against nature, to the terror of hunger and poverty as well as to political terrorism."

It's highly unlikely that our telegram was read by the two leaders. We are insignificant in the greater scheme of things. It is exciting, though, to be connected in any way with movement toward peace.

(Almost one year later, the Berlin Wall falls. All these years later, we see how the pendulum swings. Yet I still find Gorbachev's words to be noble, and hopeful.)

Wide-Eyed

Now, in the spring of 1988, *Vermont Woman* newspaper requests an interview regarding my work at Shelburne Farms and trip to the Soviet Union.

During the interview, I am asked to reflect on my future. "I don't know, at least in the future I'd like to complete what I set out to do at Shelburne Farms: for it to be financially solvent and a culturally, environmentally beautiful place for people . . . to make them part of it. I'd then like to become involved with more personal creative and spiritual discoveries such as painting and writing . . . perhaps write children's stories."

As we conclude, the reporter suggests that I read *The Way of a Pilgrim*, evidently a spiritual classic. It's the story of an anonymous Russian peasant who describes his pilgrimage in search of knowledge and wisdom through prayer. He finally moves beyond searching and dabbling to commit to a path.

I wonder whether there is a lesson for me in this story.

Silence

My return home from Russia is heavy with questions. I'm bringing my questions to marriage counseling and meditation. What of my work life? As an administrator, I have drifted away from the nature-related environmental education that had been my initial aim at Shelburne Farms. The natural world has always given me solace. Sadly, I now have less time to commune with nature.

Other questions have arisen, about marriage and the deeper meaning of relationship. I wonder how to find greater intimacy with myself, and with another. I decide to go on silent retreat. Though not a Buddhist, I've chosen Karmê Chöling, a meditation center in Barnet, Vermont. There, I will contemplate the choices I've made.

Although it may be wiser to leave books behind when on retreat, I bring *Necessary Losses* by Judith Viorst, *Celebrations of Life* by Rene Dubos, and *Jung, Synchronicity, and Human Destiny* by Ira Progoff. The latter may help to explain and validate my meditation experiences.

When addressing my earlier intestinal issues, meditations provided nonjudgmental, wise directions like "strengthen your abdominals" or "drink more water." But how does meditation work? Progoff seems to say that when we calm the mind and focus on an archetypal image, we are more capable of accessing wisdom without the clutter of our daily thoughts and emotions, our lists of to-dos.

I'm finding that, while here on retreat, silence creates spaciousness. Silence buffers me as I walk through a Zhivago-like landscape. The blackness of my long wool coat girds me for the stark chill of winter, and for my solitude.

As a stranger here, I feel free . . . and fully alive. I reimagine myself, and others, as strong in spirit.

Dream Attic

Life in 1988 is busier than ever. We are preparing for the inn's second season, hiring our first archivist, working on the mail-order catalog, and still fundraising. Educational programs are expanding beautifully with the help of Megan, our new education director.

In search of balance, I'm relying more heavily on my meditations. My personal search continues with books like *The Art of Loving, The Path of the Spiritual Warrior*, and *Love Is Letting Go of Fear*.

Alec and I are celebrating our thirteenth wedding anniversary in Vieques, with our daughters. I'm experiencing a renewed closeness. We both want that.

On the first evening of our return, Alec calls to say he won't be home for dinner. He's ordering pizza and staying late at the office. Have we done too much damage to our marriage? Is our healing process a case of too little, too late?

I take Anna and Heidi on weekend getaways, north to Montreal and south to Boston. Upon each return home, my sadness lengthens into the darkness of afternoon shadows.

I am an outsider. But, as much as I may want to blame others, my history, with so many layers of protection, likely makes me an outsider, or stranger, to myself.

I've found Jean, a new therapist who synthesizes the psychological with the spiritual. Following introductions, she queried with "Hmm. I have to ask. This may seem odd, but did you ever sleep on a cold box?" I, a bit startled, replied, "Yes, in childhood, I *did* sometimes sleep on an ice cream chest freezer." Her intuition was impressive. She had underscored a facet of my challenging childhood that I had blithely accepted.

During our sessions, I obsess over relationships. Jean delves into the psyche of ACOA, adult children of alcoholics. We discuss my childhood urge to flee by climbing a mountain. I tell her of my insistence on finding the attic of my recurring dreams, a beautiful room to which I could escape.

Tonight, in the splendor of midsummer, Paul Winter is performing on the lawn of the inn with the Russian Dmitri Pokrovsky Ensemble. An audience dots the lawn like spattered paint. Alec and I sit on blankets with our friends, taking in the beauty of the place, and its sounds. The performers' shrill and haunting songs are reminiscent of those sung by my grandmother.

I, tanned and in my prime, lean back on elbows to absorb the sight of the inn, Shelburne House. With nearly every room lit, it is the visage of a ship at sea. Guests stir behind golden windows.

How did I get here? Why me? I flash back to my recurring childhood dream of an attic, the attic found here in this grand house.

I must have landed here for a reason, but I sense that my role is ending.

Comical Counterfeits

Town and Country magazine asks to do a photo shoot. Alec and I agree, thinking the publicity will be useful. Our clothing sizes, including those of the girls, are requested. We're puzzled by that, but provide them anyway. Perhaps they want to capture our outdoor lifestyle with parkas or sweaters in colors they consider to be artistically correct.

An entire crew arrives at the inn. Several men, urban in appearance, begin to set up cameras in the ghastly Game Room with its taxidermied trophies.

A hair and makeup stylist leads us to another room where foundation is plastered onto our daughters' faces and mine. Multiple gowns and dresses are displayed with matching shoes and appropriate jewelry choices.

My hair is piled into a Gibson girl do. Anna, Heidi, and I are clothed in exquisite costumes. Alec wears a tux with velvet slippers. We *never* dress this way. Here we are, comical counterfeits, falsely portrayed as a royal family, of sorts. The whirlwind photo shoot is completed in an hour. The girls have loved every minute. Meanwhile, I wonder whether I'll be here at Shelburne Farms when the article is published.

Stargazer

Friends and family join us at the inn to celebrate my forty-second birthday. A Mozart concert is underway at the Coach Barn.

One trustee has sent stargazer lilies and requested a champagne toast. Even though deeply moved, I steal away for a quiet moment in the William Seward Webb bedroom. As I rest on a pale green chaise lounge, the window curtains gently dance on a summer breeze. I gaze toward the lake and mountains. Small birds fill the air with their celestial songs. Stars will soon appear.

Severed Ties

Alec and I vacation with the girls in New Mexico before the new school year begins. Home again, we are facing the normal turmoil associated with seasonal transitions.

My counselor Jean and I are exploring whether I am simply sabotaging my success by wanting to take a step back from work responsibility.

At a friend's suggestion, I'm interviewed by a wise woman. She analyzes my actions as stemming "from the heart." She says, "Courage is traceable to the Latin word "cor," meaning heart. Leaving your job requires much courage, much heart. I can see that you have that."

Though still working, I move to a lakeside cottage for a month. It's wise for me to step away for a while. The getaway is intended to be a retreat, a chance to gain perspective.

I can't guarantee fidelity when Alec asks. Intending to be honest, I have long since learned not to make promises like "never" or "always." Alec understandably feels threatened by this. In a matter of moments, we sever everything, including our joint finances.

We had separated before, but this time there is a sense of finality. We cry tears of pain and disappointment, but can't declare love.

Alec is holding a surprise gift for me, Santa Fe earrings. He tosses them toward me and drives away. I am numb, disoriented. His car returns. We hug and kiss goodbye. My hands feel his sinewy back. Loss and grief cloud his face. I am heartbroken, torn, but there is no turning back.

Tonight, I'm sitting alone in the cottage, feeling sharp hooks of guilt about the children, wanting to be aware of it all, sobbing. I think of missing Anna's first date or helping Heidi with schoolwork. What of my home, my kitchen, the outdoor bathtub, the garden, the beach?

Have I re-created this abyss, this aloneness, so familiar from my childhood? Is my departure doing to my children what my mother had done to me? I can't stop crying.

The girls are spending this week and weekend with me at the cottage. Anna, now twelve, is removed and in emotional pain. Only days before I left home, she had been so pleased to tell me that her "womanhood" had arrived. Some weeks earlier, we had chosen a pair of silver Navajo earrings to be given to her on that special day. What a searing collision of emotions. What pain, to have her mother leave so soon after this important passage.

Heidi, being younger, seems less affected. Each morning, I relish the few moments of watching Heidi sleep, knowing the cuddly closeness of my little seven-year-old will not last forever.

We rush from the cottage to Shelburne each day. They go to school. I go to work, to close a chapter. My desk is nearly clear. I reflect on the trustees, staff, and donors I have loved. Emotional exhaustion. Someone's wedding and the Harvest Festival will happen on Saturday. Anna and Heidi will be with Alec this weekend.

Heartbreaking Hawkweed

Am I blocking my **feelings** about Alec and all we have created together . . . children, home, SFR, a network of friends and family? I do see his beautiful qualities, but have to move on.

He asks, "But who will do what you have been doing?" I reply, "You can be president. Megan can lead the education programs and support your fundraising efforts." Megan's position had grown from intern to assistant director, and now education director. "What she lacks in polished experience is counterbalanced by her work ethic."

"Don't worry. Everyone will have sympathy. People will want to support you."

My last day on the job, except for some future consulting, has arrived. Fortunately, during the previous year, I had asked each division manager to create an operating manual, a record of basic systems and procedures.

Today, the board of trustees is honoring me with a farewell lunch at the inn. They give me a silver pendant. Someone has to remind me to open the little gift package. I'm stifled by the loss of so many meaningful relationships.

Marshall and his crew had mown the grassy roadsides, leaving patches of wildflowers along the way to and from the inn. Hawkweed in clusters of orange and yellow is a heartbreakingly beautiful detail. This feels commemorative to me, like flowers on a grave.

Buried

Alec returns from a therapy session in Santa Fe. He seems, well, buoyant. I've been meeting with individual board members to explain my decision. Each conversation is like a hands-on burial.

Alec and I are in the yard of the massive Farm Barn. We're saying goodbye, again. The barn triggers a scan of our time together, like flipping through a storybook. We cry, say we have loved the best we could, and acknowledge how much we've learned from each other. I then go on to cry with Rusty's friend Puddy, and to cry with my children. I am so very sad, but not afraid.

A call from Harvard Medical School invites me to observe Dr. Herbert Benson's work with meditation. Everything will be okay . . . in time, I hope.

Several people come forward to express their love and support. Oh, that means a lot!

Jitterbugging

My collegial relationship with Mark is becoming a friendship as we share more about our personal lives. We meet twice during my first month away. He hasn't been feeling well. His own brief marriage is falling apart.

A month later, we celebrate his birthday by seeing the opera *Il Trovatore* in New York. I'm attracted to him beyond friendship, but simply enjoy his company.

As I complete my last day of work, I run into Mark again. He comes by the following night with a pizza. I haven't seen him since. He's reconciling his own marriage, as well as a relationship that preceded his marriage.

I move to another temporary abode, closer to Shelburne. The lake is visible from my wood-heated space. On the few days that Anna and Heidi aren't with me, I walk sacred Mount Philo, read, write, and meditate in solitude. Steeped in this sweet-and-sour marinade, I have little desire for a new relationship, even with the prospect of aging alone.

During one long weekend, I attend an Opening the Heart intensive session in Massachusetts. This particular program is designed for adult children of alcoholics. We are learning to trust and love while working through past shame.

Mark drops by today. He comes bearing gifts: a black sweater, a pair of silver earrings, and blue fleece-lined slippers, possibly out of empathy for my lonely existence. It's a week or so before Christmas, so he offers to help me choose and purchase a small tree, mainly for the benefit of my daughters. I can see that he's still struggling with his two past relationships.

We don't cross paths again for several weeks, until very early this morning. Mark awakens me with a knock on the door. He steps in and asks from across the room whether I would like to join him in taking jitterbug classes. I sleepily say, "Sure," without seeing him. He leaves.

A relationship begins to grow out of friendship and jitterbugging.

Roving Ambassador

While in the process of leaving my work at Shelburne Farms, our teacher training program is approved by the national Ag in the Classroom effort. It goes on to win a Soil and Water Conservation Award. We grow a new Stewardship Institute out of those successes.

Our Inn team receives an award from the Preservation Trust of Vermont and earns the Inn of the Year Award from the Hideaway Report. Meanwhile, the inn's interior designer had submitted the project for a national award. Under President Reagan, we receive the President's Historic Preservation Award for the Shelburne House Rehabilitation.

I am allowed to bring one guest with me to the White House. Because the Lintilhac Foundation provided lead support for the project, I invite Crea, their representative.

While seated in the tiled Treaty Room, we hear a jolting clamor in the outer hall. Clicking shoes and cameras echo within stone surfaces. President Reagan arrives with a press corps and an entourage of security agents.

Grandmother Mimi had always said that it was important to have good table manners. "You might someday have dinner with the president." Although I won't be having dinner with the president, I do shake hands with him and murmur, "Thank you very much. It's an honor to meet you, Mr. President."

My generation had called him "Ray Gun." We'd disdainfully quoted him as saying "When you've seen one redwood, you've seen them all." I'm surprised that his administration is supportive of our work at Shelburne Farms.

He appears frail and much older than on television. But his air of genuine warmth and kindness is quite a surprise, as is his sense of humor.

During this time, I'm offered an executive director position at the American Farmland Trust in Washington, DC, but decline because of my children. Instead, the Vermont Studio Center, an artists' retreat, calls to ask if I will work with them. I agree to consult with them, part-time, for some time into the future. The Studio Center's cofounders encourage both creativity and meditation, making it a good place to land.

I'm becoming a roving ambassador by working with about thirty other nonprofit organizations, including Vermont Public Radio, the Stowe Education Fund, the Stern Center, and the Vermont Women's Fund. As a consultant, my work feels meaningful, I have flexible hours for parenting and am building cherished friendships.

Soulmates

While Alec's and my divorce is finalizing, I purchase a cozy condo near Shelburne Farms and the Shelburne Community School. Anna and Heidi live with me. We've adopted a calico kitten. At first, the girls spend every other weekend, Wednesday evenings, plus a week or two of vacation time with Alec.

Counseling hasn't saved our marriage, but it has eased our closure. Perhaps this is a rationalization, but I find some comfort in Jess Stearn's book *Soulmates*.

The author describes a shared calling, of working well together on joint endeavors, in a spirit of love and friendship. He goes on to explain that soulmates do not necessarily have permanent relationships once their project has been completed.

In my view, souls are immortal. Marriages may not be.

PART THREE

Softening the Heart

Mark comes by the condo today as Anna returns home from school. Agitated, Anna slams the front door, stomps upstairs, slams her bedroom door, and begins to beat on her drums. This outcry has become a pattern. Although understandable, given the divorce, I make a stern declaration. "I'm going to talk to her right now."

As I turn toward the stairs, Mark reaches for my shoulder to pull me back. "Be sure to soften your heart before you go up there." My first thought is, *I'll soften my heart, all right!* And then, *What does he know? He's never been a parent.*

I've developed quite a sharp tongue over the years. My facts are in order. Enough is enough. But I stop at the first landing and wonder: *What does he mean, soften my heart?* It's new advice that doesn't quite register. I proceed to the top landing and stand outside Anna's door.

Maybe I should try it. I close my eyes and imagine that my heart is warm and supple, open. The heart area feels a bit more expansive, less contracted. I suddenly envision Anna, my beautiful firstborn, in her entirety. My planned diatribe evaporates. Filled with a surge of love, I knock on her door. She allows me to enter.

Instead of scolding her, I tell her how much I love her, how I hope we can talk. This hasn't resolved her pain, but the door was opened. And no more harm was done.

Great Wolf

Mark's and my new relationship is turbulent. Both of us are in transition. I'm a single working mother. Each of us has a pile of personal healing and redeeming to do. Our relationship is on and off.

Our interests are somewhat different, but our values and spiritual beliefs are similar. I attempt to express these times with a poem about growth, love, and fear. I envision Mark as a great wolf on a separate wintry hill. I am drawn to him. And yet we are afraid to grow closer, until one future spring... perhaps.

Violin String

Mark is the third of four children. Like both of our fathers, he was small until the end of high school. He then grew into a tall, slender, and handsome man, a good man.

Like a violin string, or blade of grass, Mark can be taut, finely tuned, or can bend with the wind to vibrate with another. I say with a smile that "he notices like a hawk, plays like an otter, and rests like a burrowing pocket mouse."

Although he majored in English and minored in environmental studies, Mark became a carpenter after college. He now owns a construction company. His interests have grown from the restoration of historic buildings to the conservation of energy.

A palette of many buildings, some out of the ordinary, paints the story of his life's work. But I most admire Mark's kind and fair treatment of others, likely instilled by his parents.

Survivors' List

Mark's father, Bill, served in the US Navy before graduating from Yale. Mark's mother, Vivian, was a registered nurse, homemaker, gardener, and gifted craftswoman. She could sew, throw pottery, do needlepoint, crochet afghans, paint Ukrainian Easter eggs, and make teddy bears for children in hospitals.

In 1952, Bill's ship, the USS *Hobson*, collided with an aircraft carrier and sank. As sailors scrambled to disembark, he noticed that an enlisted man took a different route. Bill believed that sailor better knew the bowels of the ship. He decided to follow him through a tunnel.

Vivian, at home with three children under the age of six, received the survivors' list. She scanned the names, listed alphabetically, frantically searching the N's. Bill was not listed. Panicked, she looked more closely. Those rescued last were named out of alphabetical order, at the bottom of the page. There he was! Neagley, Lt. William C.

Covered in oil when rescued, Bill was unrecognizable in subsequent newspaper photographs. Only sixty-one sailors survived. One hundred seventy-six were lost.

Without Judgment

Perhaps it was gratitude and deepened faith that bound Bill and Vivian together, but they remained very much in love until Bill's death in 2004. Oddly to me because of my own upbringing, their children never saw them argue. I figure Mark must have needed someone like me to make his life less boring. I needed someone like him to calm things down.

Mark and I are visiting Bill and Vivian. We're telling them that we are going to marry, each of us for the third time. I brace myself for their scorn. Vivian looks at me, woman to woman, and asks, "Is this what *you* want?" I say, "Yes, it is." She continues with "Well then, we wish you much love and happiness." She offers no judgment, no advice.

On the drive back to Vermont, I quietly weep over their acceptance, their lack of dysfunction.

Husbandry

My adult life has largely been about husbandry. It's a pleasing word that implies care or stewardship, as in plant or animal husbandry. I'm fortunate to have married two good men, each of whom co-created essential chapters of my life.

Now Mark, a third good man, and I are marrying in March of 1990. The condo has become a stage set, a safe womb lit by a hundred votive candles and warmed by a wood fire. Lasagna, salad, crusty bread, and wine, a meal for twelve, is to be delivered by a caterer. Because the Episcopal clergyman's wife advised me to add ritual to the ceremony, Anna, Heidi, and I made bread for communion.

Two friends, Vicki and Sansea, are self-invited witnesses. I am deeply grateful for their presence, especially because I have no parents or siblings. They've brought pressed linens, roses, an African prayer, the *Out of Africa* soundtrack, and crystal glasses for a champagne toast. Martin and Linda have brought poetry to read.

Vivian whispers to me, "I have a good feeling about this marriage." Bill, privately, somewhat humorously, advises Mark, "Tell her she's right and tell her you love her, if you want a good marriage."

I had asked Bill early on, "What was Mark like as a young man?" He replied without hesitation, "Always pleasant and easygoing." Mark is a blend of Bill's sense of justice and Vivian's energy, along with her craftsmanship.

Anna and Heidi are fond of their new grandparents. Bill has a quietly comforting presence, like the soft-soled moccasins he wears. Vivian has positive, outgoing energy and always wears a smile. Both have gathered my daughters into their lives.

Heidi once said to Mark, "Your parents must feel so good about the family they raised." She was referring to him and his siblings, Alice, Linda, and John.

I believe we are off to a good start.

Rising Sun

Mark and I take short excursions into wooded or wilderness areas when Anna and Heidi are with Alec. This weekend we are canoeing in the Connecticut Lakes region. As we're settling into our lakeside cabin on this first night, we hear loons in the distant darkness. Their calls, both haunting and beautiful, connect us to them, and to the wilder origins of ourselves.

We head out early. With the dim light of dawn, our paddles are barely visible, but we sense motion in the water. Five or six baby otters are playfully swimming alongside our canoe. The delightful creatures look up at us with what appear to be tiny smiles. We pause to watch until they finally tire of us and disappear.

Looking eastward toward shore, the rising sun has begun to burn through a curtain of fog. Only the sound of our paddles can be heard. As the mist dissipates, a screen of green reeds slowly intensifies in color. Behind it, Canada geese appear as though painted with water.

Our serenity is soon shattered by a slurping sound. Through fading mist, a bull moose emerges, pulling mouthfuls of aquatic plants from the river bottom. He pauses, lifts his head of enormous antlers, and stares directly at us. Having little interest, he returns to his meal.

On the final day of our trip, a midday cacophonous sound comes from the lake. There appears to be a large floating raft of loons. The sound is unlike anything we've ever heard. I run to the manager's office to ask what it is. She explains, "Each fall, about twelve weeks after birth, juvenile loons are left by their parents who have already migrated. The juveniles later gather into great flocks, as they are today, now ready to head south."

Before coming here, the daily news was of disease, disaster, and violence. It now seems to me that, in the end, everything will be all right. The beauty and continuity of the natural world have dissolved my worries.

Deep Disappointment

Mark and I want to have a child. The first pregnancy happens quickly, but sadly ends in miscarriage. Soon, another pregnancy is lost.

I'm phoning Mark's mother to tell her about our second loss knowing how deeply disappointed she will be. Mark has never had a child. Thankfully, Vivian doesn't say, "Just try again" or "I know how you feel." She instead says, "We'll pray for you. Just love each other." No judgment, once again. And no pressure.

My instinct is to draw a bath. I climb into the tub, sit with my knees to my chest, and rock. I rock and cry. I moan.

There's a knock at the bathroom door. Anna steps in to ask what is wrong. When I explain, she says, "I'll bring an afghan and make tea for you, when you're ready to come out."

Imagine that. My daughter is mothering me. I had done the same for my mother. What pattern am I re-creating? Or is this only natural?

Pups

As I've said, our relationship is quite turbulent. Mark has his own issues. Mine are the same old ones as in the past: lack of trust and confidence, fear of abandonment. But today, during an argument, Mark says, "You're just like Pups."

Pups is a rescue dog that his father, Bill, adopted. Pups had been so abused that she wouldn't come to Bill for the longest time. Lured daily with treats, and with Bill's slow and steady effort, Pups began to trust. By the time I knew the little dog, she was quite old. Bill had to carry her upstairs to bed. They were seldom far apart.

Mark continues. "I'm going to stand here and tell you I love you until you believe me." *Ping!* His words strike a chord. *If I try to trust, our turbulence will lessen, or disappear.*

Howling Joy

We tried once again. Amniocentesis is scheduled. All goes smoothly, in terms of the procedure. Time passes.

At home, midday, I'm anxious to know the test results. Why not call? A woman answers. I give her my name and ask whether the results are in. "Oh yes. I just saw that folder. It's right here on my desk. Hold on for just a minute. . . . Yes, here it is. Would you like to know the gender?" Mark and I hadn't discussed this. I hesitate for a second, then say, "Yes. Sure."

"It's normal and it's a boy." I can barely breathe. "Thank you. Thank you very much. Okay. Yes. Uh-huh. Okay. Goodbye." *She said, "It's normal." What now?* I numbly pilot my way out the door and down the street to the mailbox. Mark's truck is turning onto our street. I'm surprised. He rarely comes home until the end of the workday. The truck stops next to me.

Mark lowers his window. I step closer and quietly tell him, "It's normal and it's a boy." He blinks, while taking a moment to register the words. Then, in a flash, he opens the truck door, leaps out, and rolls on the ground, making howling sounds of joy.

Separation Anxiety

It's late afternoon in March of 1992. Our son, Sam, has arrived. Both the sun and the moon are setting in the western sky. We'll tell him that the angels brought him on a moonbeam. I am forty-six, Mark is forty-one. Sam's birth does seem that miraculous.

Mark won't let Sam out of his sight. He checks his son's tiny ID bracelet whenever a nurse comes in contact with him. I'm amused by that, but Mark truly worries that someone might take our baby.

We are moved to a double room in the maternity ward. The Tierneys arrive to take a peek at Sam. As we all coo over our beautiful boy, the patient in the next bed arises. She sidles toward us. Then, in a split second, she lunges toward me, attempting to take Sam out of my arms. I'm stunned, but have little time to react.

Mark and Martin immediately restrain her until nurses arrive. The patient is moved to another room. She is out of her mind with grief over the loss of her own child. How terribly unfair that we should feel so much joy while she suffers such a tragic loss.

House Beautiful

Anna and Heidi are loving toward their baby brother. We're now a family of five, living in the crowded condo. Wanting to stay in our general neighborhood, near Alec and the public school, we search over many months for a new home. The only unbuilt house lot, three streets away, comes on the market.

Mark, being a builder, oversees the construction of what is, in my mind, a dream house. The design had earned *House Beautiful*'s Small House of the Year Award. We purchased the plans rather than offend our architect friends by choosing one over another.

The contemporary farmhouse design has a wraparound porch, a high-ceilinged living area with a fireplace, three bedrooms, and a studio apartment over the garage. The front of the house opens to a suburban neighborhood. The backyard borders walking trails that pass the same McCabe Brook my father had explored as a boy.

(A dog named Bella and a swimming pool arrive later, bringing much enjoyment to us, our children, and our grandchildren.)

Extended Family

At this time, as an advisor to the Vermont Women's Fund's and Vermont Public Radio's capital campaigns, I'm traveling throughout the state.

Meanwhile, Mark continues to work at Shelburne Farms, repairing the dairy barn and reservoir, building the new education center and tour wagons, and reroofing the enormous Breeding Barn. He is simultaneously growing his business in new directions, like energy conservation.

Family life is our priority though. Unless we're traveling, we come together every night for a healthy dinner. Extra guests, usually the children's friends, regularly join us.

Holidays and birthday dinners are celebrated with Alec and, later, Megan. (They work closely together at Shelburne Farms, and eventually marry.)

Shades of Blue

Mark is seriously ill with ulcerative colitis. One day in early September, he shows signs of extreme weakness. I take him to the hospital—against his will. Days go by. A major surgery sends him into a downward spiral. When I arrive at the hospital late this afternoon, Mark is unresponsive. He lands in the ICU with an infection.

Out of the ICU, I can now see how ill Mark is because he doesn't ask about the children or speak of returning home.

When in crisis, there's a tendency to be distracted. For protection, Juliet gave me a necklace with a miniature chime. Its tiny sound helps me focus. One part of me is numb with dread. The other part dresses and grooms with intention, mindfully preparing myself for each day. Walking to Mark's hospital room, I am conscious of every step, theoretically ready to meet each new moment as it unfolds.

Today, given Mark's progressive downturn, I realize that he might not recover. From the foot of his bed, with my arms slightly spread, I half surrender and gather whatever healing energy might exist in the world. As a last hope, I feebly project that imagined energy toward my beloved husband.

Driving home, listening to a recording of Heidi singing "Seven Shades of Blue," I sob from the depths of my being.

I try to keep life as normal as possible for eight-year-old Sam. After school, we play street hockey or watch *The Jeff Corwin Experience* while Mark's father, Bill, covers for me at the hospital. Sam appears to be taking his father's illness in stride.

Anna and Heidi don't know how serious the situation is. Heidi is away at school and Anna is a working mother. How will I tell all of them that Mark may not survive this?

Treasured Amulet

Finally, after nearly a **month**, Mark is coming home. Martin offers to bring him. I watch from the kitchen window as both of them make their way toward our front door. Having lost more than forty pounds, Mark looks as diminished as a prisoner of war. He's leaning against Martin.

Another infection sends Mark back to the hospital. With advice from our family friend Val, the infection is cured. But the same gifted surgeon must perform a second surgery, to improve upon the first.

Mark bravely begins a long period of recovery, relying on his unfailing sense of humor. Odd cravings for beef tenderloin and tapioca pudding put weight on his bones.

Perhaps, like Mark's parents, we've survived a sinking ship. We are bound together by gratitude, a treasured amulet.

Rite of Passage

As Sam approaches his thirteenth birthday, I wonder aloud, "Mark, I don't want to give you another task, but we have no traditional rite of passage for Sam. Maybe a circle of elders—" Mark raises his hand. "Stop. Say no more. I'll take care of this."

Sam and I take a brief trip to see Rusty in Captiva. Before we leave, Mark asks Sam what he wants to retain from his early childhood. He plans to renovate Sam's bedroom while we're away. Harry Potter books and fossils will remain. The dinosaur wall border and bunk beds will disappear. A full-size bed, new paint, and carpet will appear.

Mark then plans a dinner at a local restaurant. He invites men who are closest to him, including young Ave, Heidi's significant other. Each is asked to tell something about his journey into manhood.

They tell stories of honesty and kindness. One friend gives Sam a collection of Broadway musical videos. Mark gives Sam a gift of money, with the condition that he request the advice of at least one of these men before using it.

Sam's rite of passage continues into the summer. Mark is taking him, his friends, and some of their fathers camping at T Lake Falls in the Adirondacks.

Traditionally, rites of passage have a spiritual component. At this time, we are not part of a faith community, even though all three children have been baptized in a Congregational church.

As life would have it, Bill died shortly before Sam's thirteenth birthday. Sam had learned "Where Is Love?" from his lead role in *Oliver!* While Bill was in hospice care, Sam sang the tender song to his grandfather, as an eightieth birthday gift.

The family gathers around Vivian in her home. It's the day before Bill's memorial service. Even Heidi's boyfriend, Ave, has shown up. Throughout the afternoon, I've experienced an inexplicable and uncharacteristic sense of anxiety. . . .

This evening, Mark, Sam, and I are the last to retire to bed. Sam is lying on an air mattress next to my side of the bed. It's just past ten, late for us. I'm wide awake, still with a tinge of anxiety.

Mark, who falls asleep within seconds, begins to whimper. I place my hand over his heart. "Mark, what is it? Are you okay?" He mumbles, "My father just came to me. . . ." In this moment, Sam sits up. "Did you have that too, Dad?" Mark, in the fog of sleep, says he was dreaming. He explains, "Dad came toward me saying 'Everything will be all right.' Then he held me." Mark falls back to sleep.

Sam comes into the kitchen for breakfast. I ask, "What was going on for you last night, Sam?" He answers, "I decided to say a prayer for Papap," his name for Bill. "Then I focused on Papap. I had thoughts of love, then a warm sensation, not so much as heat but as a glow, like being held. Just then, Dad woke up crying from a dream where Papap had been holding him and saying 'Everything will be all right.'"

A viewing of the body is offered to the family. Only five of us, including Sam, accept the offer. Sam kneels to say goodbye to his beautiful grandfather. He softly weeps. This is his first encounter with death, so often the gateway to a spiritual journey. Perhaps Bill's death is completing Sam's rite of passage. Mark and I have benefited, as witnesses to transitions, and continuity.

Empty Nest

There's a certain amount of suffering when children leave home. The process reminds me of walking a childhood friend home after a day of play. Departing at the halfway point, both go their own way. In the darkness of night, fear of the unknown lurks behind every tree and shrub. We run as fast as we can, yelling each other's names, still connecting, feeling safer, while moving in opposite directions.

I'm poorly prepared for the departure of my children. The line that defines an end to parental guidance and support is invisibly drawn. The love, of course, never ends. Watching our children pull away is painful, but I have to let go. Like me, they need the freedom to discover their own successes and failures.

Anna moved away when her precious daughter, Jada, was in second grade. Anna and I enjoyed a trip to Baltimore in search of an apartment. The city, warmer and more diverse than Vermont, now seems to be the perfect place for them, but terribly far away for me.

Anna has since married Franklin, or Frankie, a kind and caring man whom we immediately embraced. They are partners in marriage, and in business. Jada is a marvelous young woman. I cherish her stays with us, our conversations and text messages, and her music.

Heidi and Ave married some time ago. I heartily believed he was "the one" when, as a high school sophomore, he gave her David Budbill's poem "Raymond and Ann," which speaks of love in old age.

Ave thoughtfully removed the lines about Ann's death, keeping only the words of love.

They, with their two beloved children, Fia and Holden, live nearby, in the house that Alec and I built. Heidi works for Shelburne Farms under the leadership of her father and her stepmother, Megan.

Sam first moved to Los Angeles, but is now in New York City, pursuing a creative career that involves acting, writing, and music. It is a joy to see his life unfold. We take pleasure in his performances, and look forward to his visits.

My feelings for our family remind me of a gentle man from Kenya. When he visited Shelburne Farms years ago, he shared photos of his home and family. Cooing sounds spontaneously escaped his throat. It seemed completely natural for him to spill out his love in that way.

That's how I feel when truly seeing our family. The whole is greater than the sum of its parts, in quite a beautiful way.

Letting Go

On this October day, Mark and I are heading for the Adirondacks. The atmosphere is stunningly clear. Foliage is ablaze in oranges, ochers, and reds. Based on a map's topographic contours, the trail promises to be steep from the start but not very long, a bit over two miles. We are glad for that, because Mark is recovering from knee surgery and an easy trail is generally good news for me.

The path is immediately rewarding. We pass a deeply pooled stream. At various turns, we are delighted by the spicy fragrance of fallen needles and leaves. Mark alerts me to a knoll ahead of us. Having wound our way up to it, we stand in the midst of several towering white birch trees that form a silent cathedral-like space. Moments later, and further along, we hear the trickle of water as our path periodically passes mossy ledges, echoing the music of an underground stream.

We arrive at a rocky peak with spectacular views in all directions. The temperature is perfect. Looking eastward, Vermont's Green Mountains and a portion of Lake Champlain are visible. Below us and toward the south are golden mountain ranges. Looming in the southwest is Giant Mountain, and in the north, Hurricane. Colorful deciduous trees give way to the dark greens of red spruce and balsam fir, marking the beginning of a higher, more fragile altitude, a reminder of my own fragility and rising age.

Our celebratory snack consists of homemade oatmeal cookies, two Macoun apples, and water. We pause here for a long while, absorbing the beauty of it all.

On the descent, Mark, who is always ahead, calls back to me, "Listen, it sounds like rain." There can't be rain on this blue-sky, seventy-degree day! The air is calm, without a breeze. I now see, and hear, what we have come upon.

Perhaps fifty, maybe more, maple trees are, at once, dropping their leaves. The free fall, in a flutter of yellow, makes a sacred, hushed sound upon landing. Ideal conditions, perhaps temperature, air pressure, and sunlight, must have signaled that *now* is the time to let go. Is this a metaphorical message for me?

Sunrise Service

On our twenty-fifth wedding anniversary, Mark and I are attending an Easter sunrise service. We doubt that anyone else will show up. Wet and heavy snow is falling. Yet in dim predawn light, we are surprised to find that sixty or so people have arrived. Our minister carries a wooden cross. The rest of us follow him in silence.

We take a path that meanders through a hillside cemetery, through woods, and onto a wide open field that tilts upward. Midway, one tree is etched in black against the snowy slope. A fire glows from the top of the hill ahead of us. We continue to walk in silence until we reach the fire and form a circle around it. As we conclude our prayers and songs, the sun breaks through champagne-colored clouds.

Mark and I had previously asked the minister if he would bless our marriage and our wedding rings. He gladly does so, privately, off to the side. We are inwardly pleased to celebrate twenty-five years of commitment.

Everyone descends from the hill, in full sunlight.

Greenest Pastures

Before I retired, four friends and mentors helped me embrace my spiritual life. Ron, and a team of others, asked me to bring the contemplative practice of mindfulness to public schools. Our work was enhanced by my friend Aostre and her experience with education and spirituality. Pastors Mary and Susan led me to review and refresh my beliefs.

Now, in retirement, I take more time to walk in favorite places like Shelburne Farms, Limerick Road, the Adirondacks, and Shelburne

Pond. Each season brings delightful surprises: the music of spring peepers, dancing grasses of midsummer, gray plumes of autumn goldenrod, and the silence of winter snow.

Walking is a contemplative practice, a homecoming. When I walk in communion with nature, my heart springs alive like the greenest of pastures. I enjoy walking with others but notice more when alone. And even then, I have to deliberately turn my attention outward, rather than be lost in my head.

Thoreau explained it this way. "I am alarmed when it happens that I have walked a mile into the woods bodily, without getting there in spirit. . . . But sometimes it happens that I cannot easily shake off the village. The thought of some work will run in my head, and I am not where my body is. . . . I am out of my senses."

Transitions

I awaken to a blue-sky September day. Although beautiful, this is a time of transition. A sense of emptiness lurks in me. Cooler weather limits my daily swims. Friends are heading south, both literally and figuratively. Some of us have a new preference for solitude over adventure. Others are scrambling to see the world, before it's too late. To top it off, my right thumb doesn't work well. Arthritis perhaps . . . Yes, I know. All are luxury problems.

My phone pings. Heidi is texting to ask if I might walk Duke. She adds that their apples are ready for picking. I waste no time getting to their house, my former home, only minutes away.

Lanky Duke, full of life and love, bounds toward me. Having recovered from an injury, he is again his happy dog self, thrilled to be outside.

I reach high into the Gravenstein that I'd planted so many years earlier. The sun warms my face. Branches of the aging tree bend toward me with an offering of ripe fruit. I fill a bag.

Duke and I take a walk. He trots ahead, then circles back, nudging my hand, letting me know he's near. Dozens of monarch butterflies bob in a meadow of sweet red clover. Settled on blossoms, their wings expand and contract like tiny bellows, like my breath. I sigh with relief. These lovely creatures have seemed scarce in recent years.

A shimmer appears in the distance. It's a murmuration of starlings. Their undulating movement is holographic. With rhythmic grace, they dance across the sky in unison, as though with one brain. I'm in awe. My heart is full, ready to burst.

I stop to listen. More crickets are singing than I've ever heard in one place. They sing with joy, even though summer is ending, and time is moving on.

Time Travel

Preparation for aging comes rather naturally. I am, at first, surprised to realize that I'm not *preparing* for aging. I'm already here. Eyesight and hearing have dimmed a bit. The body has grown somewhat heavier and less flexible. Tasks, like driving at night, or cooking for many, once easy, now require full concentration. More sweetly, though, I am now called Nana.

The aging process has drawn me closer to simple pleasures. Birds are astonishing. Water is mystifying. Gardens are grounding. And time spent with family and friends, or helping a stranger, matters more than ever.

My desire for challenges and travel has quieted. Writing and reading by the fire, or swimming in the pool, are as satisfying to me now as travel had been. Swimming is blissful, with underwater glints of sunlight, with rhythmic strokes and breaths. I'm now more apt to map my journey by breath. Breath is an invisible thread that connects my inner world to the outer world, like an umbilical cord.

Grandchildren and their friends sometimes spend time at the pool. I love the days of splashing and laughter, of strewn wet towels. On quieter days, I'm pleased by a few border roses and other flowers. Lulled by the flight of birds, the sound of bubbling water, I gaze upward, away from my book.

Green treetops reach for the bluest of skies. Floating clouds pass by as they did when I was a child. In such moments, I'm at ease. There's no place I'd rather be.

Dream Attic

During darker and shorter days of the year, Mark and I cherish our dinner ritual. It's a time for communion. Our table is an altar of sorts, with bread and wine, candles and flowers. We are steeped in music.

This fall day, in preparation for a long winter, I harvest the last of the herbs and mulch my roses with fresh straw. A friend helps Mark stack a wall of firewood. The fragrant logs are sawn evenly, in perfect length. End cuts of birch and ash make a tawny-cream pattern of shapes. We gaze at the beautiful woodpile, grateful for our home, our life. Home, I find, is both spiritual and physical . . . beyond time and space, yet rooted in the earth.

Irish poet and philosopher John O'Donohue reflects on the way a swallow returns to a "fragile little grass-and-mud home after its huge continental journey." He suggests that "one can undertake any voyage if the destination is home. Humble or grand, home is where the heart belongs. To be, we need to be home."

I am at home. The idealized home, the dream attic of my childhood, wasn't "out there." It was inside me all along, residing within my heart. Some part of this little girl must have known that, but most of her didn't. She had to make the long journey.

Epilogue

While concluding the first draft of this memoir, I learned that the journey continues to unfold. A man named Steven emailed me. He believed he was my half sibling, sharing the same father. My first reaction was disbelief, but after three tests I had to accept that DNA doesn't lie.

I am no longer an only child. I have a brother. My story has changed.

Steven was born in October of my freshman year of high school. At that time, my mother was in the state hospital for a second time. I was in a local hospital with pneumonia.

Fourteen months later, Dad, Mom, and I abruptly moved to Florida, en route to the Bahamas. More pieces of the puzzle, like Dad's personality change and Grammy's sudden resentment of him during those months, were coming together.

As I began to absorb the news, I felt ill, disoriented, and dirty. My stomach hurt. I wanted to climb into bed and hide beneath the blankets.

An acquaintance suggested that I read *Fixing the Fates*. The author, Diane Dewey, chronicled her inability to separate what she was responsible for from what she was not. She described the scars caused by traumatic separation from the mother: "The unloved child feels abnormal, leprous and forever condemned. The masculine archetype, manifesting as superego, then pairs with the scarred child."

I wondered, *Is my sickly response what happens when the masculine archetype is shattered?* Dad had been my rock, my primary caregiver, during those trying years of childhood. I had adored him, but now learned that he had hidden harmful secrets.

Inching along in acceptance, and grief, I soon met my brother, Steven, and his wife, Donna. He met most of my family. Mark and I later met his fine family. I could imagine a future sense of gratitude for having a younger brother, and a larger family, but I also felt trapped.

Our meetings were enjoyable, but we were beginning as strangers. We had been raised in different homes and distant places. Dad had never met Steven. Months after Steven's birth, his mother asked whether Dad wanted to meet his son. Dad did not. I wonder whether he believed Steven truly was his child, given the time lapse. And I wonder how well he knew her, the mother of his son.

Did my mother know? I now see more of the pain and complexity of my parents' relationship. My heart aches for them, in memoriam.

Why had this relationship come to light now, after so many years, and not until I was writing my memoir? *If only Dad had been honest with me*, I think. Then again, perhaps he was now revealing the truth—if one believes in metaphysics. Had writing this memoir, digging into the tangle of family roots, somehow unearthed new chapters of my story?

Or were these new chapters hidden in the attic of my childhood home? After all, Dad's violin and tennis racket were stored there in darkness, like scabs that had fallen from a wounded life. I can imagine, too, that my hopes and dreams were also stored there, beautifully arranged in a cedar-lined hope chest . . . stories . . . awaiting my future.

Acknowledgments

Juliet McVicker was my first reader. I am profoundly grateful for the constancy of her encouragement and the wisdom of her advice. I wholeheartedly thank my husband, Mark, who was also a reader, and is my pillar of support.

Other readers were: Sam Neagley, Laura M. Latka, and Susan Cooke Kitteredge. I am grateful for them and for those who kindly reviewed or heard excerpts: Anna and Franklin Taylor; Heidi Webb and Averill Cook; Jada Webb; Alec Webb; Marshall Webb; Mary Kelly; Quentyn Webb; Lisa Roberts; Emily Wadhams; Megan Camp; Jerry Leimenstoll; Martin Tierney; Eileen Growald; Lenore Follansbee; Ray Sadler; Lynda McIntyre; Sansea Sparling; Del Sheldon; Marnie Davis; David Barash; Crea Lintilhac; Victoria Fraser; Beeken/Parsons; the Miskells and the Conways; Steven Williams; Vicki Lonn; Linda Tisdale; and June Fisher.

I am deeply grateful for Penelope J. Cray, my developmental editor. Her keen insight and candor enriched the entire process. I also thank John Barstow for his work as my earlier editor.

Those who provided historical information were: Julie Edwards; Stacia Lihatsh; Cynthia Lihatsh; Victor Baskevich; Cheryl Pierce; Tom Tompkins; the town clerks of Shelburne and Charlotte, Vermont; and my mother Mary and grandmother Mimi for their photographic records.

My thanks to Bill Schubart for connecting me to Rootstock Publishing and Samantha Kolber. She and Sheryl Rapée-Adams of Cats Eye Copyediting helped bring this book to fruition.

I am grateful for the many fellow travelers who have provided support for my journey. I regret that all are not named, but you know who you are.

And, finally, I give thanks for this extraordinary planet we call home.

About the Author

Marilyn Webb Neagley has lived her life in Vermont. She is the author of two previous books and the co-editor of another. Her book, *Walking through the Seasons*, received an IPPY gold medal for best northeastern non-fiction. She has been a Vermont Public Radio commentator and has written essays for her local newspaper. Marilyn was raised in Ascutney, Vermont. She and her husband now reside in Shelburne.

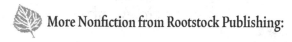 **More Nonfiction from Rootstock Publishing:**

Learn about our Fiction, Poetry, and Children's titles at
www.rootstockpublishing.com.